James Clinton
NEILL

THE SHADOW COMMANDER
OF THE ALAMO

C. Richard King

Eakin Press ✦ Fort Worth, Texas
www.EakinPress.com

Copyright © 2002
By C. Richard King
Published in the United States of America
By Eakin Press
An Imprint of Wild Horse Media Group
P.O. Box 331779
Fort Worth, Texas 76163
1-888-982-8270
www.EakinPress.com
ALL RIGHTS RESERVED
1 2 3 4 5 6 7 8 9
ISBN-10: 1571685774
ISBN-13: 978-1571685773

Library of Congress Cataloging-in-Publication Data
King, C. Richard (1924–)
   James Clinton Neill: shadow commander of the Alamo / C. Richard King.
     p. cm.
   ISBN 1-57168-577-4
   1. Neill, James Clinton, 1790-1845. 2. Revolutionaries—Texas—Biography. 3. Soldiers—Texas—Biography. 4. Texas—History—Revolution, 1835-1836. 5. San Jacinto, Battle of, 1836. 6. Alamo (San Antonio, Tex.)—Siege, 1836. I. Title
F390.N43 K56 2001
976.4'03'092--dc21
[B]   2001040836

"We share with you its good and ill,
The shadow and the glory . . . ."

John Greenleaf Whittier

Contents

Preface   vii

1. Roots   1
2. Beginnings   13
3. Indians   16
4. Public Office   22
5. On to Texas   32
6. Rumblings of Revolution   35
7. Acquiring Land   43
8. Gonzales   52
9. Forward to Victory   62
10. Bexar   76
11. March to Independence   97
12. The Twin Sisters   107
13. San Augustine   119
14. Sam Houston, President   122
15. Peace Council   130
16. Falls Treaty   150
17. Annual Indian Council   158
18. For Those Who Have Served   164
19. The Gallant Colonel Neill   169
20. Hampton McKinney   175
21. Last Will   179
22. George J. Neill   188

23.	Samuel C. Neill	200
24.	Mary Neill Price	207
25.	Miranda Neill	212

Notes 215

Index 277

PREFACE

James Clinton Neill receives little space in Texas history books. While some historians have devoted a handful of paragraphs to the man, others strain to include his name in a footnote reference. Wallace O. Chariton is an exception. In *Exploring the Alamo Legends,* he devotes an entire chapter to "What Happened to Lt. Col. James C. Neill?"

James Clinton Neill was commander of a company of artillery during the Siege of Bexar; unmilitarylike, he ignored the order of his commander in chief Sam Houston to abandon the fortifications at San Antonio and retreat to Gonzales.

It is fortunate for modern Texans that Neill could not obey the order. Neill was on leave when the Alamo—under the assumed joint temporary command of William B. Travis and James Bowie—fell.

Neill returned to military duty, taking command of the artillery at San Jacinto. Unfortunately, he was wounded the day before the skirmish. However, after recovering, he continued to serve the Republic of Texas as an Indian commissioner.

Wallace O. Chariton makes an interesting point:

> On March 6, 1836, Lt. Col. James C. Neill was still the commander of record for the Alamo garrison, and he was actively participating in the affairs of the day. The history books should all be rewritten to show Travis as acting commander out of respect for Lt. Col. Neill. . . .

Deep and sincere appreciation to Mrs. C. L. Neill; Peggy is a consummate researcher. And to Pam Cummings, whose ability to read my handwritten manuscripts is of star quality.

C. RICHARD KING

1

ROOTS

"Victory lies not in senseless armour, nor in vain din of cannon, but in living and courageous souls."

Hugh O'Neill
Speech at Battle of Yellow Ford, 1598

    To the Texas theatre of operations, James Clinton Neill, no longer a rash youth when he galloped upon the scene, brought a military record as captain of a Tennessee militia in the Battle of Horseshoe Bend and as a colonel in the Alabama Militia. Pages of his family history are filled with accounts of military deeds in fighting for independence in both Ireland and America.
    The name *Neill* comes from *ni,* meaning "a daughter," and *aille,* "a cliff." It is most probable that the name is derived from a place of residence of one of the earliest members of the family.[1]
    James Clinton Neill descended from "the largest and oldest traceable family in Europe"—a providential circumstance for which members can thank an early ancestor. The first absolute monarch of Ireland, Heremon, devised a family system of government which required "meticulous genealogical records" and deeds to prove which lands belonged to the various septs. By law, these records were presented to the council at the Hall of Tara every three years and were kept up to date. Such records provided a continuity of descent "unmatched by other clans whose beginnings so often are root-bound in obscurity." In this process of record keeping, surnames were introduced. One legend has Domnall tacking an *O* to his name and adding Niall—the name of his grandfather affectionately known as

Black Knee, who lost his life in battle in 919 A.D.[2] Domnall thus produced the first surname ever used in Ireland.[3]

Tradition says the family is traced through "a long line of kings and chieftains" from Niul—son of Phenius Pharsa, the king of Scythia[4]—whose posterity arrived in Spain and later led a colony of Milesians to Ireland.

Legend also has it that the red hand emblazoned on the family coat of arms pays tribute to a forbearer who participated in a race whereby the winner was to be the first person to lay a hand on the coast. A man named O'Neill, determined to win but realizing an opponent was outdistancing him, chopped off his hand and flung it ashore, thus claiming the land as his trophy. No details reveal how much time or what implements were involved in the surgery. Because the central figure in the Arms of Ulster is a red hand, frequently the question arises as to whether it should be a right hand or left hand. All early seals of the O'Neills show the right hand, never the left, and one authority points out that there should be "no drops of blood."[5]

It was Aedh Reamhar the Stout, King of Ulster, whose shield bears the famous red hand—the original O'Neill arms—and whose seal bears the inscription *S. Odonis O'Neill Hybernicorum Ultonie*.[6]

An authority on Irish history, Seumas MacManus, writes in *The Story of the Irish Race*, about one of the legendary figures of Neill history, Niall of the Nine Hostages.

> His reign was epochal. He not only ruled Ireland greatly and strongly, but carried the name and the fame, and the power and the fear, of Ireland into all neighboring nations. . . . Under him the spirit of pagan Ireland upleaped in its last great red flames of military glory. . . .[7]

Naturally, whenever persons gathered around peat campfires, they told stories about Niall of the Nine Hostages. By the daughter of the King of Muenster, Eochaid had four sons. His second wife, jealous and ambitious, soon realized that Niall was his father's favorite, so she arranged for him to be sent from the castle. She made certain that the boy's mother was relegated to carrying water and doing other menial tasks.

When Niall reached manhood, the poet Torna saw that he was returned to his rightful place at court, and Niall ordered his mother relieved of household duties.[8]

Legend tells that one day the five half brothers were in the smith's forge when it broke into flames. The boys were commanded to save whatever they could. Brian saved the chariots. Ailill removed a shield and sword. Fergus pulled a bundle of firewood from the forge. Fiarchra rescued the old forge trough. Niall carried out the bellows, sledges, anvil, and anvil-block, thus rescuing the very soul of the forge.

The father, who some folklorists vow set the fire to the forge as a test for his sons, observed the youths then declared, "It is Niall who should succeed me."

Another account of the five half brothers tells of a hunting trip. They became thirsty and soon discovered a well deep within the woods. The source of water was guarded by a withered hag who said she would grant a drink to the first who kissed her. Without hesitation, Niall kissed the woman. The rags fell from her; the wrinkles and blemishes vanished. She emerged a beautiful young maiden, and before the other brothers were permitted to drink, they were made to yield to Niall their rights to the kingdom and to swear allegiance to him.

Upon assuming the throne, Niall immediately set about organizing a foreign expedition to Alba to subdue the Picts.[9] From one of his expeditions, Niall brought back Succat, a young slave who was assigned to herd the swine. His name later was changed to Patrick, and he became Ireland's patron saint.[10]

By two wives, Niall fathered fourteen sons. He died in 404 A.D.[11] Some of his sons dominated the northern area while others took charge of the southern sector. Before long, the U Neill dreamed of kingship over all of Ireland.[12]

Domnall Ardmacha of Armagh was the first High King of Ireland to be styled "O'Neill," Una Neill, or "Grandson of Niall." At the time, to be the "grandson of Niall Black Knee" meant acceptance as rightful heir to the high kingship.[13]

O'Neills continued to figure prominently in Irish military history. Con O'Neill surrendered to Henry VIII on September 24, 1542, and after renouncing the title "The O'Neill," he was dubbed Earl of Tyrone. Convinced that England's main goal was the destruction of everything Irish, he denounced any ancestors who would trust in English faith and English promises.[14]

The next O'Neill to make military history was Shane, "a bad man in private life, but a born soldier, a sagacious ruler, and a believer in his own rights."[15] Shane blocked the English advance into Ireland. Queen Elizabeth I "tried to cajole him, to deceive him, to defeat him, to capture him, to murder him." When Sussex dispatched a force to Ulster, Shane and his men took to the mountains.

Elizabeth invited O'Neill to London, and he accepted. All London gawked at the Irish leader and his company of *galloglach:* "They wore shirts of mail, iron caps, bright coloured trews to the knees, leggings of leather."[16]

Shane returned to Ireland believing his land was safe from the English, and that he and the queen were friends.

For more than 600 years, this family dominated Irish history as monarchs, princes, chiefs, statesmen, and soldiers. "It would be impossible to beat their record,"[17] but perhaps one of the greatest leaders was Hugh O'Neill. The Neills who sailed into Pennsylvania and then settled in Virginia "are descended in a direct junior line from Hugh O'Neill," the line designated the Claneboy O'Neills, whose chief castle centering 3,000 acres of land near Antrim was called Edenduff Carrig, now known as Shane's Castle.[18]

In the summer of 1591, he fell in love with a nineteen-year-old English beauty, Mabel Bagenal, whose brother was Sir Henry Bagenal, marshall of Ireland. Hugh presented the woman a necklace of great value, and a month later the two were attending a luncheon with English friends. After the meal, while other guests were wandering on the lawn, Hugh and Mabel slipped away to a friend's home where they were married. After this elopement, Hugh was inaugurated *The O'Neill* on the hill of Tullaghogue.[19]

Mabel Bagenal O'Neill lived to see her husband throw off British rule and unfurl the banner with the Red Hand of O'Neill. But two years after her death, O'Neill and his brother-in-law met on the battlefield. Bagenal, as head of the queen's forces, was directed to crush O'Neill and his struggle toward an independent Ireland.[20]

Allowed by law to an army of six companies, O'Neill realized that the law failed to stipulate how these companies were to be composed. As soon as his soldiers were completely trained, the soldiers were discharged and replacements recruited. O'Neill appealed to other chiefs for help and called upon King Philip II of Spain.[21] For five years, he commanded his troops with no field guns and no siege equipment.

A story persists that Rory Dell O'Cahan, the musician in the court of James VI, was complaining one day. The courtier assured him that he had much of which to be proud. Hadn't James Stewart placed a band on his shoulder?

"A greater man than King James had laid his hand on my shoulder," the musician stated.

Puzzled, the courtier asked, "And who was that?"

Standing and stretching to his full height, the musician answered, "O'Neill, my liege."[22]

The British representative ran the St. George's Cross flag over O'Neill's ruined castle of Dungannon, of which only two stone-brick towers survive. He ordered his men to climb the hill of Tullahogue and shatter the stone chair which had served as the inaugural seat of the O'Neills. The hammer strokes tumbled the chair. There are plans to restore the Dungannon castle towers, which jot above a police impound, but the lifestyle they symbolize is gone forever.

Approximately eighty persons rallied around O'Neill in Dungannon Castle, and on September 14, 1607, he began "The Flight of the Earls," a voyage with Spain as the destination. After the party was at sea for thirteen days, a storm began to rage. O'Neill removed the cross of gold from his neck and lovingly examined it and "a portion of the Cross of the Crucifixion" it encased. He tossed this cross and other relics into the sea, and a scribe vowed they "gave them a relief."

After twenty-one days, the ship touched the coast of France, but the English ambassador prevailed upon the French king to deny permission for the Irish to travel through his country. The Spanish ambassador likewise entertained a request to deny the Irish retinue permission to journey across his country.

O'Neill, a man of determination, decided to go by horseback through Lorraine, Switzerland, and Italy. He and his party set out "well armed with arquebusses and pistols."

On May 5, 1608, the party entered Rome, where the Pope received members "with kindness, with honor and with welcome." O'Neill heard mass in St. Peter's, and "a position of honor and a fitting place was selected for them close to and near the Pope."

O'Neill watched his years in exile pass with no promise of military aid. One of his spies wrote that often in the evening, when O'Neill was warm with wine, "his face would glow and he would strike the table" and sing out that there would be a good day yet for Ireland.

Unfortunately, he did not live to see that good day. He died on July 20, 1616, and was put to rest in the Spanish National Church of San Pietro in Montorio.[23] San Pietro was erected on Janiculum Hill, on the site where legend has it that St. Peter was crucified. Rebuilt in the 15th century, it contains a single nave with paintings by Sebastino del Piombo and Peruzzi.

A nephew of Hugh's, the red-headed Owen Roe O'Neill, had never ceased to hope that he could have a hand in freeing his homeland. After winning military distinction in the Spanish Netherlands in 1642, he stepped off a ship in the north of Donegal. With him marched a hundred soldiers.[24]

Word spread. "Owen Roe is come!"

Owen Roe O'Neill was handed command of the northern army and began to train troops. At Benburg, where the river passes between green slopes before being funneled into a gorge, he smashed the opponent.[25]

Cromwell landed in 1649, and Owen Roe marched again, hoping to meet the great cavalry master. O'Neill, however, fell ill—mysteriously, suddenly. Legend persists that a poisoned nail had been planted in his shoe.

The portrait of another Neill, the third Baronet of Killeleagh, Lord Lieutenant of Armagh who raised the O'Neill Dragoons for King James II,[26] is in the Tate Gallery of London. The subject was wounded in the Battle of the Boyne and died at age 32. Artist Joseph Michael Wright, however, painted him in 1680, showing "a great Irish noble in his national dress of that period; with his 'wild Irish,' fringed cloak, curious but beautifully adorned Erse apron, long red hose, pointed brogues, Celtic dirk, bask-hilted broadsword, great oval shield of studded leather, gold-tipped black javelin, and elaborately-tooled, leather conical cap with the flowing plumes of an Irish chieftain.[27]

Dorothy Till, a "low sized" woman, must have spent hours looking at the cathedral spires dominating the town of Exeter, England. She remained proud that she had been born in France, and the stocky Norman towers reminded her of that heritage. Her husband, Robert Reford, "bred to the woolen manufacture," no doubt took equal pleasure in the community's guild hall, its ceiling supported by beams resting on figures of bears holding staffs. He and Dorothy settled on a small estate between Honeystone and Chimney, not far from Exeter, and the property soon boasted a corn and fulling mill.

Through marriage the family became associated with Sir Hugh Clotworthy, who, eager to establish trade at Antrim, Ireland, persuaded the Refords to locate their clothing factory there. His widow Dame Mary Clotworthy and a son, Sir John, continued to grant the Refords leases and encouragement.

The Refords had two daughters and a son. The third child, Esther, born in 1675, became the bride of John Neill in 1694. The son of Thomas and Elizabeth Neill, he was a native of Enniskillen and later lived in Largan, County Armagh, and Clare, County Down. John and Esther Reford Neill began opening their home to meetings of the Quakers.[28]

In 1654, the Society of Friends had held a meeting in the home of William Edmundsen in Lurgan. Edmundsen, a native of Westmoreland, had served as a captain in Cromwell's army and settled on land in Ireland.[29]

The following year a meeting was called in Cavan and among those attending was William O'Neill. Obviously impressed, O'Neill joined the organization and as evidence of his new faith began writing his name without the *O*. Although the Society of Friends flourished in northern Ireland, members suffered persecutions, so in 1730, Lewis, John, and William—three brothers who followed their grandfather's custom of writing their names without the *O*—took passage from Lurgan. After docking in Pennsylvania, they settled near Lancaster, but finding the lands already taken and opportunities scarce, John and Lewis Neill, in 1733, moved into Shenandoah Valley—which was settled by Scotch-Irish immigrants and Friends under the patronage of Alexander Ross. John Neill built his home near Spout Spring in Clarke County, Virginia. Lewis settled approximately a mile and a half away on a point known as Burnt Factory. Lewis made his home in a small cave until he could erect a "large, old-fashioned hipped roof house," which became recognized as "the finest in the country."[30] He constructed a large grist mill near the home, operated a mercantile business, and dabbled in the slave market.[31] He was elected sheriff in April 1751, and in September the commission of "Lewis Neill, gentleman," was renewed. In 1759, through Lord Halifax, he complained to the crown that a neighbor had drawn too much water and his plantation was suffering. He requested some grafts of Golden Pipin, Nonpareil, Aromatic, and Medlar apples for his orchards.

In speaking with the crown, Lord Halifax made it clear that Lewis Neill had requested his grants and those of his brothers should "be made separate," but by this time John and William had joined him.[32]

A man holding large estates, mills, and other property, Lewis Neill was "industrious in business, upright and fair in all transactions," and "firm and courageous in his convictions of right and justice."

A second brother, John, also became prominent in colonial affairs, serving one time as Gentleman Justice of the Peace. Through the terms of his will he left a plantation to his son Lewis, two town lots in the town of Winchester—then known as Frederickstown—to his daughter Sarah, and a farm to his daughter Elizabeth in partnership with her brother Lewis.

William Neill, the third brother to come to America, was born April 21, 1711, in Clare, County Down, Ireland. His name and that of a son appear on early Clinton Tavern Petitions of Chester County, Pennsylvania. The General Land Office in Richmond, Virginia, however, shows that "William Neill of Frederick County was granted 400 acres on the north side of Opeckon Creek, and on the west side of Abraham's Creek, October 7, 1750." A two-page deed in tedious Spenserian script is on file in Rowan County, North Carolina, by which the second John Karl Granville transferred the title to 630 acres of land to William Neill, land described as existing on both sides of Lambert's Creek.

By 1752, three brothers—Andrew, James, and Captain William—appeared in Rowan County, North Carolina. They settled on both sides of Lambert's Creek, which later took the name Neill's Creek.

William, a later Neill, was married to Mary (Polly) Clinton, daughter of Archibald and Sarah Clinton, whose will was dated September 5, 1746, in "London Britain in the county of Chester and province Pensilvenia." Being "weak and sick in body but of a sound mind and perfect memory," he directed that his daughter Mary was to receive "the sixth part of my personal estate or household goods & stock to be improved for her and eleven pounds six shillings & half pence to be paid for her one year after she is come of age for her part of the plantation & I order she live with her brother William till she come of age. . . ." Also named in the will were William, James, John, Mary, and Elizabeth.

William Neill and Polly Clinton exchanged wedding vows in Delaware on May 3, 1750, although the license shows both to be residents of Chester County, Pennsylvania. The walls of their home long rang with children's laughter, for they were the parents of William, James, Andrew, John, Archibald, Gilbreath Falls, Robert, Hannah, Alexander, Samuel, Polly, Sarah, and Elizabeth.

Concern filled Polly's heart as she watched her husband, Capt. William Neill, and four sons take their rifles from the mantelpiece and march to join the American forces opposing British soldiers. Capt. William Neill served in the Battle of King's Mountain, fought in October, 1780. When the British began retreating, Colonel Campbell, realizing that his footmen might yet be needed, selected Captain Neill, "an officer of much energy or character," and his cadre "to do everything in their power to expedite the march of troops."[33] Late in the afternoon, the detachment under Captain Neill and the main force were reunited and set up a bivouac on an abandoned plantation. Here grew "a sweet potato patch sufficiently large to supply the whole army."[34]

Captain Neill had four sons take part in the American

Revolution. One, Lieutenant William, died in 1790 in the Battle of Ramsour's Mill. In September 1828, heirs of Lieutenant Neill appointed Samuel Ragsdale of Monroe County, Mississippi, their attorney "to take into possession, occupy and use to sue for and equit and recover of the Trustees of East Tennessee College" 2,560 acres of land on Big Hatchie River. The land had been granted by military warrant December 26, 1822, to Lt. William Neill and his heirs. Heirs authorized Ragsdale to sell and convey the land and to lease as he thought proper.[35] Robert Neill, on December 2, 1831, testified that his brother James "came to my fathers during the Revolutionary War in America and said that they was just from the battle at Ramsour's Mill." He continued in his testimony, "James brought my brother William's clothing to my fathers and said that he was killed in the Battle."

The second son to participate was Andrew Neill. At age 85, he submitted a request for a pension for service as a private in the company commanded by Capt. Thomas Kennedy in Col. Charles McDowell's regiment. He was unable to remember the exact date, but "in the spring or early part of summer," he had marched from Burke County, North Carolina, to Pacolet, South Carolina, for "an engagement against the British and Tories at that place." At different times he was engaged in scouting "after the Indians along the frontier." Sometime "after the frost had killed the potatoe (*sic*) vines," he served under Capt. Joseph McDowell and marched from Burke County to Wilmington, North Carolina. He also served three months under his father Capt. William Neill. At the time of his pension application, he admitted to being "very old and frail."[36]

He testified that all records in his father's books were lost when Cherokee Indians robbed the residence and "destroyed his books among other things." At the time Andrew submitted his application, he was residing in Marshall County, Tennessee, "near the Big Spring formerly in Bedford County."[37]

The third son was Gilbreath Falls Neill, who filed for a pension on June 21, 1833, from Iredell, North Carolina. He died January 29, 1834, and his widow qualified for the pension. He served in a militia company commanded by his uncle, Capt. Gilbreath Falls, and volunteered in the summer of 1776, for three months to protect the frontier against Indian attack. He became sick before the period ended and returned home, but in the spring he again volunteered as a lieutenant under Captain Falls. Again he became ill and returned home. Once more, in the spring of 1779, he joined Captain Falls and marched to Augusta, Georgia. He took part in reconnoitering expeditions in the neighborhood of Rock River, North Carolina, and was in the Battle of Ramsour's Mill.

The fourth brother seeing service in the American Revolution was John Neill, whose widow, Cynthia Forgy Neill, on February 24, 1854, applied for a pension. John was in the Battle of Ramsour's Mill and served under Colonel Shelby or Colonel McDowell in the Battle of Kings Mountain.

While her father and four brothers were meeting their patriotic responsibility to the American cause, Sarah saw her husband shoulder his musket. Sarah on August 13, 1778, in Rowan County, North Carolina, had exchanged marriage vows with a cousin, James Neill, the son of James Neill and his second wife, Agnes Snoddy. In 1832, while living in Union County, Kentucky, Sarah's James had applied for a pension for his Revolutionary War service, stating that he had been a resident of Rowan County until 1796, when he had moved to Kentucky. In 1828 he had relocated in Illinois, but in 1832 he returned to make his home in Union County, Kentucky.[38] He "enlisted or found the Militia company commanded by his uncle, Capt. Gilbrath Falls." He also had been a private in a regiment commanded by Col. James Rutherford in the North Carolina line, and in 1781 volunteered as a private in Captain Nelson's company.

James Neill, Captain William's son, was married to Hannah Clayton, daughter of George and Sarah Lambert Clayton.[39] Hannah was proud of her family's residency on the east coast since 1635, eleven years after Virginia had become a Royal Colony. Her grandfather was John Lambert, a plantation owner in the Catawba River Valley. From her mother, Sarah and her two sisters Elizabeth and Hannah had each inherited a Bible and shared an estate consisting of 149.1.10 pounds, a plantation, and 100 acres in western New Jersey. They had been "committed for their education and bringing up to the care of the executors."[40] Sarah Lambert had married George Clayton in 1744, and for a time the couple lived in Mecklenburg, North Carolina.

George received 738 acres from his father and inherited additional acreage from him.[41]

"In a sick and low condition but thanks be to God being in perfect mind and memory," George Clayton wrote instructions for the disposition of his property. To each of his beloved daughters, Hannah included, he left five shillings.[42] His widow lived until the autumn of 1800, and through the terms of her will, she bequeathed "unto my son George Clayton one armed chaise. I leave to my son Lambert Clayton one pare (*sic*) stilyards.[43] I leave to my daughter Henrietta Davidson one spice mortar. I leave to my daughter Hannah Neill one coffey (*sic*) pot. I leave to my daughter Ann Cook one puter (*sic*) dish. I leave to my daughter Margaret Neill one set silver tea spoons.

"I leave to my grandson Lambert Oliphant one bed striped homespun tick with the furniture belonging to it. I leave to my grand daughters Ann and Betty Neill all my gees. I leave to my grand daughter Sarah Scott Neill one feathered bed and furniture, likewise five pounds in cash. I leave to my grand daughter Sarah Clayton one half dozen Delf plates."[44]

Sarah Clayton concentrated on the will she was preparing. Had she overlooked anyone? She had mentioned her sons George and Lambert. And her daughters—Rebecca, who had married Lambert Oliphant, and Henrietta, the wife of Davidson. Margaret was Mrs. Robert Neill, and Hannah was the wife of William James Neill.

2

BEGINNINGS

"In the beginning . . . ."
Genesis

James Neill, the third son of Capt. William Neill, exchanged wedding vows with Hannah Clayton in Rowan County, North Carolina. A son, George Clayton Neill, was born in 1783 and given a middle name to honor his maternal grandparents. Three years later, another son, William David, arrived.

George Clayton was six years of age and William three when a third son was delivered in the log cabin belonging to James and Hannah Neill.

"Hannah, it's another boy," Neill said as he held the newest member for his family and wife to see.

"James Clinton Neill," Hannah said, her voice barely more than a whisper. "James for his father, and Clinton for his Grandmother Polly Neill's family."

"James Clinton Neill it is," the father said, his voice filled with pride.

Two years later on June 30, 1790, the Neill household welcomed another son, John Lambert, and again the mother went to her family for a middle name—Lambert, honoring her own mother and her brother, Lambert. With regularity the family continued to increase—Andrew, Samuel, Mary, Jane, and Alexander.[1]

By the time Alexander arrived in 1800, the seventeen-year-old George Clayton was edging toward the rim of the nest, avidly watched as he did so by William. Alert to the eagerness George and William experienced but also sensitive to the apprehension his mother and father displayed, James Clinton Neill awaited his turn to go out on his own.

Like a great number of his fellow North Carolina veterans of the Revolutionary War, to whom grants of land were available,[2] James Neill tramped over the south central region of Tennessee. He found Duck River with red soil in the cedar area; on the south side of the river he admired the black soil—soil that would produce rich yields of corn, cotton, and potatoes. The rich grasses tickled the belly of his horse, and the vast forests of beech, gum, oak, hickory, and maple, promised a rich source for logs when the time came to build. His stripling sons would furnish labor for construction.[3]

Redbuds and dogwoods appealed to the romantic nature of James Neill; he thought they looked light and airy like ladies of his youth dressed in their pink-and-white cotillion gowns.

He found the canebrakes thick, almost inpenetrable, and challenging; to clear them would occupy him and his sons for many months to come.

He found some springs bubbling clear, refreshing water, and around them James Neill and his family set about raising a log cabin in 1807.[4] Later his brothers Alexander and Andrew erected homes not far away.[5]

Soon other settlers were hacking their way through the cane or traveling along the river banks to look over the area. John Reed opened a small farm not far from the springs. Neill welcomed the John Dysarts when the family located only a short distance away. James Neill and John Dysart had many memories to share—their role in the Revolutionary War, their part in the Indian War, and their experiences in the Maine Creek skirmish prior to King's Mountain Battle.[6] On West Rock Creek, Allen Leiper, a cane cutter, built a watermill. John Shaw soon brought his family from North Carolina, and Allen Leiper's brother, James, established a settlement on the headwaters of Rock Creek. When Benjamin Simmons from North Carolina arrived, he brought an eight-year-old slave boy with him. Throughout the area George McBride gained a reputation; if someone put a violin in his hands, feet around began stomping and heads began nodding.[7]

Known for a long time as Neill's Gap,[8] the area around the Neill holdings became Farmington, a village of farmers.[9]

Information on James Clinton Neill's years in Tennessee is scarce. It is possible, and highly probable, that he became a member of a Masonic Lodge, A.F. and A.M. while living here.

He married Margaret Harriet, whose maiden name escapes genealogists. It's possible that when the two families assembled to celebrate the union of James Clinton and Harriet, they invited neighbors to a barbecue, and it is just as possible that George McBride tucked a fiddle under his chin and another neighbor began "calling."

3

INDIANS

". . . in bitterness and in tears."
Andrew Jackson

August 1813. The 535 residents of Fort Mims, Alabama—white, Spanish, mixed bloods, soldiers and settlers—could smell the tenseness in the atmosphere, heavy as incense. On the surface, however, the swampland that had been fenced to enclose the large frame house of Samuel Mims was serene. A fresh supply of whisky had been carted in to the stockade the day before, and the men inside the fort had sampled it. Maj. Daniel Beasley and some of his volunteer officers studied their cards carefully, leisurely, and soldiers sprawled on the ground or participated in their own poker games. Young residents of the cantonment were more energetic; they danced.[1]

Major Beasley appeared relaxed. Erased from his mind were the messages Gen. Ferdinand Leigh Claiborne had submitted following an inspection of the fort. The general had instructed Beasley "to strengthen the pickets and to build one or two additional blockhouses,"[2] reminding him about the explosive potential of the region. He suggested that scouts frequently reconnoiter the surroundings and cautioned Beasley to keep the gates locked.[3]

On August 30, two black men reported they had seen a party of Indians, their faces smeared with war paint. Beasley ordered the men flogged for the announcement.[4]

Later that same day, Jim Cornells rode to the fort along the riverbank and as he approached, he observed a gathering of Indians. Jabbing spurs into his horse's sides, he rode within shouting distance of the fort and called a warning to Major Beasley.

The major shrugged. "He's just seen a herd of red cattle!"

Lighthearted Beasley returned, "That gang of red cattle'll give you a terrible kick before dark."

His back on the open gate, Beasley ordered Cornells arrested. The rider, however, again kicked his horse with his spurs and dashed toward Fort Pierce to warn residents that Indians in the area were on the move.

Beasley soon realized that, unfortunately, Cornells and the two blacks had been accurate in their reports. The realization hit when approximately 1,000 Creeks stood in the ravine approximately 400 yards from the open gate.[5] The major ordered volunteers to shut the gates, but first the men had to scoop away deposits of drifted sand. Members of the home militia and other soldiers scurried from card games to grab their rifles and man their posts. Women volunteered to help by loading guns and hauling pails of water from the well.[6]

At noon, Beasley tried to reach the gates, but fell when a dozen bullets lodged in his chest.[7] As he hit the ground, a swarm of Creeks poured into the fort. They captured a few half-breeds and some blacks; thirty-six persons managed to escape, and soon the fortress was ablaze. The Indians turned their backs on a pile of ashes and bodies.[8]

News of the Fort Mims massacre spread. Horrified, settlers along the Natchez settlements listened to accounts. Officials in Washington feared the British had an ally in the Creek warriors, and the Spanish governor and the British emissaries at Pensacola, who had furnished the Indians with weapons, rubbed their palms, satisfied with the results.[9]

News of the fort's fall rang throughout Tennessee like a clear recruiting call. Residents of the area, long aware of the Creek disturbances, had watched the prices climb on cargoes delivered to New Orleans. They questioned the possibility of a shortcut going to the Gulf through the port at Mobile. Although claimed by the United States as a result of the Louisiana Purchase, Mobile was occupied by Spain. Andrew Jackson, gaining public attention, declared the harbors and rivers of west Florida "indispensable to the prosperity" of the people of Tennessee,[10] and criticized the Indian raids on white settlements.

The Tennessee legislature called for 3,500 volunteers for a state militia that would be organized like two armies, one under Jackson and the East Tennessee force under John Cocke.[11] These Tennessee volunteers took to the field, many repeating the words they had heard Jackson utter, "Long shall they remember Fort Mims in bitterness and in tears." James C. Neill was among those recruits, enlisting as a private in Capt. William Dooley's company in Col. Thomas McCrory's regiment of militia. On October 4, 1813, he signed papers for a three-month enlistment, his name appearing on the papers as the recruiting officer pronounced it Nail. He agreed to payment of eight dollars a month and received an allowance for fourteen days of rations at thirteen cents per day when the roll was signed at Nashville. A note explaining that "non-commissioned officers, musicians, and privates travelled 212 miles in marching to place of musterin, and in returning from Fort Strother to residence, Columbia, Maury County," was printed on his service record.[12]

In 1816 Neill, then a resident of Bedford County, Tennessee, appointed John Taylor his lawful attorney "to demand, receive and receipt the paymaster of the United States at Nashville all the money due for a tour of duty for three months in the Creek Nation under the Command of Gen. Andrew Jackson and in Capt. Duly's (*sic*) company." Neill wrote the authorization in his own hand, branding it with the characteristic Napoleonic *N* in the word Nashville and in his own name.[13]

When the enlistment ended, Neill, like his ancestors in the American Revolutionary War, signed for another period of service as a private in Capt. John Chitwood's company of infantry in Col. Robert Steele's Regiment of Tennessee Militia. In Fayetteville, he drew a pay voucher for $18.40 for the two-month nine-day term beginning January 28, 1814. On April 6, he transferred to the artillery.[14]

He enlisted as a private in Capt. Joel Parrish Jr.'s company of Volunteer Artillerists on March 1, 1814, serving one month and eleven days and drawing a paycheck of $10.83. After an expedition against the Creek Indians, the company was discharged in Nashville on May 16, 1814.[15]

Residents of Mississippi and Georgia, like their brothers in Tennessee, also heard the bugle call, picked up enlistment pay from the drum head, and prepared to march against the Creeks.

On March 9, Jackson with 1,200 infantrymen and 800 cavalry left the Battle of Talladega, where 400 Creek warriors had been slain. Jackson buried 100 of his followers. After caring for the wounded, Jackson ordered his men to return to the depot on the Coosa River that he called Fort Strother. Supplies, however, had not arrived as he had anticipated, and some of his men who had enlisted for brief periods decided to return to their homes. For two months, Jackson remained inactive.[16]

Early in the new year, Jackson welcomed 800 recruits. Determined to give them little time for discontentment, Old Hickory left a small force at Fort Strother and sent supplies down the Coosa River to the mouth of Cedar Creek. He established a camp called Fort Williams, and with approximately 2,000 men began marching across the ridge separating the Coosa from the Tallapoosa. It was at a location across the neck of a peninsula that covered approximately 100 acres of marshland the Indians called Tohopeka, that the Creeks had erected a breastworks of logs.

General Jackson constructed his plans carefully. The Cholocco Litabixee—the horseshoe—had been well chosen by the Red Sticks,[17] for it was "adapted by nature for security is well guarded."[18] Jackson realized that it also was vulnerable. Warriors of the Hillabee, Ockfuske, Oakchoie, Eugaulahatche, New-Yauca, Hickory Ground, and Fish Pond had concentrated into the huts of the village. They had secured hundreds of canoes to the low, swampy banks.

Jackson's plan was to send John Coffee, a native of Virginia who had located in Tennessee sixteen years earlier,[19] with his troops augmented by friendly Indians to cut off the possible retreat of the Red Sticks. As instructed, Coffee and his men forded the river two miles below the log breastworks that jutted five to eight feet out of the water.[20] As a signal that he had taken his position, Coffee and his men set fire to some of the houses.

As soon as the smoke began curling upward, Jackson marched the remainder of his force toward the breastworks and only eighty yards from the Indian concentration planted pieces of artillery.[21] At midmorning Coffee's men moved canoes across the river to where troops boarded them. Jackson's men opened a brisk fire. Whenever an enemy attempted to approach or even revealed himself, he was cut down by musket or rifle fire.

By noon, a company of spies and some of the friendly Indians under Col. Richard Brown crossed in canoes and ignited a few of the Indian buildings. They began firing on the Red Sticks manning the breastworks.[22]

Muzzle-to-muzzle combat ensued, and by nightfall 557 Red Sticks were dead.[23] Jackson and his troops were mourning the loss of thirty-two comrades and bandaging ninety-nine wounded.[24] Among the injured was Sam Houston, a gangling youth who had attempted to scale the logs while "arrows, and spears, and balls were flying, swords and tomahawks gleaming in the sun."[25]

In midafternoon, Jackson gave the Red Sticks a chance to surrender, but they were convinced that by some twist of fate victory would be theirs. Jackson ordered his men to continue pouring volleys of fire into the village.

The battle ended. Andrew Jackson, "standing . . . as high as any man in America," returned home to prepare for an hour on the national political stage.

Sam Houston, never fully recovering from his wounds, also faced a new role—to later find in Texas a new theatre in which to star. In vaulting a barricade at Horseshoe Bend, he had received an arrow deep in his thigh. He called for an aid to assist in removing the barb. As blood gushed down his leg, two rifle balls later struck him in the right arm and shoulder, and he fell. One surgeon removed a ball near the shoulder, and a second surgeon ruled it would be useless to torture the man by attempting to remove the second ball. Houston was left on the wet ground, given up for dead.[26]

In 1841 Houston's part in Horseshoe Bend became an

issue when he was a candidate for president of the Republic of Texas. Colonel Neill's account of the Raven "bleating like a young cub" was twisted in the political mill.

Like Houston, Neill found a new theatre in Texas. Although his service papers reflect no injury, the story circulated in Texas that Neill arrived in Austin's Colony bearing "the scars of wounds received in service under General Jackson" in the Battle of Horseshoe Bend.[27]

James Clinton Neill, on March 15, 1815, ended his enlistment period, which had begun on September 20, 1814. For 203 days Captain Neill of the Separate Battalion was entitled to three rations a day, a total of 609 rations at twenty cents per day, or $121.80. From that figure, however, $35.40 was deducted, and on July 9, 1815, Neill received $86.40 from Joseph Caliman, a district paymaster. He certified the account "accurate and just" and vowed he "did not draw rations in kind, or money in lue (*sic*) thereof from the United States for any part of the time."[28]

During this time, he had commanded the James C. Neill Company of the Battalion of Tennessee Militia Infantry, under the leadership of Maj. William Woodfolk. Neill signed the roll in Fayetteville to receive $40 per month, and for this service drew $268.[29]

At Neill's release in Fayetteville, Brig. Gen. John Coffee certified he had "performed a tour of duty of seven months in the service of the United States—that his good conduct, subordination, and valor, under the most trying hardships, entitle him to the gratitude of his country, and he is hereby honorably discharged. . . ."[30]

By 1820 Neill had moved from Tennessee to settle on a farm in Greene County, Alabama. Major Woodfolk, likewise, had sought a change. He was among a group of settlers who located in Cotton Grove,[31] and when Madison County was organized two years later, Woodfolk was a member of the first court.[32]

On March 20, 1820, Neill was commissioned a colonel in the Alabama Militia, commanding the 19th Regiment; he signed papers in December certifying the results of the November 18 election, but resigned his commission on June 18, 1824.

4

PUBLIC OFFICE

"The drought ... has indeed lessened our agricultural prospects...."
State of the State Address,
Alabama Assembly,
November 20, 1826.

The first Alabama legislature whittled a new county from Marengo and Tuscaloosa counties, which had been formed only the year before.[1] The new political division was named in honor of the Revolutionary War hero, Gen. Nathaniel Greene.[2] In the west central section of Alabama, the county is in the fork of the Tombigbee[3] and Black Warrior rivers; its northeast section is hilly, its southwest section undulating with only an occasional rise of land. Pine, oak, hickory, ash, and gum grow from its loamy soil, and along the river banks, poplar and other hardwoods thrive.[4]

Israel Pickens[5] of Greene County occupied the governor's office and in 1823 gained a second term after withstanding the challenge of Dr. Henry Chambers of Madison.[6] Residents of the young commonwealth began to express concern over the prices public lands had drawn in sales in Huntsville and St. Stephens in 1818 and 1819. Some unimproved land had sold for $60 and $70 an acre, one-half paid down with the remainder due in three annual payments. The purchasers now owed $12 million, and the federal government finally offered relief to save many residents from bankruptcy, but only after the Alabama General Assembly prepared a memorial for officials in Washington.[7]

The name Andrew Jackson continued to ring like a chime. Some Alabama residents recalled that the general had attended the land sale in Huntsville, and when he had bid for a tract between Tuscumbia and Florence, no one dared submit a competitive bid. He, therefore, had won the land for the minimum price, $2 per acre. Many Alabamans also remembered how solidly the state had supported Old Hickory in his campaign for the presidency;[8] all five electoral votes had been cast for the Tennessean and for John C. Calhoun as his vice-president.

In 1824 General Lafayette of France visited the capital of Alabama as guest of the state and of Governor Pickens. With true southern hospitality, Alabama citizens cheered the Frenchman as he made his way toward New Orleans.[9]

Neill became justice of the peace in Greene County, and after presiding over weddings of young persons in his community, he signed entries in the county wedding book, beginning each with his characteristic Napoleonic *N*. He wrote that the bride, Eilenor Riche, and groom, Martin Castleberry, were "both of age."[10] He performed the wedding of Joseph Huges (*sic*) and Martha Fox on August 9, 1826, and noted that the couple had the "consent of parents."[11] Joseph Auger and Martha Fox appeared before Neill on August 9, 1826, and were united in marriage with "consent of parents." It was August 26, however, before Neill made entry in the wedding book.[12] The couple Nathan Baker and Amanda Hutchins—having approval of their parents—were married by the justice of the peace on August 12.[13] Elisha T. Horn and Matilda Richardson exchanged vows on September 1, 1826, with Justice of the Peace Neill presiding.[14] Margaret Strait and Price Cuthbert, both of age and with parental consent, appeared before Neill on December 20, 1827.[15] James T. Crowley and Jane Knox were married by Neill on December 17, 1827.[16]

In 1825 Governor Pickens, upon completing his second term, relinquished the gubernatorial duties to John Murphy of Monroe, who had campaigned without opposition. While the Greene County resident was packing his personal effects to leave the statehouse, other Greene County men were unloading their valises. Julius Sims was back as representative after a term's respite. Zachary Merriwether, who had represented Greene from the county's beginning, was now in the senate, and two newcomers prepared to take their oaths as representatives—R. H. Warren[17] and James Clinton Neill.[18]

On December 9, 1825, a spokesman for the committee on divorce and alimony, which had been reviewing the proceedings of the circuit court of Tuscaloosa County in the case of *Will Bryant v. Rhody Bryant,* offered a bill approving the divorce.[19] Neill, a freshman legislator, listened attentively.

He also heard arguments for a bill authorizing Caesar Kennedy to erect a toll bridge, provisions of a bill seeking incorporation of the town of Summerville, and one seeking relief for James Frazier, former tax collector of Franklin. Neill heard sections of one act designed to prevent more effectually the trading of slaves, and one designed to reimburse county clerks the costs of printing advertisements for certain stray animals.

A joint session of both houses of the assembly listened to a report on the opening of several crates in the Cahawba[20] arsenal. After examining the cartridge boxes, straps, and arms in several crates, and determining that they had been used during the visit of General Lafayette, members approved an investigation of public arms belonging to the state.

On December 10, 1825, the committee on divorce and alimony perused the record and chancery jurisdiction notes in the case of *Nancy Gillespie v. Andrew S. Gillespie.* A bill approving the divorce was read for the first time.

Neill focused his attention on a proposal that would alter the boundaries between Madison and Jackson counties. The judiciary committee proposed a bill restricting officers from taking commissions on fees collected on executions. It passed on December 31, 1825. Neill, a member of the committee on military affairs, was especially alert throughout the discussions.[21]

The assembly focused attention on permanently locating

the seat of state government. James Delett,[22] a large man with a talent for public speaking, moved that the bill be referred to a select committee, but legislators rejected such a move. Neill voted with the majority. The group then approved to refer the bill to a committee of the whole house.

On motion of Thomas Coopwood, a bill instructed the military committee to inquire "into the expediency of revising, consolidating, and reducing into one, all the militia and patrol laws of the state."[23] The measure called for furnishing each captain and commissioned officer of higher ranks with a copy of the proposal.

Another item pertaining to the military, drafted by William B. Martin of Lauderdale,[24] instructed the judiciary committee to inquire into "the expediency of passing a law authorizing the qualified voters in each battallion (sic) in the several regiments of this state, severally, to elect two, or some other suitable number of commissioners of roads and revenue; and that said commissioners be householders, residents, in their respective battallions (sic), and over the age of twenty-five years." The proposal was rejected.[25]

The group authorized Isaac Jordan to emancipate a slave and listened to arguments for and against abolishing the office of county treasurer.

In December, Nicholas Davis[26] of Limestone County and Neill were added to the committee on divorce and alimony. Neill studied the man who received the assignment with him. Tall and robust with light hair and blue eyes,[27] Davis was an eloquent orator with a magnetism that swayed fellow legislators. He was practical and candid, and his Virginia-styled hospitality won friends readily. Neill heard that Davis was deeply interested in horse racing.[28]

The legislature listened to proposals to open a public road over Sturtevant's Creek in Butler County, extending the thoroughfare to Black's Bluff in Wilcox County.[29]

Neill introduced few resolutions his freshman year. He did present a petition for Benjamin Jones, asking for "privileges of a citizen,"[30] and introduced a bill entitled "an act more effectually to prevent Sabbath breaking"[31] and a petition of "sundry inhabitants" of Greene County who asked passage of a law allowing them to lease the 16th section.[32]

The Alabama House began its eighth annual session in Tuscaloosa on Monday, November 20, 1826. Julius R. Sims, James C. Neill, and Matthew F. Raney,[33] representatives of Greene County, were certified to take their seats.

During the opening session, James I. Thornton, secretary of state, delivered a note to the speaker's chair then withdrew from the room. The message, a state of the state, was read to the legislature:

> During the past season, although we have not been exempt from disease, in particular places, we have no where suffered its most violent and fatal influences.
>
> Neither famine, pestilence, or the sword are permitted to ravage our land. We enjoy the bounty of the seasons, the rich fruits of the earth, domestic comfort, and public harmony. The drought which prevailed in many places in this state, in common with our sister states adjacent, has indeed lessened our agricultural prospects, but has not deprived us of the essential recourse of bread. If we have not abundance, we are blessed with plenty, and should the begnignant Disperser of all good gifts see proper, only to give us food and raiment, we ought to learn with pious submission to be therewith content.

Turning to education, the governor mentioned, "No people can rise to the highest standard of moral and civil refinement, without the enlarging and correcting effects of suitable education." He continued:

> Every consideration urges the propriety of enlightening the minds, and improving the morals of the whole body of the people . . . . The liberal policy of the General Government has provided us a munificent resource, for the establishment of an Institution to perfect the education commenced at the primary seminaries. The most judicious application should be made of the fund thus committed to us for the establishment of a State University, providing, by a safe and just economy, for the greatest effect which such an amount can be made to produce.

Members of the legislature listened carefully as the reading continued. "It will be for your wisdom to determine whether the moment may not have arrived, when efficient operations ought to be commenced; the institution to be located, and preparations made for the erection of the edifices." The message went on, "It will be for your wisdom also to devise means of encouragement for primary seminaries. There must be nurseries to supply the literary vineyards . . . ."

Legislators were aware of a change in subject matter, for there was a long pause before the reading continued. "The means necessary for the defense of the state will always engage the attention of the representatives of the people who have confided their safety to the mass of the population armed and disciplined." Neill found his interest mounting suddenly. "It is obviously essential, under such a system that arms should be provided, and the attainment of discipline secured. Such is the present situation and habits of the people, that we are in less danger of not having arms, in any emergency, than of failing to have the discipline which alone can give efficiently to arms."

Neill quickly asked himself if the governor were easing into a condemnation of the militia, a special interest Neill long had felt.

In a discussion during the 1819 constitutional convention, assembled in Huntsville, Alabama—prior to Alabama's becoming a state—the question of a militia had been raised. Members of the session felt that the presence of Indians "made effective defensive measures necessary," and that it was "the duty of the assembly to provide for the raising and training of an effective militia." As a result, "all able-bodied men were made subject to militia duty," although those who "held conscientious scruples against bearing arms" were eligible for exemption by paying for a substitute. The lawmakers agreed that the organization of a militia should be left under complete control of the assembly, which "within certain limits," would provide the "manner of electing or appointing the officers."[34]

The distribution of colors or standards to each militia company or regiment, would no doubt have a beneficial tendency. This measure, indeed, would coincide with the most natural expectation. If the state requires its citizens to assume the character and discharge the duties of soldiers, shall they not be furnished with standards under which to assemble? The distribution among the officers, of the militia laws, which you have already directed, the rules and articles of war, and connected with the whole, a plain and simple director to perform the most necessary elementary evolutions, which would be attempted with great advantage. Perhaps the small progress which the militia make in military knowledge everywhere is principally owing to the circumstances that the officers commanding them are not expert in their duty, and are therefore averse before their friends and neighbors, to make blunders in teaching to others what they do not themselves perfectly understand. Hence, very little is attempted to be taught and still less acquired. It will be worthy of your consideration whether it be or not be expedient to provide in instructing the officers whose duty it is to impart instruction to others.

We ought not only to preserve, but to incite, among our citizens the moral sentiment, that they all are and ought to be soldiers in their country defense.

With enthusiasm, Neill stood and joined his associates in applause.

In the last session, the body had authorized a digest of the militia laws. General Farrar had attended to the "duty with alacrity and promptitude," but difficulties in printing had brought delays in distribution. The governor promised a copy of the digest soon would be available for inspection.

The governor's message then focused on opening Muscle Shoals "to admit the more convenient transportation of a large portion of our produce to New Orleans, and the cutting of a canal, so as to convey, as our interest may direct, the same produce to the waters of Mobile Bay." Legislators, as "the guardians of the resources of the State," were urged to carry through with these projects.[35] He mentioned that the Tennessee offered "good stream navigation from the upper end of the shoals to the mouth of the Hiwasse" and could be connected by a canal with the waters of the Coosa.

The committee remembered that the governor had recommended "sparing the three per cent fund appropriated to the improvement of roads and navigation," until it could accumulate an annual interest of ten thousand dollars.

The House met Wednesday, November 22, 1826, and in implementing the body's organization, a committee on inland navigation was appointed to study the Muscle Shoals issue. Named were William Fluker of Morengo, Henry S. Rhodes of Morgan, Matthew F. Raney of Greene, Zaddock M'Vay of Lawrence, Joseph Powell of Limestone, John Martin of Jefferson, John Massey of St. Clair, and Neill.[36]

Neill borrowed $500 from William M. Lewis and Dennis Hopkins on March 8, 1827, and afterward signed a promissory note. "Desireous and willing to secure the note," Neill turned over to Lewis, who was instructed to pay Hopkins, "one rone mare, 1 bay horse, one rone mare and one bay colt one year old, 4 cows and 4 calves, one year old steer, two two year old steers, one 2 year heiffer and 2 heiffers one year old each, one barren cow all the stock marked with a crop off of the left ear" and his "farming utensils together with all my crop of cotton & corn now growing in the ground." It was agreed that Neill would remain "in peaceable possession" of the property until December 1. Parties understood that if Hopkins were not paid at the end of four months, Lewis would sell the holdings "to the highest bidder for ready money." The sale could be scheduled in "some public place in Springfield" after public notices had been circulated ten days. The document was signed by Frances T. Scott and John C. Roden, justices of the peace.[37]

On March 7, 1830, Neill was called upon with Joseph Sanderford and Benjamin Carpenter to witness as Hardy Hopkins signed his will. Hopkins provided for his wife Mary, his three children, Joseph Carpenter Hopkins, Archiband Henderson Hopkins, and Elizabeth Hopkins, and for the child his wife was then "pregnant with." To Mary, Hopkins bequeathed "her Negro woman named Lile," plus his "stock of horses, cattle, hogs, and household and kitchen furniture."[38]

Signs of a severe drought began settling over the western edge of Alabama. The moisture from dew and rain that normally pulled fragrance from the wild honeysuckle and pushed crops toward the sun failed to appear. Neill tilled the soil, preparing it for cotton and corn; as he did so, he frequently looked to the sky for clouds that might promise moisture. None appeared. The skies remained blue and clear.

Hoping again to see his name on a government payroll to alleviate his dwindling estate, Neill announced as candidate for sheriff. An advertisement in the Greene County *Gazette* shows him in a five-man race with B. F. Beazley, J. White, J. A. Beal, and M. F. Raney, his associate from the Alabama Legislature.[39]

Checking the *Gazette*, published in Erie, for news of the area that might help in campaigning, Neill was intrigued by a brief item concerning Texas. A letter printed in the Nashville *Republican* and originating in Stephen F. Austin's colony on the Rio Brazos de Dios, February 25, commented on the "highly prospering condition" of Texas.

"Prospering!" Neill no doubt focused on the word. He continued to read that "emigration in the last three months has been greater than in any three years before." Many settlers were arriving by the land route, and three or four vessels were docking in Texas ports at the same time, "laden with passengers."[40] So Texas was prospering and developing while Greene County was drying up with a drought.

Of interest to Neill as a Mason was the notice inserted by Theodore Noel, secretary pro tem, that Lafayette Lodge No. 26[41] would celebrate an anniversary on June 24 with an address by John Gayle.[42] If circumstances had been different, Neill would have had time to attend the meeting.

Alabama citizens eagerly prepared to celebrate the anniversary of American independence. July the Fourth, Neill knew from experience, was a day for candidates to present themselves to voters. Jefferson C. McAlpin would give an address at Erie.[43] Citizens would spend Sunday preparing the brush arbor, and on Monday they would barbecue a beef. At night he could watch the couples dance as he recovered the strength from campaigning. More than 300 persons would attend, he anticipated.[44]

During the final days of the campaign, Neill had little time to read his newspaper, but he observed that editor J. J. Cribbs had run another brief item on Texas. He would read it carefully when the election was over.[45]

A disheartened Neill learned the election results. He had finished collecting only 139 votes in the county. Except for Springfield and Canton, each of which had awarded him thirty-five votes, Neill received only a smattering of ballots elsewhere. Results showed Beal, 491; Raney, 600; Beazley, 242. There was no count reported for White in the *Gazette*.[46] Raney won the run-off.

The election results crushed Neill's spirit just as the drought had dried his cash flow. He read in the *Gazette*:

> Our country at present exhibits a discouraging aspect. We have been visited by a long and scorching drought which has disappointed the hopes of the husbandman and with him, the hopes of the community.

The article mentioned that the drought was felt throughout the state and farmers could hope for no more than "half a crop of corn."[47]

Again, Neill's attention fell on a story about Texas. Perhaps the Lone Star was his star of hope![48]

On November 15, 1830, "J.C. Neill & Wife for the sum of one hundred dollars & fifty cents" deeded eighty acres of land "in the district of lands sold at Tuscaloosa" to Moses Lewis.[49] Joseph Ricks and John W. Jenings attested that "James C. Neill & Harriet, consort" personally appeared before them to sign the deed and that "Harriet privately examined apart from her husband," acknowledged she had signed the deed.[50]

The couple prepared a list of supplies required for a move to Texas as they read the *Gazette*. T.H. Herndon advertised that his warehouse contained "7,000 pounds of Tennessee bacon in prime order" as well as sugar and coffee.[51] John Meeks of Tuscaloosa, was making stoneware jugs, jars, and other "crockery items."[52]

5

ON TO TEXAS

". . . The best men, the best kind of settlers."
Stephen F. Austin

James Clinton Neill arrived in Texas as part of a flood of immigrants. No doubt, he was one of the contacts Austin had made with residents of Alabama, those people the empresario regarded as men of comfortable circumstances. In March 1830, Austin wrote his brother-in-law, "You have no idea at all of this country, not the great emigration that is daily coming to it, nor of the character of the emigrants. We are getting the best men, the best kind of settlers. . . ."[1]

The Texas landscape was lead colored when Neill arrived in February 1831, and the mood of Texans matched their skies. From Stephen F. Austin in San Felipe, Neill learned that John Davis Bradburn,[2] a renegade Ketuckian, had arrived on upper Galveston Bay with troops and plans to construct a fort and customs house.[3]

Appointed by Gov. José María Viesca, Juan Francisco Madero[4] had established a town council at Liberty, where he began recording titles. Texians chatted that the commissioner seemed to violate the national decree of April 6, 1830, which had restricted Anglo-American settlers. Bradburn arrested Madero and placed him under martial law, and Texians grew tense.

In San Felipe to learn more about his claims to a headright,

Neill studied Austin's secretary, Samuel May Williams, who resembled the empresario in many ways. Both were short and frail. Austin had dark wavy hair and hazel eyes; Williams looked at Neill with piercing blue eyes from under a head of reddish blond hair. Neill evaluated Austin as the type who would try to please everyone; he labeled Williams as brusque—the explosive type of individual who would alienate many of his fellow Texians.[5]

Neill learned that Williams once had turned over his duties in recording deeds to the ayuntamiento. He submitted neatly bound record books compiled from loose sheets, insisting that each page he had copied be checked against the original.[6] John G. Holtham[7] had worked as secretary of the ayuntamiento only a brief time before resigning, and officials again pressed Williams into service.

Waiting to deal with Austin and Williams, Neill realized he faced a new system of land measure. Settlers who called at San Felipe spoke of *varas*, and Neill soon learned that the *vara* was the chief unit of linear measurement, much like the English yard; it was divided into three feet or *tercios*. For longer distances, the Texians talked about *legua* or league, the equivalent of 5,000 varas or 177.1 acres. A *labor of land* was regarded as sufficient for one family to farm. A league, containing 25,000,000 square *varas*, or 4,428.4 English statute acres, was an impressive estate.

While in the ayuntamiento office, Neill heard one of the settlers discuss a *sitio de ganado minor*, a ranch for small stock such as sheep or goats. Another mentioned a *sitio de ganado major*, a ranch for cattle, a square league.[8]

Even after selecting his land, Neill was not convinced circumstances were idealistic in this Eden called Texas. He began completing the forms, listing his name and place of birth as North Carolina. The year of birth he recorded was 1780. He indicated that he had arrived in Texas with a wife, Harriet, thirty-four years of age, two sons, George Jefferson and Samuel Clinton, and a daughter, Mary Harriet.

Austin withheld consent for Neill to settle on a parcel of land he had chosen unless the colonist gave up a portion of his right to that location. Neill refused to do so.[9]

The political situation in Texas was clouded. In November 1831, Teran visited the fort on Galveston Bay and reinstated

George Fisher[10] to collect customs. Fisher ordered all vessels, including those already in port, to clear their papers with him at Anahuac. Two captains who had disposed of their cargoes and were loading at Brazoria for the return to New Orleans objected to the inconvenience such procedure would entail. Jeremiah Brown, captain of the *Sabine,* attempted to bribe officials. His schooner then ran past the garrison, exchanging cannon shots with the troops.[11]

As he reviewed the personal and political scene, Neill must have pondered his wisdom in leaving Alabama for Texas. The drought might have eased by this time.

Austin returned to the state capitol in Saltillo in 1832, leaving Williams to handle colonial affairs. Neill had received Austin's consent to make a selection in any part of the colony, and he did so. When the survey was completed, he submitted the field notes to Williams.

Details of what happened are not recorded, but Williams and Neill disagreed. Years later, Neill recorded that "Samuel M. Williams, who with abusive language said to your petitioner that he should never have a foot of land in the colony." Neill immediately went to the Colorado River, where he located a headright.[12] It was November 1832, before Neill received title to a league in Austin's Fourth Colony. Two-thirds of the holdings was situated in Washington County and one-third in Lee.[13]

6

RUMBLINGS OF REVOLUTION

*"As honorable men seeking our individual welfare
and happiness..."*

With eagerness marked by a slight spasm in the stomach and a touch of tension, James Clinton Neill kicked his boot heel into the mount as he approached San Felipe. His riding partner, William Robinson, was relieved that Neill wasn't one to dally. He was happy for a respite from surveying chores and, were he pressured for the truth, the widower would call the business ahead a peaceful break from the ten dependents in his home.[1] He welcomed the opportunity to revisit his former home to see what changes had come to the community.

As the two men neared the cluster of buildings on the old Atascosito Crossing of the Brazos River, Neill was aware of the excitement that seemed to grow with each yard of prairie land he crossed; ahead lay the site Austin had chosen as headquarters of his colony. Ahead for Neill lay responsibility. His two terms in the Alabama House of Representatives flashed through his mind, and he recognized he was eager to use the mental powers in something as challenging as resolutions. Something more lasting than guessing whether a heifer had been covered or where the guinea hens had secreted their eggs. Clearing new land was back-breaking, repetitive, and he was like an old war horse, chomping at the bits to see action.

"Quite a village," Neill commented. "Tailor shop. A smithy. Even a newspaper plant."

Robinson shook his head. "And two hotels. I'd recommend we try Angelina Peyton's place."[2]

"Not a widow, is she?" Neill chided. From under his broad-brimmed hat, he looked obliquely at his associate.

Again, Robinson shook his head before speaking. "Nope. Not a widow, but an artist of a cook."

As they were signing the guest register in the San Felipe Inn, Neill and Robinson met Mrs. Peyton, who bustled around the inn like a bandmaster. Each chorus of hoofbeats from the San Felipe streets reminded her that only six months earlier in October 1832, a similar convention had assembled, and some of the delegates had taken room and board with her. She recalled the discussions that mixed with tobacco smoke and ale as the delegates weighed possible governmental reforms. Finally, delegates had resolved to seek an extension of tariff exemption for three years, to ask for more general immigration from the United States of the North, to seek the appointment of a commissioner responsible for issuing land titles in East Texas, to recommend that the government donate lands for the maintenance of schools, and to press for permission to organize a state government separate from Coahuila. Mrs. Peyton remembered that William H. Wharton[3] and Rafael Manchola[4] had been instructed to deliver the resolutions to Mexican officials.

That first convention had ended October 6, but somehow the resolutions it adopted never reached Mexican officials. For one thing, the district of San Antonio had neglected to send a delegate, and some of the men attending believed that such neglect might impress officials that only the Anglo-Americans were dissatisfied. Stephen F. Austin, who had presided over the convention, openly denounced a request for separate statehood as premature, arguing that Antonio Lopez de Santa Anna, to whom the Texians had pledged their support as president, had not yet taken over reins of federal government.

Six months passed. Red berries had fallen from the yaupons, and the leaves on the spikes of these shrubs were lined with tender yellow- and green-hued leaves. The prairies were oceans of bluebonnets with redcaps of Indian paintbrushes.

Again, delegates were riding into San Felipe for another convention. Some of the leaders expressed the hope they could shake this conclave into definite action, strengthening it where they recognized weaknesses in the earlier sessions. Some of the more impatient Texians pressed for this convention to open April 1, 1833, the very day on which Santa Anna would accept his vows as leader of Mexico. They would cover bets that the new leader would approve their request for separate statehood.

As Mrs. Peyton hurried to the kitchen, Neill and Robinson watched with interest the arrival of their fellow Viesca[5] representative. Still in his twenties, Leonard Waller Groce,[6] only recently returned to Texas from school in Augusta, Georgia. He was now looking after family interests.

When the sessions opened in the alcalde's offices, Neill realized there were two factions—the conservatives backing Stephen F. Austin and the war party supporting William H. Wharton—and he reckoned that while Austin's constitutional following was doomed, it had strength enough to prevent the radicals from carrying the convention over a deep precipice. His assessment proved accurate when the convention rejected Austin for the presidency, placing the gavel, instead, in the hands of Wharton.[7]

Even in April, a chill filled the alcalde's offices in a double log cabin behind Whiteside Hotel. The absence of chinking in the rough-hewn walls pulled the wind, whistling, into the room.

When it became clear that the question of slavery would be brought to the floor, Neill was surprised by the turn of events. A slave owner himself, with a plantation heritage, he judged a majority of delegates to be of southern stock. Naturally, he enjoyed watching the reactions of his fellow representative, Groce. The young man had recalled that not more than ten years earlier he had helped his father prepare for the move to Texas. Jared Groce had operated a plantation, Fort Groce, in Alabama until 1821, when he decided to relocate in Texas. He had called Leonard home from school to help organize the train that included fifty wagons, a number of slaves, cattle, and all the farming equipment necessary to convert grassland prairie into productive cotton fields. Entitled to eighty acres of land for each slave, the senior Groce had been granted ten *sitios*[8] by the Mexican government, and after settling in Texas, he avidly sought more.[9]

Neill recognized that Groce would confess slavery was his way of life, and so would other men in the convention hall.

From the floor, David Burnet reported that a vessel had docked in Galveston Bay. "Direct from the Island of Cuba, this vessel was laden with Negroes recently from the African coast," he said.

Burnet offered a resolution. "We do hold in utter abhorrence all participation, whether direct or indirect in the African Slave Trade; that we do concur in the general indignation which has been manifested throughout the civilized world against that inhuman and unprincipled traffic; and we do earnestly recommend to our constituents, the good people of Texas, that they will not only abstain from all concern in that abominable traffic, but that they will unite their efforts to prevent the evil from polluting our shores." [10]

The hall was hushed as the speaker continued, ". . . and will aid and sustain the civil authorities in detecting and punishing any similar attempt for the future."

Proponents of the resolution freely declared "the . . . shameful violation of law . . . was perpetrated by transient foreign adventurers."

One delegate, however, declared "that trade of any sort . . . with Cuba, which was a Spanish possession, was treason to Mexico." [11]

As a rest from political matters and a change from the scene of the deliberations, Neill and several of the delegates probably walked to the well on the town square.[12] Even during the walk, however, they talked about issues, and they agreed there would be little, if any, opposition to the resolution calling for repeal of the eleventh article of the decree of April 6, 1830, forbidding the further immigration of North Americans into Texas.

"The act's not just; it merely perpetuates a wild, savage state of the country," one said.[13]

"We'll need to modify the tariff laws if we're to encourage immigration, agriculture, and commerce," suggested another.

Almost unanimously the convention approved a constitution drafted by a committee headed by Sam Houston, the delegate from Nacogdoches. Serving with Houston were Robert M. Williamson, James Kerr, Oliver Jones, Luke Lessassier, and

Henry Smith.[14] The document had been composed by the committee, reported to the convention, discussed, amended in minor ways, and adopted.[15] It was similar to the document written in Massachusetts in 1780.[16]

Unquestionably Anglo-American in character, the document asked for a bicameral legislature.[17] Texas would be divided into eleven senatorial districts with one representative for each 100 votes. The executive branch would be composed of a governor, who must be at least twenty-seven years of age and a resident of the state for three years preceding the election. He would be eligible to serve "no more than four years in a given period of six years."[18]

A bill of rights, with twenty-seven articles, included the guarantee of trial by jury, the improvement of a mail system, and the establishment of free schools.[19]

A debate on a banking clause brought some of the widest rifts in the session. Branch T. Archer[20] favored the proposal; Sam Houston opposed it. The convention eventually declared that "no bank, no banking institution, or office of discount and deposit, or any other moneyed corporation or banking establishment should ever exist under the constitution," and nothing but gold, silver, and copper coin should be legal tender.[21]

Another committee, under the leadership of David G. Burnet, sat around the lamp deep into several evenings to draft a memorial to the Mexican Congress seeking separate statehood from Coahuila.

"After all, this is the specific and sole purpose of this convention, isn't it?" The delegate who presented the question appeared flippant.

His question, however, opened the way for other delegates to touch on suggestions of diplomacy.

"As a state of the federation, Texas would form an essential and integral portion of the body social of the Mexican nation," one mentioned, "consequently its union would be as binding and intimate . . .

"We're acting as faithful Mexican citizens who understand our duties and aspire to fulfill them . . . as honorable men seeking our individual welfare and happiness.

"But, there can be no harm in pointing out some of the deplorable situations of this country in regards to internal affairs . . . our suffering . . . and of those threatening."

Another jumped to his feet. "Certainly we can bring out the general and particular advantages that would result from the formation of a separate state."

Spotted cheers filled the hall.

He continued, "Whatever we do, we must make no charges or accusations against Coahuila for failure in its intentions . . . or for bad faith . . . in regard to us. On the contrary, we must attribute to it the merit of having desired to serve the interests of Texas in general." Again, the speaker observed the audience reaction before continuing. "But, we can point out the differences in climate, situation, products, occupations, character of inhabitants, and we can mention the distance which separates one people from another.[22]

"Don't forget to mention that the laws are printed in Spanish now, and that's a language practically unknown to many of us."

As the three Viesca delegates downed a glass in the tavern following the April 13 adjournment, they speculated on what lasting contributions might come from the convention before the conversation wheeled to personalities.

"Quite a galaxy here," one observed.

"You can say that again," another agreed. "Amazing, isn't it, how a frontier like this can have so much brain power, so much experience . . . ."

"And you might add such accord overall. Not too much dissention."

"Just look at the mental giants here. Take Branch Archer. He practiced medicine in Virginia. Served two terms in the House of Burgesses before coming here . . . ."[23]

"If you're talking about giants, Three-Legged Willie won't take a second to any man."

The three agreed that Robert McAlpin Williamson was a man to be reckoned with. Williamson was a teenager when illness crippled his right leg, but he had strapped on an artificial limb and proved that his physical handicap had not damaged his mental powers. Admitted to the bar when he was nineteen, he had practiced law in Georgia.

"He's not a bad journalist either. Least, I take the *Texas Gazette* to be as good a journal as you'll find published between here and the Carolinas." [24]

"You don't want to overlook Burnet. Old Dave showed his ability when he drew up the resolutions for separation." [25]

"Not only a mental giant but something of an adventurer too. You heard about his enlisting in Miranda's expedition to free Venezuela from Spain. First American to join the expedition."

Neill recounted what one of the delegates had told him about Burnet. "Burnet was riding on the banks of the Colorado one day when he fell from his horse. Comanches were waiting for him. Practically had their hands under his horse to cup up the body when it struck the ground. Anyway, these Indians nursed him back to health and after about two years released him. Just let him go."

"Nestor Clay[26] would have to be considered, too."

The associates looked surprised.

"He was another who had served his state in the legislature before moving here. Kentucky. And I'd say that experience was obvious. His speeches are incisive and clear, showing perfect familiarity with the condition of affairs and displaying the comprehensive views of a statesman."

The remarks recalled to Neill his own days in the legislature, and he wondered how many of his associates were aware he had been a lawmaker in Alabama.

"Remember, if you will," Neill said, "that Clay was on the committee to draft the constitution. Sam Houston was committee chairman."

"Clay's the gifted nephew of a gifted uncle," another said. "Educated. Brilliant. A perfect master of the English language, and adept at retort."

"But . . . ."

The speaker continued, "I've seen him sit and talk politics. . . ."

"When he couldn't rise from his seat. So drunk."

"Well, you know the story they tell about him, don't you?"

Members of the conversation crew nodded.

"Someone said to him, 'Oh, you're drunk, Clay.' And he answered, 'Is that so?' The person assured him it was. Then Clay said, 'Well, then are you not a fool to be arguing with a drunk man?'" [27]

"While we're talking about giants, we cannot overlook Houston," Robinson spoke.

"Ink isn't dry on his citizenship papers yet.[28] I've known him in Tennessee and Alabama, and I'd say we won't be able to forget him." His friends were not sure how Neill meant his statement.

By April 13 delegates had finished their works. Neill, realizing that his cattle and crops needed him, galloped away from San Felipe. No doubt during the saddle trip home, he mulled over the actions, puzzled what accomplishments would result from the deliberations, and reflected on personalities.

A committee of three commissioners, Stephen F. Austin, James B. Miller, and Don Erasmo Seguin, had been instructed to carry the proposals of the convention to the Mexican Congress. An outbreak of cholera in San Felipe prevented Dr. Miller from accepting the assignment. Don Seguin flatly rejected the commission. Austin, alone, set out to deliver the resolutions which never had received his enthusiastic endorsement. Nevertheless, the frail, lone figure turned toward Mexico City early in May 1833.[29]

7

ACQUIRING LAND

". . . to settle and cultivate . . . ."
James C. Neill
June 1, 1835

Benjamin Rush Milam had his thick brows set. As agent for Arthur Goodall Wavell, he was determined to make a success of the colony the two planned to establish along the Red River. Milam assured the English investor that the colony would appeal to natives of Ireland, Scotland, and England who would direct their interests in agriculture to "culture of articles little known in Great Britain."[1] Reports labeled the soil of the colony "superior to any on the face of the earth," capable of yielding "products most valuable in both American and European markets." There were occasional fevers, true, and the rivers did rush from their banks during certain seasons.[2]

Wavell, who claimed to have recommended Ben Milam for Mexican citizenship and to have provided him with a horse and funds, insisted he return to Texas and tackle administrative work on the colony.[3]

Milam had completed the surveys on the project when the Mexican government issued the April 6, 1830, decree halting immigration from the United States.[4] Another problem grew over the question of authority along the Arkansas frontier; a committee was appointed to determine the boundary line of Arkansas and Texas.[5]

Navigation of the Red River—the artery that fed the

colony—also puckered Milam's brows. Rafts in the upper part clogged the stream, making navigation impossible, but Milam resolved to clear the log obstructions so that a steamboat could call on settlements along the water. He bought a $2,100 steamboat, the *Alps,* and was able to pilot it through the Red River.[6]

At the same time he was working on Wavell's colony, Milam, a man with irons in a number of fires, faced the problem of settling the land he had been granted on January 12, 1826—that fertile valley between the Colorado and Guadalupe rivers. Under the terms of a contract with the Mexican government, he agreed to settle 300 families on this green strip within a period of six years.

On November 26, 1832, James C. Neill applied for title to one league of land on Yegua Creek, the property joining C. R. Stephens' plantation.[7] Although Milam colony officials delayed in delivering the title, Neill and his family settled on the property and began clearing the brush. Two years earlier, Neill's son, George Jefferson Neill, had received one-third league from the colony commissioners.[8]

When the ayuntamiento for the city of Mina assembled on August 18, 1834, with R. M. Coleman presiding, members included Joseph Rogers,[9] Jessie C. Tannahill,[10] and James Smith.[11] An important item of business was recommending persons for the four judgeships of Mina. The ayuntamiento named James C. Neill, Andrew Rabb,[12] Samuel Wolfenbarger,[13] and Coleman.

Neill was beginning to make friends in the region, and they, hearing stories of his part in the Battle of Horseshoe Bend, held the man in high esteem. A neighbor, John Holland Jenkins, wrote that Neill received a "hearty welcome in our midst."[14]

On August 19, 1834, the ayuntamiento passed a resolution that any citizen of the community was entitled to a twelve-acre lot and two small lots in town at the present minimum price. The owner would be required "to improve and cultivate" such property and should make his selection by the third Monday in September. The ayuntamiento also provided that any person holding more than two small lots be required to erect a building worth at least $300 on each, construction on such buildings to be completed within a year of the date of the deed.[15]

Neill submitted a petition to the ayuntamiento "praying to be allowed to enter lots in the Town of Mina and at the present minimum price." Minutes show that "after mature deliberation on the subject," officials agreed that he was entitled to the building lots and a twelve-acre farm tract provided he became a citizen of Mina within a reasonable time.[16] In the same session, officials approved Thomas Henny's request for property on which to erect a grist mill, provided he have the mill in operation within a year.[17]

The ayuntamiento also debated relocating the public square, agreeing unanimously to make the move "to a more eligible site." Members agreed, therefore, on Main Street as commons for the town.[18]

Although some settlers like Neill moved into the Milam Colony, the area was not as accessible as other regions in Texas, and the empresario recruited only fifty-two families to claim land, and these settlers did not receive titles until 1835.

Like his neighbors, Neill fretted over failure to receive documentation giving him claim to the property. Finally, Robert M. Williamson established an independent law office in San Felipe, and Ben Milam asked Williamson to serve as land agent for the colony.

Williamson—aristocratic, poised, and refined—took up the matter of deeds with the Supreme Government of the State of Coahuila and Texas. Dressed in a coonskin cap with coontails flapping, he asked that settlers receive possession of their lands. The government answered that "the contract celebrated between the government of the state and the Empresario Benjamin R. Milam, expired by its own limitation on the 25th day of January 1832."[19] The government, therefore, did not recognize the people in the colony as belonging to it. Talbot Chambers, living in the vicinity of San Felipe de Austin, had been appointed "to put the same families in possession of their lands in conformity with the sixteen articles of the said law of March 24, 1825."[20]

A copy of the title in the Bastrop County courthouse shows that Neill was introduced by R. M. Williamson, acting as agent.

After Neill had agreed to settle in the colony on the Colorado River, he bound himself "to settle and cultivate" and obligated himself to erect permanent structures. The 4,428 acres were "measured by surveyor Bartlett Sims"[21] and described as "above the mouth of Cedar Creek on the west side of the Colorado River, then up the river with the meanders." The league was staked, identifying points including an ash twelve inches in diameter, a box elder nine inches in diameter with an *N* notched in the trunk, and mesquites measuring eighteen inches and fifteen inches in diameter. Neill signed the agreement on June 1, 1835.

Williamson brushed back his long, black, wavy hair before affixing his signature, then addressed the commissioners. "I say to you that James C. Neill is a colonist introduced by me as the agent of the Empresario Benjamin R. Milam and that he is a man of family . . . ."[22]

Uneasiness like fog blanketed the western fringe of the republic. Clearly, the wild tribes of Indians felt hostile toward the white settlers residing along the Colorado River. The Caddo leader, Canoma, was employed by the white people residing at the Falls of the Brazos to travel among the wild tribes to recover two white children and at the same time plant and nurture the idea of maintaining peace among the Indians and settlers.

Leaving two of his children as hostages, Canoma rode among several tribes. He returned, however, to report the Indians he had visited were willing to keep peace with the settlers on the banks of the Brazos, but adamantly opposed entering friendly relations with settlers on the banks of the Colorado. Canoma announced that even at the time of visit a band of hostile Indians was preparing a foray in the direction of the Colorado settlements.

Settlers at the Falls dispatched Samuel McFall to Bastrop to warn residents of the danger, but before the rider reached the new village, tragedy had struck.[23] A trader, Amos Alexander, and his two sons were guiding their animals, tugging at a loaded wagon, through Goacher's Trace[24] when they were ambushed. Settlers discovered the bodies of the three wagoners several days later. Upon learning of the incident, Edward Burleson and a squadron of men buried the victims and began combing the territory to determine the strength of the raiding party, the direction members had taken, and the identity of the group.

With all signs indicating that the raiding party was small and without mounts, the Burleson squad followed the trail for approximately 100 miles. Eventually, however, signs faded, and posse members puzzled over what to do.

Several Burleson men volunteered to scout the area. During the hunt, John Bate Berry[25] came upon a single Caddo he immediately hauled before his leader. The Caddo informed Burleson that members of his tribe were camping in the region.

"Show us where they are," commanded Burleson. Hastily, the leader and men mounted to follow the Indian, who directed them to Canoma's camp.

Alerted by the approach of men and mounts, the Caddo Indians broke camp and took refuge in the woods. So intent on escaping, they neglected to untie their horses. Burleson's men examined the animals and concluded that because they were so well shod and because they were so neatly groomed, they belonged to settlers. The Burleson men found evidence that the Indians had been involved in the assault on the Alexander family.

Burleson interrogated the leader, a glass-eyed Caddo called Canoma, who handed him a sheet of paper certifying that he had been employed by white settlers to ride among the Indians urging them to make treaties.[26] He begged Burleson to ride with him to the Falls, only thirty miles away, where settlers would vouch for him. Burleson was inclined to grant the request, but his men doubted the Indian's story.

Canoma related that shortly after McFall was sent with his warning, some settlers at the Falls employed him to recover horses that had been stolen from them. The Caddo set out with his wife and son and a statement that he was working for the settlers. He rounded up the animals on the Three Forks of Little River but was in no rush to return to the Falls. Leisurely, he had stopped to hunt when the Burleson men had ridden into his camp.[27]

Burleson's men voted to kill the captives. Canoma and his son were tied to trees and shot.[28] The squaw was spared to return to her people; she did so hastily, spreading the word of her husband's death. Choctaw Tom, the principal man in the Caddo band, predicted that all Indians soon would make war on the Colorado settlements.

Robert M. Coleman[29] and some of his associates volunteered to kill the captives. They scalped the Caddo men. The skin was peeled from the back of one Indian and made into a razor strop.

Burleson, however, continued to brood over the fate of Canoma.

Major Coleman soon raised a squadron of eighteen men to raid a village of Waco Indians on the Navasota River. He planned carefully, but barking dogs alerted the Indians before the attack. Fierce fighting ensued as the white settlers struggled against an entire tribe.[30] J. W. Wilbarger, in *Indian Depredations in Texas,* indicated that Coleman and his troops rode into a Keechi camp on the Navasota River. Although the Indians pretended to be friendly, "they were in fact most consumate thieves, and were constantly depredating upon them." Wilbarger says Coleman had authority to ride into the village and induce the Indians "to discontinue their theft." Alerted to Coleman's approach, the Indians fortified their camp by digging pits into which they could retreat.

Without waiting for a powwow with Coleman and his men, the Keechi jumped into their pits and opened fire on the white settlers, well exposed as they approached the camp on open ground.

After one of his men had been killed and three injured, Coleman ordered a retreat.[31] After falling back to Parker's Fort, he sent an express requesting recruits.

Growing concern over the Indian depredations motivated members of the Committee of Safety to meet in Mina on May 17, 1835. With Samuel Wolfenbarger in the chair and J. W. Bunton taking notes as secretary, they commented on anecdotes that fueled the growing apprehension, then discussed arrangements for protecting themselves and their families. Someone proposed sending recruits to help Coleman at Parker's Fort; the idea met with enthusiasm.[32] As companies were being formed by Robert M. Williamson and Captain Coheen elsewhere, Mina men organized under Dr. George W. Barnett.[33]

Neill, although only briefly established in the area and with much work to do about his plantation, remembered his role in the Battle of Horseshoe Bend. He was ready to ride. His appointment with axe and pine and cedar could wait; the grueling hours grubbing stumps to clear the land for cultivation and to provide logs for cabin building seemed not so pressing. Colonel Neill heard the bugle, and like a war-horse he chomped at the bits to ride with his neighbors.

Mina recruits, after electing Col. John H. Moore commander and James C. Neill adjutant, reined their horses to join Coleman.[34]

When the combined forces marched against the Waco village, they found it deserted. Corn—the shucks swelling in the July sun and the ears golden and plump when stripped—had been left unharvested, evidence of a hasty departure.

Coleman's troops followed the trail for at least a hundred miles until they approached a small encampment. The white settlers immediately began firing. Three Indians fell in battle, and half a dozen were captured. From them Coleman learned that the main Indian force was camped some distance away. Advisers suggested the white troops wait until morning before pursuing the enemy.

Coleman's men found the large camp as predicted. Cut stake ropes again suggested the Indians had left hurriedly.

The men scouted the country as far as the forks of the Trinity, then passed over the Brazos, still without encountering more than several Indians.[35]

Coleman called a conference, and his men agreed that because they and their mounts were nearing exhaustion, it would be well to head toward home.

Among the captives returning with the Coleman force were a squaw and a three-year-old child. Jenkins recalled that she was "not only bright, but very pretty." Naturally, the whites settlers—many of them fathers separated from their own daughters—paid attention and petted her.

One night the squaw, using a knife she had obtained in secret, killed the child and attempted to take her own life. She was near death when discovered the following morning. Oliver Buckman volunteered to kill the woman as a deed of mercy.

Jenkins recorded the incident: "Taking her to the water's edge, he drew a large hack knife, which he had made himself. As she gazed unflinchingly into his face, he severed with one stroke her head from her body, both of which rolled into the water beneath." [36]

Emotionally disturbed, the force continued homeward. Two participants pointed out two Indians "making for a timber," half a mile away. Some of Coleman's men dug their spurs into their mounts and went in pursuit. The braves outran the horses, reaching the thicket in time to hide in the yaupon brush.

Before long, one brave was located and shot.

Smith Hornsby soon caught sight of the second brave. He took aim, but missed. The Indian also fired, striking Hornsby in the shoulder. Hornsby struggled from the thicket, yelling, "Here's the Indian!"

William Magill, mistaking the white man for an Indian, fired and "tore the unfortunate man's arm literally into pieces."[37] A physician examined the wound and called for an amputation, but Hornsby rejected the idea, vowing he preferred death to life with only one arm. He remained in great pain a day or two before he died. The body was placed in the ground, the earth returned and packed, then "smoothed above the body until perfectly level, then a fire was kindled upon the spot and left burning." Such a custom, Jenkins wrote, was "to prevent Indians from digging up the bodies and taking their scalps." [38]

During this foray, Neill was accused of using a "barbarous method of sending destruction upon the Indians." He vaccinated one of the captive warriors with smallpox virus and released the Indian, believing he would transmit the disease to the tribe. "Nothing was ever heard as to the success or failure of this project," Jenkins commented.[39] Still puzzling is where Neill obtained the vaccine. A physician, James H. C. Miller,[40] was on the expedition, and Dr. George Barnett had organized the Mina men who made the Indian chase.

By midsummer, Neill and his companions were back in their homes, recovering from their days in the field and planning their schedule of autumn work on the farms. Whenever former associates of the Indian expedition got together, they no doubt talked about Dr. Miller, who upon returning from the raid had written that he believed Mexican authorities should arrest the chief agitators who were causing problems in Texas. The busybody, they declared, had been responsible for the arrest of Robert Williamson, William B. Travis, Samuel Williams, and F. W. Johnson.

"We will not give up any individual to the military authorities" came the answer from a public meeting at Columbia.[41]

Slapping their rifles, the associates vowed, "Men who fight Indians can also fight Mexicans!"[42]

8

GONZALES

"Come and Take It!"
Gonzales Flag
1835

Before summer passed, Texian emotions, like the weather, steamed. Throughout the country, colonists generally agreed on the need to elect delegates from each municipality to assemble in San Felipe in October. Lorenzo de Zavala, who had served as a member of the Mexican Congress and as governor of the state of Mexico, had bought a well-drained farm between Buffalo Bayou and Old River. Even before his family could join him in the new home, Zavala was attending public meetings to speak "against the imperialistic tendencies of Santa Anna."[1] In August he had been invited to address inhabitants of Harrisburg, but illness prevented his appearing in person. His letter reviewing current affairs in Texas was read before the gathering, and its contents published in *The Telegraph and Texas Register* on October 26, 1835.[2]

Columbia residents elected a fifteen-man committee to promote the calling of a consultation, and members of the Committee of Safety and Correspondence resolved they would "not give up any individual to the military authorities," but would use all means in their power "to secure peace and watch over our rights."

Within ten days, every municipality in Texas had learned of the action of the Columbia citizens, and Texians, in most instances, were relieved that the step toward "harmonious and organized opposition to the impending depotism" had been made.[3]

Elsewhere in Texas, a detachment of Mexican soldiers reopened the customs house at Anahuac,[4] but citizens of San Felipe resolved that the Anahuac troops be disarmed. In June 1835, William Barret Travis and twenty-five Texians besieged the garrison, and the Mexican leader agreed to march off Texas soil.[5]

Other disturbances were taking place in the colony Green DeWitt had established in the Guadalupe River valley. On January 7, 1831, DeWitt had petitioned military officials in San Antonio that if an artillery piece could be lent the colony, it would be of great help in defense against troublesome Indians. He agreed, of course, to return the cannon if necessary.[6] Two weeks later, Gen. Altonio Elosua, senior military commandant in Bexar, approved transfer of an artillery piece to Gonzales,[7] but it was March before DeWitt dispatched James Tumlinson[8] to Bexar to remove the cannon "if it is not too heavy for his wagon."[9] Tumlinson presented the Mexican Commandant a letter from DeWitt, loaded the artillery piece, and signed a receipt for "one bronze cannon, in order to take it to the villa of Gonzales." He dated the receipt March 10, 1831.[10]

When Col. Domingo de Ugartechea, military commandant of Coahuila and Texas in charge of the Bexar post, learned of the disturbances at Anahuac, he became concerned about the cannon in Gonzales. Fully aware that the artillery piece had little military value, he, nevertheless, decided to seek its return so there would be no arms within reach of the colonists that were now beginning to flex their muscles against Mexican authorities.[11] To Cpl. Casimiro De Leon, Ugartechea gave the orders: select five soldiers, ride to Gonzales, get the cannon, and return.

Corporal De Leon tried to obey, but Gonzales residents failed to cooperate. Were the Mexicans determined to disarm them, to leave them defenseless? The danger of Indian attacks had in no way subsided from the time the colonists had requested the weapon. For some residents, the appearance of the small band of Mexican soldiers struck fear; some deserted their homes to seek safety elsewhere; some crossed the river to be closer to the town of Gonzales; and some, concluding that Gonzales, midway between Bexar and San Felipe, would be the site of military activity, loaded their families and belongings into wagons and urged their teams to withdraw from the arena of possible conflict.

Alcalde Andrew Ponton, holding $1,000—probably belonging to the ayuntamiento—feared the Mexicans might demand the money.[12] He apologized to Corporal De Leon for delaying an answer to Ugartechea, but explained that he understood the cannon had been given in perpetuity so that the residents of the colony would be able to defend themselves against possible Indian raids. Too, he had received no orders from James B. Miller, *jefe-politico* of the Department of Brazos, to surrender the piece. Certainly a military man would understand the alcalde's reluctance to break a chain of command; Ponton would not turn over the cannon until he received orders from Miller.[13]

Corporal De Leon cooled his heels on the west side of the river. Ponton, meanwhile, composed a letter to the political chief:

> I received an order purporting to have come from you for a certain piece of Ordnance which is in this place. It happened that I was absent and so was the remainder of the Ayuntamamto when your dispatch arrived in Consequence the men who bore sd dispatch were necessarily detained until to day for an answer. This is a matter of delicasy for me nor do I know without farther information how to act this cannon was as I have always been informed given in perpetuity to this Town for its defense against the Indians. The dangers which existed at the time we received this cannon still exist and for the same purposes it is still needed here—our common enemy is still to be dreaded or purposed against.
>
> How or in what manner such arms are apportioned throughout the country I am as yet ignorant but am led to believe that dipposition of this nature should be permanent at least as long as the procuring cause exists. I must I hope be excused from delivering up the sd cannon until I have obtained more information on the subject—as well to act without precipitation—as to perform strictly and clearly my duty and I assure you, that if, after a mature deliberation on the subject, I find it to be my duty & in justice to your self—I obligate my self to comply with your demands—and will without delay send the cannon to you.

Ponton probably grinned as he penned the final line, "God & Liberty." Then he affixed his signature, Andrew Ponton, Alcalde.[14]

Meanwhile, the eighteen male citizens remaining in Gonzales organized under Capt. Albert Martin, a merchant. They wheeled the six-pounder to the peach orchard owned by George W. Davis,[15] dug into the rich loam, and planted the artillery piece, careful to level and spread the soil upon it.

Alcalde Ponton, who had been in office less than nine months, began preparing letters to neighboring communities. To the residents of Bastrop he wrote:

> I am directed by the Committee of Safety of Gonzales to address you for the purpose of procuring immediate assistance to repel an expected attack of the enemy . . . . A demand at the instance of Ugartechea, has been made for a piece of cannon, which has been in this town upwards of four years. This cannon is not needed in Bexar, for they have eighteen pieces, all unmounted, besides those which they have mounted; this piece was given us unconditionally, as we are informed, for the defense of the colony. From every circumstance and from information we are justified in believing that this demand is only made to get a pretext to make a sudden inroad and attack upon this colony for marauding and other purposes. . . .[16]

Bastrop leaders scanned the message. Gonzales neighbors needed help. Word circulated among those men who had made an Indian expedition in the summer, and soon a force assembled. Neill looked at the men riding with him under the leafless trees. Heading toward Gonzales were Robert M. Williamson, John H. Moore, Robert M. Coleman, and others. When they had asked Neill if he were willing to ride again, he was terse. "Never been discharged."

"Never been discharged?"

"Nope."

"Sure you have," Colonel Moore declared.

"Mean you haven't received your discharge papers yet?" one of the riders asked.

"Nope. Enlisted July 25 and haven't been discharged yet."

Colonel Moore looked at Neill to see if the man were serious or jesting. Once he determined Neill meant what he said, Moore explained that he had signed discharge papers which apparently had been lost.

A paper dated Houston, May 30, 1837, and signed by J. H. Moore, colonel, commander, corrected the mistake. This paper shows that Neill entered the service of Texas "on an Expedition against the Indians as adjutant of my Command on 25th July 1835 and served for the term of fifty-five days." The document, now in the Archives of the Texas State Library, replaces an original honorable discharge, "the other being lost or mislaid."

His associates, like Neill, had been quick to answer the call. Like him, they had required only minutes to sling a rifle over their shoulders, tie bedrolls behind their saddles, bid farewell to families, and mount their horses.

Once they reached Gonzales, they were joined with men from Old Caney, Brazoria, Columbia, and Victoria—men who had heeded the call from Ponton.[17]

A dozen Texians had slipped across the Guadalupe River on September 28 and attacked a small Mexican detachment under Corporal De Leon. Surprised and disarmed, the Mexicans surrendered and were rowed across the river to Gonzales. One soldier, who had been permitted to round up the Mexican horses, escaped. As he made his way toward San Antonio, he rode upon a detachment of 100 Mexicans under Lt. Francisco Castaneda. Colonel Ugartechea had sent the lieutenant to take the cannon. Do not ask for it; take it, the colonel had barked. If there is resistance, use force. Arrest the alcalde, if necessary. And if any colonists resist, punish them.

Approximately half a mile from Gonzales, Lieutenant Castaneda met a cart driver the Gonzales troops had released. He informed the officers that for two days Anglo-American reinforcements had been galloping into Gonzales. Some were DeWitt colonists returning to town after having safely lodged their families; others were from other communities answering the alcalde's call for assistance. Stressing that the army was growing steadily, the soldier estimated the force at 200. Additional men were anticipated later in the day.[18]

Alerted to the approach of Castaneda and his troops, the Texians had anchored the ferry and all boats on the east side of the Guadalupe and stationed guards to watch over them. These guards withheld their fire when they saw the Mexicans on the opposite bank. They listened as they heard orders shouted to make camp in a less exposed site.

Lieutenant Castaneda sent word he would like to confer with the alcalde but learned that Ponton, not in town, was anticipated to return the following day. Castaneda agreed to wait.

On September 30, two of Castaneda's soldiers swam across the river[19] carrying documents seeking an appointment with the alcalde, and although Ponton remained absent, the Mexican officer crossed the river at 4:00 P.M. Joseph C. Clements, regidor of the ayuntamiento, and three other Gonzales officials met with him. Clements assured the officer that the ayuntamiento had authorized him to deal with the matter.

Would he turn over the cannon?

Indeed, he would not. Clements read a prepared statement, "I cannot nor do I desire to deliver up the cannon.... The cannon is in the town, and only through force will we yield."

Castaneda insisted the officials had no right to retain the artillery piece, lent only as a favor.

An adamant Clements answered that until the ayuntamiento received orders from the *jefe-politico* at San Felipe—until instructions came from that source—he and members were responsible for the cannon and would not surrender it. "We are weak and few in number," he said, "nevertheless, we are contending for what we believe to be just principles."

Castaneda's mission had taken on a different complexion. When he had left San Antonio, he anticipated his assignment would be nothing more than a gallop to Gonzales, a brief encampment while he submitted his request, and then the return to Bexar with the six-pounder bounding behind his troops. Now he was uncertain. Personally, he had no way of estimating the number in the Texian camp, and word continued to sift in that recruitments were arriving steadily.

The Mexican tried a different approach. He castigated the ayuntamiento members for holding Corporal De Leon and his troops as prisoners. "An outrage," he termed the offense.

Clements resorted to his prepared statement. Residents of Gonzales were not willing to surrender the cannon.

Realizing he was getting nowhere with the stubborn Texians, Lieutenant Castaneda hastily reviewed the matter: his orders from Colonel Ugartechea were simple—return with the cannon. Castaneda, however, decided to remain a while. On September 30 he wrote his commander that he would move his troops upriver, hoping to find a place to ford the stream. He was not convinced that such a large force was stationed in the town; otherwise, how could it have remained hidden from him? He ordered a camp on DeWitt property approximately 300 yards from the bank of the river.[20]

While the Mexicans camped on the west side of the Guadalupe, the Texians on the east decided to organize. They elected John H. Moore commander and J. W. Wallace[21] lieutenant colonel. Several physicians in the group elected the Rev. W.P. Smith, M.D., their president, and he served as surgeon of the army and chaplain.

Several men hastily resurrected the cannon and joined Lt. Almeron Dickinson in servicing it.[22] Jacob Darst, Richard Chisholm, and John Sowell cleaned the weapon, scoured it, and mounted it on wooden trucks.[23] They caressed the weapon, they christened the flying artillery, and joyfully accepted contributions from Gonzales women—sad irons, skillets, kettles, even the spindle of a spinning wheel for ammunition. The older men and boys brought in plows and hoes.[24]

The Texians tugged the cannon to a high clearing, plainly visible from the opposite bank of the river. The site was the "prairie bluff below the town watering place just above where the timber bottom begins."[25] Here they erected a rude fortress and fluttering above it was "a breadth of white cotton cloth about six feet long, in the center of which was painted in black a picture of the old cannon, above it a lone star and beneath it the words, "COME AND TAKE IT."[26] The battle banner had been created by Evaline DeWitt and Cynthia Burns.[27]

The Texians sprawled beside the gun. Creed Taylor, a participant, said they realized that "loaded as it was, with slugs and scrap iron, when once fired at close range it would carry slaughter to the ranks of the enemy." Those persons not killed by it probably would be "scared off the field by the outburst."[28]

Colonel Moore called a council of war on October 1. He

and his staff officers declared it would be too much for each of the men to bear his own expense and ride the distance some had without engaging in a fight. "We will hoist the flag of liberty and attack the Mexicans in their encampment on tomorrow morning at daybreak," shouted the commander. Neill and other soldiers cheered the announcement.

Orders came for the army, taking up a line of march, to cross the river, and await orders on the west bank. Before midnight the Texians forded the stream to form a hollow square. Colonel Moore, Lieutenant Colonel Wallace, and Dr. Smith, remaining in the saddle on his favorite mount, addressed the crowd: "Fellow Soldiers: To cap the climax of a long catalogue of injuries and grievances attempted to be heaped upon us, the government of Mexico, in the person of Santa Anna, has sent an army to commence the disarming system. Give up the cannon, and we may surrender our small-arms also, and at once be the vassals of the most imbecile and unstable government upon the earth."

Texians mumbled their agreement.

"But will Texas give up the cannon?" Smith questioned.

"No," the soldiers answered as if in chorus. Some shook their heads for emphasis.

"Will she surrender her small arms?" Again a chorus sounded negatively.

"Every response is no, never! Never will she submit to a degradation of that character!"

Dr. Smith reminded Texians that their cause was "just, honorable, and glorious." They were, Smith said, like the soldiers of '76 fighting for their liberty. "Having waited several days for the Mexican Army to make an attack upon us, we have now determined to attack them on tomorrow morning at the dawn of the day. Some of us may fall, but if we do, let us be sure to fall with our faces towards the enemy. Your humble speaker has had the pleasure of examining the contemplated plan of attack. It is judiciously arranged; and to show you that he has had some opportunity of judging, he would simply say that he was with Generals Jackson, Carroll, and Coffee in the great battles at New Orleans in 1814-15."

Dr. Smith had ignited enthusiasm within the soldiers, now eager to face their Mexican opponents.

"Fellow soldiers, let us march silently, obey the commands, front to the enemy. Victory will be ours! We have passed the Rubicon, we have borne the insults and indignities of Mexico until forbearance has ceased to be a virtue. A resort to arms is our only alternative; we must fight and we will fight."

Like a cheerleader, Dr. Smith whipped the Texians into a frenzy. When he said, "March with bold hearts and steady steps to meet the enemy," he felt that the troops emotionally were prepared for battle. When he concluded with Patrick Henry's words to the Virginia House of Burgesses, "Give me liberty or give me death," Smith—himself emotionally spent—slumped in his saddle, observing the soldiers silently march into position.[29]

With the esteemed cannon in the center, unmounted men on each flank, the Texians prepared for battle. Fifty cavalrymen rode directly in front of the artillery piece, under the direction of Colonel Neill. A small group of foot soldiers acted as a rear guard. The group pressed forward.

A Mexican picket fired. Heavy fog shielded each side from the other, so firing was by sound. The opponents were three hundred yards apart when the fog lifted. Five A.M. October 2.

The Mexicans were on higher ground when the Texians opened fire.

Lieutenant Castaneda tightened his lines before agreeing to meet with Colonel Moore.

The two leaders advanced on the open prairie. The Mexican questioned why his detachment had been attacked. Colonel Moore suggested the reason was obvious: the Texians did not want to surrender their cannon, the colonists were resisting attempts to destroy the system of government set up by the Constitution of 1824. Colonel Moore assured his opponent that his forces were fighting to uphold that constitution.

Castaneda asserted that he was an officer of the republic bound by duty to obey the laws. He had no intention of killing colonists. He wanted only the cannon.

"Why not join us in the struggle to preserve the constitution?" Moore was earnest in his proposal.

Castaneda answered that he must obey orders.

Both leaders wheeled their horses to rejoin their troops.

Castaneda rode back convinced that the colonists had superior numbers. His best tactic would be to withdraw.

Texians, however, had other plans.

Colonel Moore looked at Neill, who was behind the cannon. Colonel Moore gave the signal, "Fire!" James Clinton Neill ignited the cannon.[30] It roared. The war for Texas independence was on. Texians charged, yelling as they advanced.

The Mexican line, like thin toast, crumbled, and the troops began retreating toward Bexar. The Texians did not pursue but returned to Gonzales. Jubilant and victorious, they were ready to see their war for independence carried to a successful conclusion. The fact that they had not lost a colonist in this battle convinced them they were ready for the conflict.[31]

9

FORWARD TO VICTORY

"We must go forward to victory...."
Stephen F. Austin
to Texas Army at Gonzales

Their only artillery was a brushed cannon.

Their arms were Bowie knives and long, single-barreled, muzzle-loading flintlocks. A few had pistols.[1] Some had created lances from files picked up on Gonzales and attached to hoe and rake handles or cane shoots harvested from the banks of the Guadalupe River.[2]

Their canteens were Spanish gourds—"a curious specimen of the gourd family having two round bowls, each holding near a quart, connected by a short neck, apparently designed for adjusting a strap about."[3]

Their mounts were varied—"a nimble Spanish pony . . . a half broken mustang . . . a sober methodical mule."[4]

Their bedrolls ranged from shaggy brown buffalo robes to "gainy checkered" counterpanes, from "bedquilts" to "store blankets."[5]

Their uniforms—anything but uniform—were described by Noah Smithwick, a participant, in this way:

> Buckskin breeches . . . and there was wide diversity even there, some being new and soft and yellow, while others, from long familiarity with rain and grease and dirt, had become hard and black and shiny. Some, from having passed through the

process of wetting and drying on the wearer while he sat on the ground or a chunk before the camp fire, with his knees elevated at an angle of eighty-five degrees, had assumed an advanced position at the knee, followed by a corresponding shortening of the lower front length, exposing shins as guiltless of socks as a— Kansas' Senator's. Boots being an unknown quality; some wore shoes and some moccasins. Here a broad sombrero overshadowed the military cap at its side; there a tall "beegum" rode familiarly beside a coonskin cap, with the tail hanging down behind, as all well regulated tails should do.[6]

These 250 Texians, ill equipped though they were, wanted to march on Bexar to chase the Mexican troops. They realized they had to weld their local bands into a Texas army. Molding bullets, repairing rifles, and fashioning lances left little time for military tactics, but they recognized the value of training. As Smithwick expressed it:

> . . . to learn to act in concert, the most important maneuver being to fire by platoons and fall back to reload. We had neither swords nor bayonets and few of us had pistols, and we knew that, if we all fired at once, the Mexican cavalry would be upon us with sword and lance before we could reload, and then our only resource would be to club our rifles, a very effective mode, however.[7]

Because so many individual groups supported their own military leaders when the troops attempted to elect officers, soldiers acknowledged that no compromise candidate could be selected. Some companies threatened to leave if their "favorite son" were not commissioned. Finally, the units agreed to invite Stephen F. Austin to Gonzales to head the army.[8] General Austin began reorganization as soon as he arrived. Very ill, probably with tuberculosis, he could barely remain in the saddle as he addressed the troops.

"Retreat is now impossible," Austin said. As soon as he had recovered from a coughing spasm, he continued. "We must go forward to victory or die the death of traitors."[9]

The Texian troops cheered.

William H. Jacks[10] also spoke, giving a "fervid appeal to

passion and chivalry" as opposed to Austin's "statesmanlike review of the situation."[11]

Ben Milam, fresh from a Mexican prison, joined the army in Gonzales. His clothes were in tatters, but he rifled through some captured stores and stuffed his six-foot frame into a pair of pantaloons at least six inches too short.[12]

Recruits began to pour in until Austin's command numbered approximately 600 men—eager to move toward Bexar. Then came the order. The old cannon flag fluttered over the artillery piece, now mounted on two wooden wheels and pulled by horses. Smithwick described the wheels as "traverse sections of trees with holes in the centers, into which were inserted wooden axles."[13] Soldiers took turns riding behind the cannon, and when the dray animals were slow, Texians prodded them with their lances until the horses broke into a trot. Neill, astride his Tennessee walker, kept watch over the cannon although Lt. Almeron Dickinson was in direct charge.

When the horses had been prodded too enthusiastically and were trotting, one of the wheels bumped over a rock, leaving a crack in the wood. The animals slowed their pace and halted, and Neill was quick to examine the damage. Soldiers poured water over the wheel, hoping to tighten the wood.

"Don't be too generous with that water," Neill warned. "Keep your own thirst in mind. Never know when we'll be able to fill our gourds."

Neill suggested using tallow on the wheel, but without success. The rent remained. Dickinson complained that a stronger, more substantial carriage had been needed all along.

Neill took another look at the wheel and nodded his head. The crack was too severe. The "Come and Take It" cannon would have to be abandoned. To refashion a wheel replacement would require too many hours; the need was to press forward. A number of men dropped by to look at the wounded cannon.

"Wouldn't be of much use, anyway," Milam said. "Unless we had a supply of ammunition, and where are we gonna get that?"

"We just gonna leave it? Ride off and abandon it?" a soldier asked in disbelief.

"Nope," Neill answered. "We'd better bury it—hide it—you never know when the enemy might be this way."

The small band around the cannon scooped a shallow hole in the soft river bank and rolled the artillery piece into the grave.

"Old gun must like dirt by now," a soldier said. "First that peach orchard at Gonzales and now this river bank."

"Too bad it can't roll on to Bexar with us," Neill said.[14]

Years later, Smithwick recalled the interment at Sandies Creek. "The old cannon was abandoned in disgrace," he wrote tersely. Creed Taylor, however, recalled that brush and leaves had been burned over the site to make it look as if a campfire had been there. He could not recall whether the flag had been left leaning against a sapling, whether it had been used some other way, or whether it had been a winding sheet for the cannon.[15]

Men were sprawled on their bedrolls around camp when a messenger reported a picket force stationed at the Cibolo crossing. Austin sent twenty-five men, under cover of darkness, to dislodge the pickets. The squad crossed the river below the ford and slithered along the opposite bank, alert to the snapping of twigs and to the hooting of owls. As the men neared what was reported to be the Mexican camp, one soldier whispered, "Boys, I don't like this. If there's a big force of 'em, they'll whip us."

"Shut up," hissed a Pennsylvania Dutchman in the group. "Don't say they'll whip us, or you're already whipped."

The other scouts smothered their nervous laughs and continued their mission. They failed to turn up any pickets and returned to the main camp.[16]

At the Cibolo, James Bowie, accompanied by several Louisianians, rode into camp. Texians stopped cleaning their rifles and sharpening their Bowie knives to stare as the living legend strode to Austin's tent. The sandy-haired Bowie had brawled—remember the Sand Bar Fight in which he had killed his opponent; had made fortunes—remember his profitable slave trade and his Arkansas land deals; had married the richest girl in San Antonio—remember Maria Ursula de Veramendi; was an adventurer—remember his search for the San Saba silver mines; and here he was, walking among the soldiers.[17] Austin appointed him aide-de-camp.

On October 26 Austin prepared to relocate his camp near Mission San Francisco de la Espada.[18] From the banks of the San Antonio River, he wrote to the council. Pulling his coat closer around his frail body, Austin began, "I shall move with the Army today to the Mission, and press the operation as fast as my force will permit." He coughed then continued to write that the Texas Army's effective strength was 400. General Cos, he had learned, had a force estimated between 800 and 900.

"We need reinforcements," he wrote, beginning a plea that would send refrains throughout the San Antonio operation. "My health is very bad—There has been skirmishing daily but no loss on our side. . . ."

Austin sent James Bowie, James Fannin, Robert Coleman, and ninety men to reconnoiter the area with the purpose of selecting another site, one nearer Bexar but still on the river—a site from which to conduct operations against the garrison.

Faced by a party of Mexicans who fired at long range then retired, the Texian scouts soon pitched camp in a bend of the river, a quarter of a mile from Mission Concepcion.[19] They anticipated Austin and the main army soon would follow.[20]

At sundown, the scouts heard a cannon ball buzz through the air then bury itself in the earth only rods from their camp. Other cannon balls hissed overhead. Then the area became quiet. At dawn, while the area was still clothed in fog, the Texians were pulled from their bedrolls by musket shots and pickets sounding an alarm. Henry W. Karnes[21] was wounded when his powder horn exploded, and a close comrade, Jacob H. Shepherd, was burned slightly. Smithwick remembered, "Another fell as soon as we got into camp, and we thought he was killed, but on examination found that his only injury consisted in a sick stomach caused by a bullet striking and breaking a large Bowie knife which he carried stuck under the waistband of his pantaloons."[22]

Although unable to estimate the strength of the enemy, the Texians took positions that would enable them to cross fire on the enemy. Fannin's unit occupied one arm, and Coleman's men were situated on another. A six-foot bluff and beyond it heavy timber secured them against an attack from the rear; in front were several companies of infantry and a field piece. Across the river were two companies cavalry. The Texians hugged the ground while their position was raked by cannon fire and balls that swept through the pecan trees, showering the ripe nuts upon soldiers, who welcomed the supplements to their rations.[23]

"Keep under cover, boys. Reserve your fire. We haven't a man to spare," Bowie shouted.

When the Mexicans began forming for a charge, Bowie called for Coleman to support Fannin. So eager for a shot that they became foolhardy, some of the Texians mounted the bank and ran across it, fully exposed to enemy fire. Smithwick took a less dangerous route, and when he caught up with the others, he saw Richard Andrews[24] of Mina. Sweat, like pearls, formed on his ashen face. A hole in his left side, below the ribs, discharged blood.

"Are you hurt?" a stunned Smithwick cried out upon seeing his injured friend.

"Yes, Smith," came a faint reply. "I'm killed. Lay me down." Smithwick did what he could to make the man comfortable, but the order—fire—from his commander pulled Smithwick back into the battle. The Mexican forces charged three times; the Texian platoons were prepared. Panic then swept the Mexicans, who jumped on the mules that had been attached to the caisson. They dug their heels into the animals, urging them to retreat.[25]

Smoke of the battle still mingled with the haze of fog when the main Texas Army arrived at noon.[26] Austin happily reported results of the skirmish to the council. "The overwhelming superiority of force, and the brilliance of the victory gained over them, speak for themselves in terms too expressive to require from me any further eulogy."

Hastily, the Mexicans rode from the field, leaving behind a brass six-pounder, still loaded, the bodies of fifty fallen soldiers, and a number of wounded. Neill learned of the cannon with joy. He was an artilleryman and too long without artillery. He had felt like a jockey without a horse. He could remember visiting the tracks in Tennessee and seeing the dejected riders on the rails because they had no mounts for a contest. He had been like that—on the rail during much of this conflict. Now he had a cannon with which to carry out his part of the fight for independence. Like his comrades, he mourned the death of Richard Andrews and sorrowfully watched some of the man's friends bury the body at the foot of a pecan tree.

Each morning Austin scanned the eastern horizon, hoping that reinforcements and a larger cannon sent from another Texas port would bolster his strength and morale. On November 1 he sent a note to General Cos, asking him to surrender. Cos answered that his official duty prevented accepting any official communications, and he must return Austin's communique unopened. He did, however, send a priest with the oral message that Mexican orders were to fortify Bexar and to hold the city at all costs. The following day Austin moved a part of his force to the mouth of a dry gully on the Alamo Canal, approximately one mile from town. While camped at that location, he learned that the Mexicans were sending approximately 900 surplus horses to Laredo with twenty men riding herd. Austin ordered Travis to select fifty fighters to ride with him in capturing the mounts. The duty performed, Travis, without losing a man, returned to the camp with 300 spirited animals.[27]

On November 2 Austin called a council of twenty-six officers to decide whether to attack or impose a starving-out policy on Bexar, hoping reinforcements and an eighteen-pound cannon would arrive. The officers supported delaying; only one voted to storm immediately.[28]

The following day, both units of the army were united, establishing camp at the Old Mill, approximately 800 yards from the Alamo.[29] To the representatives in San Felipe, Austin wrote that to take Bexar would require 1,000 men and at least one battering cannon. He reported, "Our army has so far done wonders. It has confined a superior force within strongly fortified walls; It has beaten the enemy in every contest and not a day passes without skirmishing within the reach of the enemy grape shot." If necessary, to raise funds to supply the army, the Consultation had permission to mortgage all his estate.[30]

Austin, who never claimed to be a commander, began to face serious problems. On November 22 he issued an order to storm Bexar at daylight, but only half his men were willing; the order was rescinded. With relief, General Austin received word that the Consultation had appointed him a commissioner to the United States, and on November 24, he delivered his farewell address to the army.[31]

Delegates for the Consultation re-assembled in San Felipe on November 1, 1835, and early arrivals twiddled their thumbs three days before a quorum could be counted. They named Dr. Branch T. Archer of Brazoria president. Archer, they were aware, knew how to take charge of a meeting; he had been speaker of the House of Delegates of the Virginia Legislature. In his opening address, Archer proposed establishing a provisional government with a governor, lieutenant governor, and council. He urged members to give immediate attention to the militia. He said, "You have an army in the field whose achievements have already shed lustre upon our arms; they have not the provisions and comforts necessary to continue their service in the field . . . Sustain and support them . . . But neglect them—Texas is lost."[32]

Henry Smith, who had farmed, been a district surveyor, taught in the Brazoria canebrakes, been wounded in the Battle of Velasco, and served as political chief of the Department of Brazoria, drew up plans for the civil government and Almanzon Huston for the military; the Consultation accepted them with only slight modifications. On November 12 the Consultation elected officers, naming Henry Smith president, thirty-one votes to twenty-two over Stephen F. Austin. James W. Robinson of Nacogdoches received fifty-two votes to become lieutenant governor.[33]

Smith took the oath then delivered his inaugural, saying in part:

> Our country is involved in war. Our foe is far superior to us in numbers and resources. Yet when I consider the stern materials of which our army is composed, the gallant and heroic men that are now in the field, I regard not the disparity of numbers, but am satisfied that we could push our conquests to the walls of Mexico. I earnestly recommend that you adopt the most prompt and energetic measures in behalf of the army; that you forthwith provide all the necessary munitions of war, so that our army may not be cramped or impeded by any remissness on the part of the government, and that you be careful to select agents of known skill and science to purchase artillery and other munitions.[34]

By unanimous vote Sam Houston was elected commander-in-chief of the Texas Army. Earlier he had introduced a resolution expressing appreciation to General Austin, Colonel Bowie, Captain Fannin, and their troops for "heroism, gallantry and valor."[35] He held his right hand high as he took the oath, administered by Archer:

> In the name of the people of Texas, free and sovereign: We, reposing special trust and confidence in your patriotism, valor, conduct and fidelity, do by these presents constitute and appoint you to be major-general and commander-in-chief of the armies of Texas and of all others who shall voluntarily offer their services and join the army . . . .[36]

Almanzon Huston proposed that the Consultation elect three commissioners to the United States. Delegates deliberated but briefly before naming Branch T. Archer, William H. Wharton, and Stephen F. Austin. An express was dispatched immediately to notify Austin and Wharton of their appointments.[37]

Col. Edward Burleson was elected commander when Austin departed for San Felipe to accept appointment as U.S. Commissioner.[38]

Approximately 100 men commanded by Colonel Bowie were riding outside of San Antonio on November 26, when scouts reported approximately 200 Mexicans approaching from the west, the animals in their pack train apparently loaded. After sending a runner on to General Burleson in camp, Bowie and his men pressed forward, believing the enemy to be Ugartechea's men with silver to pay the garrison troops.

To prevent the Mexicans from drawing closer to town, Bowie ordered an attack. The enemy sought cover in a dry gulch. The movement had been observed by watchmen in Bexar, so Mexican reinforcements soon arrived. Close behind came units from the main Texas army.

The enemy began to retreat, and Texians looked happily over the seventy head of horses they had captured. Eagerly they tore into the packs they also had taken, but happiness quickly soured. The sacks were filled with hay. They had captured a forage squad returning from cutting hay on the banks of the Medina River.[39]

While the skirmish, later known as the Grass Fight, was taking place near San Antonio, Don Carlos Barrett[40] of Mina was composing a letter to Gen. Sam Houston recommending the appointment of James Clinton Neill as a major in the artillery corps. "A gentleman, high in the esteem of his fellow citizens—brave and patriotic," Neill was mentioned as a man with age and experience that "would seem to justify his first commission as a field officer." Barrett felt his appointment would be in the interest of the Texas service.[41] When he had finished the letter, Barrett instructed the bearer to await an answer.

San Antonio—its thick stone walls catching rays of sunlight—shone like a glittering trophy, a Cibolo. Neill and his friends looked at the village as they, as youths, had looked beyond the rail fences at a bay-colored filly. Attractive. Alluring. But beyond reach. Men from the United States joined their ranks, filling the gaps of volunteers who had returned to their firesides and families. Bexar—or San Antonio as some preferred to call it—was the goal that cemented the New Orleans Grays in their uniforms and the frontiersmen in their buckskin together; although some of them were miserable, they had fought for weeks with the idea of reaching Bexar, but now there were rumors of a retreat.

Men likewise heard talk that a company of volunteers would be dispatched to capture the house belonging to Jose Angel Navarro.[42] A second force would charge through the village to the home of Antonio de la Garza,[43] and a third force would take control of the Veramendi palace.[44]

The desire for storming Bexar again flamed as men listened to details of the plan. Eagerly the Texians awaited morning, when the attack would begin.

Following a conference in General Burleson's quarter, Texians were told to turn out for a parade. Some companies, disturbed over gossip that a retreat would be ordered, refused to appear on parade grounds. Those men who did "fall in" heard that the attack would be postponed. As explanation, officers mentioned that one of the scouts, Hendrick Arnold,[45] had not yet returned to camp, and there was general fear that word of the planned attack had leaked. Baggage wagons, the soldiers learned, already had been loaded.

Soldiers were suffering from disappointment when two things happened. Arnold galloped into camp, and a Lieutenant Vuavis, who had deserted the Mexican Army, walked among the Texians, asking to confer with the commander. General Burleson began questioning him. As the lieutenant described how disheartened and how hungry men in Cos' army were, Texians turned the tragic masks on their faces into comic ones, and chatter filled the ranks.[46] The Mexican officer denied the enemy had had any suspicion of an intended attack that morning. Strength of the Bexar garrison, he assured Burleson, had been greatly exaggerated.[47]

Adjutant General Frank Johnson, who had urged continuing the siege, listened with interest; he urged Texians to storm the fortress. To Ben Milam, standing beside him, Johnson whispered that perhaps there were volunteers willing to carry through the plans for an attack. Milam's dark piercing eyes appeared to dance.

Caught in the excitement, Milam shouted, "Who will go with old Ben Milam?" Louder he again called, "Who will go with old Ben Milam into San Antonio?"

Arms holding long rifles shot up.

"Then fall in line!" The man calling the order was a 200-pound Kentuckian who stood 6-foot 1-inch tall.[48]

Approximately 300 men obeyed Milam's order and promptly elected him commander.

"I wouldn't mind going with you fellows," one soldier said. "But I have no gun."

"No gun?"

"My horse fell with me yesterday and broke the stock of my rifle."

"Never mind. We'll take you along to cut bullet patchin'."

"Meet at the Old Mill after dark, and we'll complete the organization," Milam suggested.

Darkness covered Bexar, and the volunteers assembled at the Old Mill. They established two divisions. Colonel Milam would head one, and Col. Frank W. Johnson, assisted by Colonels

James Grant and William T. Austin, the second. Colonel Neill, it was decided, would make a feint on the Alamo to divert the enemy's attention while the other units marched into position in town.

What had been a crystal starlit evening turned into a night of heavy fog; the mist was so thick that forms could be distinguished only a few feet away. "Ideal," Colonel Neill thought as he prepared to direct his men, selected from the Nacogdoches Independent Volunteers under Capt. John S. Roberts. Pulling their single artillery piece, the men waded across the river and silently, like figures in a pantomime, took a position "commanding the Alamo."

"Fire," Neill called, and his men began squeezing the triggers on their long rifles and in ramming the cannon.

Caught unprepared, the Mexicans were pulled from their bedrolls by a bugle sounding wildly and by a roll of drums.

The Texians began cutting down the sentinels and as they darted into town, Neill's men could hear the roar of enemy artillery. They were exposed to heavy grape fire and musketry. For two hours the guns "played upon the fortress," allowing the main force to enter Bexar.[49]

By 7:00 A.M. Bexar echoed with piercing rifle fire, and the discharge of a cannon near the Alamo sounded as musical as church chimes to Neill, for it was the signal that his ruse had succeeded. A bugle from the garrison cut into the early morning; drums began to roll. Mexicans scurried to their posts at the Alamo. Then the cannon blared, streaming blue puffs of smoke.[50]

Milam's troops, having broken through the pickets, were now in Bexar pressing toward the De la Garza house.

Johnson's force, taking a route approximately a block north of Milam, was able to take over the Veramendi palace. These residences were on the east side of each of the two streets, approximately a hundred yards from the town's main square.[51]

The town filled with smoke, the air sharp with pings of rifle and booms of cannon.

On the following morning, Texians learned that the enemy had taken over the tops of the houses between their sites and the plaza. From loopholes in the parapet walls atop these structures, Mexicans poured a steady, brisk rain of small arms fire.[52] Texians found some cloth in one of the houses from which to make sandbags for their protection.[53]

Meanwhile, Ugartechea had managed to slip back into Bexar with reinforcements, swelling the Cos force to 1,300 men. Texians could count only 500 among their number.

Yet, a squadron of Texians took possession of the house on the right of the Garza dwelling, extending the Texas Army line toward Military Plaza.

On the morning of December 7, the Mexicans began firing from a trench they had opened, but by 11:00 A.M. the trench had become quiet, the aim of the Texians having proved deadly accurate. Henry Karnes, armed with a crowbar, began attacking the houses that separated the Texians from the plaza. He soon forced an entrance, permitting his comrades to take over the building.

Colonel Milam, in passing from his position to confer with Colonel Johnson at the Veramendi house, was struck in the head and died instantly upon entering the yard. Texians grabbed the loss as an incentive; they set out on foot to capture the Navarro house, situated on the north side of Main Street, a block west of the plaza. When the enemy attempted to hold them off by firing through the loopholes in the roof, Texians returned fire through the same holes.

By December 8 the Texians focused on capturing Zambrano Row.[54] Despite a cold, wet day, troops broke the thick partitions that separated room from room and were able to fight their way from house to house. By nightfall, they commanded the northwest portion of the enemy's main defenses, and later in the night they captured the Priest's House, a strong building commanding the plaza. In destroying the wall that surrounded the building, Texians put fear into the enemy. Learning that the Texians were so near, the Mexicans retreated to the Alamo.

To produce a diversion, the Mexicans had sent out fifty men from the Alamo to advance upon the Texas camp. As they did so, they were raked by fire of a six-pounder. Colonel Neill had not retired to his bed roll after completion of his feint but had put his squad to priming the artillery piece.[55]

At 6:30 A.M. on December 9, Cos flew the flag of surrender and Johnson, who had taken command upon Milam's death, notified General Burleson.

On December 11, 1835, commissioners from both sides agreed to terms. The Mexicans would return to their country with their arms and private property. They would not oppose the re-establishment of the Constitution of 1824. Public property would go into the hands of the victors.[56] General Cos and a sufficient number of men were allowed six days to take an inventory of the Alamo and to deliver the stores to the Texians.[57]

On the day that General Burleson endorsed Colonel Johnson's report and forwarded it to the governor, Cos and 1,105 men left Bexar. They camped at Mission San Jose and the following day began a march toward the Rio Grande.[58]

10

BEXAR

"I will fight as long as I can and then not surrender . . . ."
J. C. Neill
to Gen. Sam Houston

A committee of the Consultation temporarily governing Texas debated plans for the army, and by early December recommended a regular force of approximately 1,200 men. In the organization there were to be two regiments, one of infantry and one of artillery with a group of rangers to guard the frontier against Indians. In pay, the army would be modeled after that of the United States of the North; Texas soldiers, however, would be awarded land bounties for service. On December 7 field officers were named by the committee on military affairs to include J. W. Fannin, colonel of the artillery; J. C. Neill, lieutenant colonel of the artillery; P. A. Sublett, colonel of the infantry; Henry Millard, lieutenant colonel of the infantry; and William Oldham, major of the infantry. Additional officers were elected the following day, including: D. B. Macomb, lieutenant colonel of the artillery; William B. Travis, first major of the artillery; and T. F. L. Barrett, second major.[1]

Travis, at Mill Creek when he learned of the appointment, was not pleased. On December 17 he wrote James Robinson, vice president, that he thanked the Consultation for the honor intended, but he believed he could be of greater service elsewhere. He apologized for rejecting a commission for which he officially had not been notified,[2] and he suggested that Francis W. Johnson, "an old settler" with "many claims to the favorable consideration of the council," be named. He requested Robinson refrain from reading his letter to the council but relay its contents.

As Travis had suggested, Johnson was commissioned major.[3]

Travis expressed surprise that the council had overlooked a corps of cavalry, which he considered "indispensible to the services of Texas during the present struggle." As he expressed it:

> Do you wish to get the information of the movements of a distant enemy? It must be done by cavalry—Do you wish to escort expresses? Guard Baggage while on the road? Charge a defeated & retreating enemy? Cut off supplies of the enemy? Harass an invading army by hanging upon his rear, or forming ambuscades in his front? Do you wish to carry the war into the enemy's country as has been indicated? Do you wish to take him by surprise, or perform any other movement requiring celerity & promptness? All these things must be done by cavalry—and cavalry alone.[4]

The council considered the matter and later approved a committee report along the lines Travis had proposed.[5]

By December 16, Governor Smith had ordered General Houston to establish headquarters of the Texian Army at Washington-on-the-Brazos.[6] Once the relocation was accomplished, Houston turned his attentions to placing troops and supplies at key points in Texas.

General Houston dipped his quill into the office ink bottle and began a letter to Colonel Neill in San Antonio. "On receipt of this you will take command of the Post of Bexar," he wrote, ordering the lieutenant colonel to "make such disposition of the troops" as he deemed proper "for the security & protection of the place." The commander asked for reports—"the quality of ammunition & the number of arms & together with a list of property taken from the enemy as well as the statement of the force under your command." He directed Neill to call upon G. B. Jameson to survey "the different articles necessary for your Command & the number of Cannon & other munitions of war

& also of provisions clothing &c—& you will immediately detail some capable officer to assist in fortifying the place in the best manner possible."

Neill obeyed orders; he assigned Jameson and Lt. Almeron Dickinson—the young Tennessean who had nursed the Gonzales "Come and Take It" cannon in the early stages of the march to Bexar—to remount the guns and strengthen the defenses of the Alamo fortress. By the middle of February, Jameson could report that despite a "scaricity of Tools," men had "done well in mounting & remounting Guns and other necessary work."[7]

Neill scanned the inadequate supplies and armaments and in frustration shook his head. He was aware that organization of the defense of the place must begin immediately. Many of his men spent their time in San Antonio, but Neill determined that the defense—if it became necessary—would have to be made from the Alamo. The old mission-compound contained a large collection of artillery, but the ammunition supply was sadly inadequate. The church of San Antonio de Valero—the Alamo—was begun in 1744 but not completed until 1757. The twin towers, arched roof, and dome had collapsed, and the debris was left littering the floor of the building. The church was abandoned.[8] The village surrounding the mission had attracted thirteen families from the Canary Islands in 1731, and in 1794 the Alamo lands were divided among village residents. Some Americans then located in San Antonio, but the village remained Mexican dominated.[9]

With his message to Neill, Houston enclosed instructions for the officers in the recruiting service, a blank for the commander's use in listing names of volunteers, and a list of officers in the regular army. He requested Neill notify those who had not received word of their appointment.

Lapsing into third person in his letter, Houston wrote Neill, "The Commander in Chief in depositing the high trust of the Command of Bexar to Col. J. C. Neill feels assured that the confidence is not misplaced & that he will always be able to respond to the country in defense of its rights."[10]

General Houston made other appointments. Col. William Barret Travis of the First Regiment of the Infantry took over the recruiting station in San Felipe, where he spent the time in seeking enlistees and handling legal affairs. Later, however, Travis was appointed lieutenant colonel of the cavalry. Col. James W. Fannin was assigned to Velasco.[11]

In the middle of December 1835, Lt. Tony Fitch approached Colonel Neill about an appointment in the regular army, and one of the first acts Neill performed after taking over Bexar was to compose a letter indicating if Fitch did not receive an appointment, the young man would leave the armed forces. Neill wrote D. C. Barrett, his old Bastrop neighbor, concerning the appointment, saying that "in the siege of Bexar, Fitch had acted like a soldier and a man." The lieutenant, who had been in the regular army of the U.S.A., was filling the post of drill master with credit, and Neill suggested that Barrett approach General Houston and the executive council with the matter. He wrote:

> It is my wish for him to remain as he is of great utility & the Army is inexperienced & awkward & he is experienced and can train them. I wish you to send me a copy of the Infantry tactics & the regulation of the Army & a copy of Salmans—Artillery discipline.
>
> [Requesting haste in responding, Neill scrawled his signature.][12]

It was December 30 before Houston notified Fannin that Colonel Neill had assumed charge of the Bexar post.

Dr. James Grant—never a Texas resident, nor owner of lands in Texas—proposed to carry operations to the south of the Rio Grande to wage war on the enemy's own territory. His target would be Matamoros, the major Mexican city on the border. Texas soldiers, exhilarated by the victory over the Mexican forces at Bexar, listened eagerly as Grant outlined his plan. The Scot, who had lived the last ten years in Mexico and who more recently had served as Edward Burleson's aide-de-camp during the siege, spoke convincingly.[13]

Why Matamoros?

Smoothly, the well-educated Grant explained. Matamoros

had approximately 6,000 to 8,000 inhabitants, many of them English and American traders who had located their headquarters and residences in the community.

Grant could sense the excitement growing within the troops as he talked. He could not keep from thinking of the Hacienda of the Furnaces near Parras, Coahuila, that he had purchased in 1825 and which the government of Santa Anna had confiscated. He would not, however, mention his loss lest it sound as if his reasons for hitting Mexico were for personal revenge.[14]

"A number of the Mexicans dissatisfied with the present government will join us," Grant said. "As soon as they see Texians of some force approach, they will flock to our side."

"And think of the señoritas," someone yelled from around the campfire. There was a stir of interest.

"Those black-eyed beauties . . . ."

Grant ignored the interruption but continued to tell of the damage that could be wrought if Santa Anna faced war in his own arena.

Some of the soldiers, once thinking themselves tired, began to feel refreshed and ready for activity. Like good harness horses, they were ready to move.

"Matamoros is the principal city of Tamaulipas—not far from the mouth of the Rio Grande. It's a shipping center. Said to have a revenue of more than $100,000 each month," Grant said. "That's right. You heard me correctly. More than $100,000 a month."[15]

Col. Frank Johnson, commander of Bexar, and Dr. Grant enlisted 200 men from the San Antonio forces and began their march. Their target—Matamoros, Mexico.

After a time, Colonel Johnson and Dr. Grant decided they should apply to the Texas government for permission for their raid. Grant galloped into San Felipe, seeking permission from the general council and the governor. Grant heard some opposition. General Houston agreed there could be some advantages to a hit-and-run operation only if the Texians had sufficient strength. He believed James Bowie was the only person qualified to direct such a maneuver. Before long, council members were disagreeing among themselves. Governor Smith, General

Houston, and some who had little interest in Mexican politics opposed the idea of moving the entire army south. Some council members, however, favored the proposal.

Eventually the council authorized Dr. Grant and Colonel Johnson to direct the foray. At first Johnson declined the appointment, and in his place the council named James W. Fannin, Jr. Then Grant convinced the council that General Burleson had voiced plans to pass the command of volunteers to him, so the governing body of Texas named him commander in chief of the volunteers. Because a majority of those serving in the Texas Army were volunteers, the appointments made Fannin and Grant mutually responsible.

The following day, after Johnson had expressed his change of heart, the council appointed him. Unfortunately, the council neglected to inform Houston, commander in chief of Texas forces, of the appointments.

Governor Smith vetoed the appointments, but the council outvoted him on the matter.

In speaking to the council, Colonel Johnson answered questions about the Bexar forces. "This force I consider to be barely sufficient to hold the post," he said, "and it will require at least fifty additional troops to place it in a strong defensive position. I have ordered all the guns from town into the Alamo and the fortification in the town to be destroyed." [16]

He neglected to mention he had stripped the fortress of men and supplies in order to conduct his Matamoros expedition.

Neill, although miles away, agreed with Johnson's assessment that the Bexar garrison was insufficiently manned and equipped. He composed a succinct report expressing his feelings on the conditions of his command as of January 6—"104 men and two distinct fortresses to garrison, and about twenty-four pieces of artillery." He followed the report with a plea:

> You, doubtless, have learned that we have no provisions or clothing since Johnson and Grant left. If there has ever been a dollar here, I have no knowledge of it. The clothing sent here by the

aid of patriotic exertions of the honorable council was taken from us by the arbitrary measures of Johnson and Grant, taken from the men who endured all the hardships of winter and who were not even sufficiently clad for summer, many of them having but one blanket and one shirt, and what was intended for them given away to men, some of whom had not been in the army more than four days, and many not exceeding two weeks. If a divide had been made of them, the most needy of my men could have been made comfortable, by the stock of clothing and provisions taken from here.[17]

Neill reported approximately "two hundred of the men who had volunteered to garrison this town for four months left my command contrary to my orders and thereby vitiated the policy of their enlistment." The commander expressed a wish to have 200 men at Bexar at all times, but believed 300 men could garrison the place until "repairs and improvements of fortifications are completed."[18]

From his office in Washington, General Houston wrote Governor Smith, attaching the report from Colonel Neill and respectfully requesting the executive to "render to the cause of Texas and humanity the justice of bestowing upon it your serious attention, and referring it to the general council of the provisional government, in secret session."[19]

Houston rode from Washington on January 8 for Goliad, where, on January 14, he was met by a courier who handed him Neill's desperate message. After reading the note, Houston ordered James Bowie to give relief to the Alamo force. Bowie put his 6-foot-1-inch, 180-pound frame into his saddle and rode out immediately "with a few very efficient volunteers," who had joined him only two weeks earlier.

Only minutes before Bowie set out for San Antonio, Houston wrote Governor Smith:

I have ordered the fortifications in the town of Bexar to be demolished, and, if you should think well of it, I will remove all the cannon and other munitions of war to Gonzales and Copano, blow up the Alamo and abandon the place, as it will be impossible to keep up the Station with volunteers, the sooner I can be authorized it will be for the country.

Houston, with more than 200 men, then set out for the Mission Refugio to await orders from the chief executive.[20]

An ambassador of the Comanche Indian tribe appeared in the Bexar headquarters on the morning of January 8 to inform Texians that "an attitude of hostilities" existed between the two peoples. The Indians, however, were willing to put aside their concerns for twenty days and proposed a meeting. The ambassador suggested that five Texas commissioners meet with an Indian delegation to draw a "Treaty of Amity, Commerce & Limits."

Neill listened to the ambassador and forwarded the information to the governor with the suggestion that Francisco Ruis[21] and Don Gasper Flores, men "familiar with the Comanche character" because they had served as negotiators earlier, be named commissioners.[22]

Acting governor James W. Robinson named Francisco Ruis, Edward Burleson, John W. Smith[23] and Neill commissioners to meet with the Comanche Indians. On January 17 Robinson directed the four to "repair to the City of Bexar & meet and treat with such deputation" as would be present. They were told to call the meeting at a place and time they deemed "best calculated to effect the object of the mission." The acting governor warned commissioners "to avoid direct acknowledgment of any national rights" and "to make and fix no definite boundary." Commissioners had the power to give the government's consent for the Comanches to hunt and fish within certain boundaries.

The acting governor also instructed:

> You will impress them with the sentiments of the Texans, that they are friendly to them, but its continuance depends upon their conduct, that if they remain our friends, we will aid them if the centralists of Mexico make war upon them, but if they are determined upon war, impress them with a just dread of the horrors we can inflict upon them, by giving them to understand & be informed of the aid in men and money that we can get and are daily receiving from the United States. . . .

The acting governor suggested commissioners remind the Comanches that the Shawnees, who defeated the Comanches near San Antonio, were friends and would be "arrayed against them in battle with us." Robinson told commissioners to promise extermination of the Comanche tribe if members engaged in war.

He warned commissioners that if circumstances made it necessary for them to use their own judgments, they were to remain aware of the "present exposed condition" and the future importance of the right of soil "over which the tribe may wander but to which it had no right or claim other than that of hunting temporarily at our pleasure."

Robinson reminded commissioners that "immediately on concluding a treaty," they should send a copy of the agreement to the general council. Likewise, word was requested should the treaty attempts fail.

The council appropriated $500 for the commissioners to conduct the conference.[24]

On January 14 Neill wrote the governor and council about reports "the enemy is advancing on this post, and from the number of families leaving town today, and those preparing to follow; among which, is that of John W. Smith, who has this evening engaged wagons to remove his families into the colonies." Intelligence was that the enemy was on the Rio Frio, but because of the shortage of horses, Neill was unable to "gain any information, not being able to send out a small spy company."[25]

Colonel Neill expressed another concern in his letter. Volunteers who had enlisted for two or four months—those who had signed under Burleson or Johnson—understood they were to be paid monthly. Payment had not been made, and as a result, several soldiers left the post January 13. As Neill wrote, ". . . I have not more than seventy-five men fit for duty, and afraid that number will be considerably reduced in a few days." Unless reinforcements arrive, he wrote, "we must become an easy prey to the enemy, in case of an attack."

Giving vent to the impatience he felt, Neill continued to write:

> My frequent repetitions of the subject of our distress, and the apprehensions of an enemy, arise partly from the interest I feel for my country, and a wish to preserve those lands she has acquired in the infant stage of her campaign; and being well convinced as above stated, that the enemy may be nearer than rumored, without a power of ascertaining it through our own men on whom we depend, and would, if necessary, ascertain the movements of the enemy, however distant, had we but a few horses.
>
> In this extremity I will assure you, that as far as our strength goes, we will, till reinforced, use it both in spy service, and if drawn within the walls, will defend the garrison to the last.[26]

At the same time, Neill submitted a requisition to the committee of safety at Gonzales, asking for as many men and horses as available.

Growing more impatient as he added a postscript to his message to the governor and council, Neill concluded:

> I shall not again make application for aid, as considering it superfluous, but wait the result of either receiving aid or an attack before it should arrive; in which case I will do the best I can with the small force I have, understanding that my commanding officer was under marching orders, and not knowing his destination, I have been induced to make my situation known to you, supposing it the chance through which I, as well as the country, may receive most immediate assistance.[27]

On December 16 the council recognized that the troops garrisoned at Bexar were "without the necessary provisions and clothing for their support and comfort" and admitted "the probability of its being some time yet before the necessary supplies from our agents in the United States for the support, subsistence and use of the army will be received." Council members agreed that is was "impossible to drive beeves—and procure provisions for their use, without horses." The council resolved:

> That Lieut. Colonel Neill, commandant at Bexar, be, and is hereby authorized and empowered to employ as many Mexicans, or other citizens, for the purpose of driving up beeves, and procuring provisions for the troops under his command, as may

be required for their support; and that this Government shall respect the drafts of said commandant for the pay of the said men in his employ, as aforesaid; provided, that the said commandant cannot offer them any more money for their services as enlisted soldiers, or volunteer troops, than the existing laws prescribe.

Council members approved $20 per month as pay for the Mexicans "employed by the commandant at Bexar" and authorized John W. Smith "to collect the sum of one thousand dollars of the public dues, or any money to that amount belonging to this Government in the department of Bexar, and to give the same to the commandant of that place" for use in supporting the troops. James W. Robinson was directed to forward a set of resolutions to Neill.[28]

William R. Carey, writing his brother and sister from Bexar, mentioned that the forces were commanded by Lieutenant Colonel Neill, "who has quarters in the Town which is called the left wing of the forces and your brother William has the command of the Alamo which is called the right wing. I am subject to the orders of Colonel Neill but he thinks a great deal of my judgment and consults me about a number of the proceedings before he issues an order."[29] Carey had been with the troops who marched to Gonzales in the fight for the Come and Take It cannon and had been appointed second lieutenant in October 1835. He had received a wound to the scalp while attending a cannon. Popular with his company, which he called the Invincibles, he was elected captain and had charge of the Alamo while Neill commanded the town. On January 14, 1836, Neill located his entire forces in the Alamo. He continued, however, to assign tough tasks, even the duty of military police, to Carey's company.

Sometime in December 1836, Neill signed discharges for several men who had been with the Texas Army approximately two and a half months. In turn, they signed over any "title, claim or right of property" to any land for which they might be entitled because of the military service.

Neill decided to pen another message to his commander in

chief, describing the men who had been in the field for four months:

> They are almost naked, and this day they were to have received pay for the first month of their last enlistment, and almost every one of them spoke of going home, and not less than twenty will leave tomorrow, and leave here only about eighty efficient men under my command.[30]

Neill then relayed rumors that 3,000 men under the command of Gen. Joaquin Ramirez y Sesma had arrived at Laredo. A letter received in Bexar the night before indicated that 1,000 of the troops were destined for Bexar, the remaining 2,000 to march toward Matamoros. Neill wrote:

> We are in a torpid, defenseless condition, and have not and cannot get from all the citizens here horses enough to send out a patrol or spy company. . . . I hope we will be re-inforced in eight days, or we will be over-run by the enemy, but, if I have only 100 men, I will fight 1,000 as long as I can and then not surrender . . . .[31]

Reinforcements arrived.

Col. James Bowie galloped ahead of his column of thirty men as he again entered Bexar on January 19. In his saddlebags were orders from General Houston telling Colonel Neill to leave San Antonio—to destroy the Alamo, to salvage the artillery pieces and military stores, then to retreat to Gonzales or Copano.

Neill warmly welcomed Bowie and his troops into the mission-fortress, and the newly arrived officer anxiously looked over the situation. Was it as desperate as Neill had pictured in dispatches to Houston, the governor, and the council? Neill had written that he was determined to fight the Mexicans no matter the odds. He would not surrender.[32]

Bowie had been doubtful, but the more he saw of the Alamo, the more he agreed with Neill. The situation was not pleasant. After a time, Bowie, his blue-gray eyes set, asked Neill what he thought about strengthening the Alamo and making it into an adequate garrison.[33]

And the men? Bowie knew these soldiers under Neill had turned down the chance to participate in the Matamoros expedition. They had courage, he knew. Later, Bowie wrote of them:

> All I can say of the soldiers stationed here is complimentary to both their courage and their patience. But it is the truth and your Excellency must know it, that great and just dissatisfaction is felt for the want of a little money to pay the small but necessary expenses of our men. I cannot eulogise the conduct & character of Col. Neill too highly; no other man in the army could have kept men at this post, under the neglect they have experienced. Both he & myself have done all that we could; we have industriously tried all expedients to raise funds; but hitherto it has been to no purpose. We are still labouring night and day, laying up provisions for a seige, encouraging our men, and calling on the Government for relief.

Although Bowie could count only 120 men and was aware of persisting rumors that 2,000 Mexicans were on the banks of the Rio Grande, he was determined. "Col. Neill & myself have come to the solemn resolution that we will rather die in these ditches than give it up to the enemy." [34]

Bowie's spirits seemed to climb. Neill, on the other hand, grew more depressed and frustrated. Over and over he had requested recruits and supplies. Over and over these requisitions had gone unanswered. True, some supplies had trickled in—43 head of cattle, 100 bushels of corn, and some ammunition for the 18-pound cannon.[35]

Shortly after the arrival of Bowie and his contingent, Neill and Deaf Smith left San Antonio for the interior. Purpose of the trip was for Neill to purchase wagons and teams to move the supplies and artillery pieces from the Alamo in carrying out Houston's orders.[36]

Meanwhile, an express arrived in San Felipe de Austin on January 18, carrying Colonel Neill's report that a force of men had been sighted near Laredo and 1,000 of them had "advanced as far as the Rio Frio, eighty miles from San Antonio." An immediate attack was anticipated, yet there were "only seventy-five in the Alamo and provisions were scarce."[37]

James Robinson, who had been named governor when the council had removed Henry Smith from office,[38] issued a proclamation urging Texians to help defend the fortress. He said:

> Will you go? I regret to call upon you at this time of the year, when your domestic affairs demand your care and attention; but I am onstrained by the imminent danger that threatens your brethren in arms, and by the danger to which the frontier inhabitants would be exposed, by neglecting to defend them, and by the disgrace and ruin of the country, consequent upon delay.
>
> Rally then my brave countrymen, to the standard of constitutional liberty, and join your united energies, and spread the mantle of your courage over your defenseless country. Your homes, your families, your country call, and who can refuse to obey? Your homes and your friends are assailed; will you refuse to defend them?

As if caught up in his own rhetoric, Governor Robinson continued:

> March then, with the blessing of your household Gods, to the western frontier, where you will be organized for a short, but glorious campaign. March then, where victory awaits you, and the genius of freedom spreads her banner, and will crown her sons with imperishable laurels. Roll back the crimson stream of war to its source, and make the tyrant feel the fiery sun of blazing, burning, consuming war; and since he has driven you to take up arms in your defense, give him 'war to the knife and knife to the hilt. . . .
>
> March, then, united, and without delay and you will erect a monument in the affection of your admiring countrymen, and, of the world, that will stand as firm on the pyramids of Egypt 'mid surrounding ruins, that shall continue while time shall last, and only perish 'amid the war of elements, the wreck of matter, and the crush of worlds.

He prayed that the "God of war guide you to victory, honor

and peace," and signed his proclamation as acting governor of Texas.[39]

On January 23 Neill wrote two letters to the governor and council. The first informed officials that Jose Antonio Navarro had received a message from his brother Eugene in St. Louis Potosi saying Santa Anna and 3,000 troops had reached Saltillo and in the town of Rio Grande were an additional 1,600 troops. Neill continued:

> ... that he is instructed by the Government to raise forthwith Ten Thousand in such manner as he may think proper and proceed against Texas, which he says he will reduce to the State it originally was in 1820.

Neill learned of plans from Colonel Bowie, who had been told by the priest of Santa Anna's plans to "attack Copano and Labahia first and send but a few hundred cavalry against this place at the same time."

Reversing his stand of not surrendering so long as he had men, Neill wrote that if teams were available so that he could remove the cannon and public property, he would "destroy the fortifications and abandon the place, taking the men I have under my command here, to join the Commander in chief at Copano, of which I informed him last night.[40]

When Henry Smith received the letter from Neill that Grant and Johnson had stripped the Alamo of essential supplies, artillery, and food in order to begin the Matamoros expedition, he raged. The governor demanded an apology from the council and threatened to dissolve the body if members did not cooperate with him. He called the council's attention to the situation:

> You will find there a detail of facts calculated to call forth the indignant feelings of every honest man. Can your body say that they have not been cognizant of and connived at this predatory expedition? Are you not daily holding conference and plan-

ning co-operation both by sea and land? Acts speak louder than words, they are now before me, authorizing a Generalissimo with plenary powers, to plan expeditions on the faith, the credit, and I may justly say, to the ruin of the country.

The governor continued his blistering attack on members of the council:

You urge me by resolutions to make appointments, fit out vessels, as government vessels, registering them as such, appointing landsmen to command a naval expedition by making representation urgent in their nature, and for what? I see no reason but to carry into effect by the hurried and improvident acts of my department, the views of your favorite object by getting my sanction to an act discouraging in its nature and ruinous in its effects. Instead of acting as becomes the counsellors and guardians of a free people, you resolve yourselves into low, intriguing, caucussing parties, pass resolutions without a quorum, predicted on false premises, and endeavor to ruin the country, by countenancing, aiding and abbeting marauding parties, and if you could only deceive me enough, you would join with it a piratical co-operation. You have acted in bad faith, and seem determined by your acts to destroy the very institutions which your are pledged and sworn to support.[41]

When Governor Smith threatened that he would not call the council into session, members retaliated by impeaching him. They charged he had "retained and embezled"[42] that he had libeled the army, calling it "a mob nicknamed an army," that he had called the governing body the "damned corrupt council," he had withheld correspondence of a public nature from the acting governor and general council and he continued to act officially after he had been suspended, issuing army orders to Travis, Neill, Houston, and others.

Acting governor Robinson wrote commissioners Stephen F. Austin, William Wharton, and Branch T. Archer that the impeachment grew from the Matamoros project, with Smith "being opposed to it and council in its favor."

A pessimistic Robinson urged commissioners that "without

money and provisions speedily we cannot predict or imagine the disastrous consequences to our unhappy and distracted country." He prodded, "do for God and your countries sake effect a money." He insisted that they:

> send it to the Treasury or to the Gen. Council, for if Henry Smith gets it there is no knowing what he may do with it. $5000 was handed him a few days ago, and he utterly refused to put it in the Treasury or under the control of the Genl. council, it was a gift to Texas from Mr. Hill of Tennessee. . . .[43]

The day after Robinson wrote the commissioners, January 24, Colonel Neill pulled his lap desk into position to write a report. The garrison, he noted, had a strength of only 100 men. Many individuals were leaving at will, and those who remained were with "neither arms nor supplies" and had not been paid for more than a month. As he wrote, Neill could not keep from thinking that he did not have enough money to have his shirt washed. Nevertheless, he begged the government officials for more men and supplies, and he urged that the Alamo be held at all costs.[44]

In his second letter dated January 23, Neill requested the governor send "a writ of Election for the volunteer Army now under my command to authorize them to Elect two delegates to the Convention to be held in Washington." Neill pointed out that not a man under his command would have a voice in the election otherwise. "Such men should be represented in the council of their Country and that too by men chosen from among themselves." Neill closed his request, saying, "You have the highest regards of the whole Army and you shall be sustained by your firmness and Philanthropy."[45]

Officers and men stationed in Bexar soon forgot the impending convention, which would result in the drafting of the Texas Declaration of Independence; instead, they gathered in groups to discuss the news a messenger had delivered. They learned that in a closed meeting, the executive council had impeached Governor Smith and had ordered the land offices temporarily closed until a general convention could be called. Of concern to them was the charge that $5,000 that the people of the United States had sent for paying the soldiers of the Bexar garrison had been used by council members "to their own purposes."[46]

Soldiers and civilians assembled on January 26 to discuss "recent movements at San Felipe," and they invited Neill to chair the session. They voted H. J. Williamson secretary. As they discussed matters, they focused their wrath on the "private and designing men" in San Felipe who were content to leave the men in the garrison half naked and hungry. Members of the council, they agreed, had embarrassed the governor, "the legitimate officer of the government."

What could they do about affairs? Almost to a man, they called for a set of resolutions, which after much discussion and publishing, they adopted. These documents had been prepared by a committee of J. B. Bonham, James Bowie, G. B. Jameson, Doctor Pollard, Jesse Badgett, J. N. Seguin, and Don Gasper Flores, saying:

> That we will support his Excellency Governor Smith in his unyielding and patriotic efforts to fulfill his duties, and to preserve the dignity of his office, while promoting the best interests of the country and people, against all usurpations and the designs of selfish and interested individuals.
>
> Resolved 2nd.—That all attempts of the president and members of the Executive Council to annul the acts of, or to embarrass the officer appointed by the general convention, are deemed by this meeting as anarchical assumptions of power to which we will not submit.
>
> Resolved 3rd.—That we invite a similar expression from the army under General Houston, and throughout the country generally.
>
> Resolved 4th.—That the conduct of the president and members of the Executive Council in relation to the ungrateful, we cannot be driven from the post of Honor and the sacred cause of freedom.
>
> Resolved 5th.—That we do not recognize the illegal appointments of agents and officers, made by the president and

members of the Executive Council in relation to the Matamoros Expedition; since their power does not extend further than to take measures and to make appointments for the public service with the sanction of the governor.

Resolved 6th.—That the Governor Henry Smith will please to accept the gratitude of the army at this station, for his firmness in the execution of his trust, as well as for his patriotic exertions in our behalf.

Resolved 7th.—That the Editors of the Brazoria *Gazette,* the Nacogdoches *Telegraph,* and the San Felipe *Telegraph* be requested, and they are hereby requested to publish the proceedings of this meeting.[47]

When he wrote the president and members of the executive council on January 27, Neill could not ignore personal feelings regarding the "disorganized situation." "Such interuptions in the General Council of Texas," he wrote, "have bad tendancies—they create distrust & alarm, and at this critical period of history are much to be lamented." He enclosed a copy of the proceedings of the meeting he had chaired to "convey to you some idea of the feeling of the Army."[48]

On the same date, Colonel Neill wrote Governor Smith, saying he had received from the council "a copy of resolutions... empowering me (as said therein) without giving me the means to do sundry acts to my own relief as commander of this post." An impatient Neill wrote:

> In my communication to the Executive I did not ask for pledges and resolves, but for money, provisions and clothing. There has been money given or loaned by private individuals expressly for the use of the army, and none has been received.... We can not be fed and clothed on paper pledges. My men cannot, nor will not, stand this state of things much longer.[49]

Meanwhile, on January 8, Houston—as ordered by the governor—had left headquarters to take command of the volunteers and to avert the Matamoros expedition. He reached

Goliad on January 14, accompanied by Col. George W. Hockley, inspector-general, and several other staff members. Houston learned that Dr. Grant had left Goliad three days earlier, taking with him all the horses.

Houston spoke to the Texian forces preparing for the Mexican march. As he recalled:

"I remonstrated with the officers in a friendly manner, representing the great difficulties they would have to encounter—the futility of the project—and the disasters attendant on failure."[50]

To his dismal predictions, soldiers answered with "bantering scorn." He rode with the men to Refugio, hoping to meet Fannin and his volunteers, but Fannin was not there. Again Houston talked informally with the men, and several joined him, leaving the Matamoros troops numbering only fifteen men.

That evening Houston reported to Governor Smith that word of what he considered his dismissal as commander in chief of the Texas Army had reached him. He sincerely feared the acts of the council would extend the war for years, costing Texas "more useless expenditure."

In answer, Governor Smith granted Houston a furlough to March 1, "for the purpose of adjusting your private business, preparatory to your necessary absence, hereafter, from home in the country's service."[51]

When rumors spread that Texian volunteers had refused to submit to Houston's commands, the editor of the *Red River Herald* called them "utterly without foundation." An explanation followed the denial—that a treaty with the Indians in East Texas "required immediate attention.[52] Only months earlier, Houston, John Forbes, and John Cameron had been appointed commissioners to make a pact with the Cherokees "and their twelve associate bands."[53]

On January 28 Neill concluded that the enemy had begun the march toward the Texas border, and he planned to send a spy to look over the situation. "On the arrival of Col. Travis and his men I shall also dispatch them to cut off their supplies, a policy I conceive to be at this juncture more expedient as by depriving the enemy's troops of their provisions & of the means of progressing they will become discouraged and be induced to return," he wrote the provisional government, and continued:

> I shall instruct Col. Travis to cut down the bridges over the Leona and Nueces to embarrass the enemy in crossing those streams. . . .
>
> Fellow citizens, the time has now arrived and a second epocha is to be from this date dated in the affairs of our adopted country in which domestic dissentions should be hushed and rancour should be the watchword United, the attempts of the enemy can be baffled even if Santa Anna with his 3,000 men do come on. Texas ought and must again arouse to action, another victory will secure us forever from the attack of Tyrany and our Existence will no longer be doubtful but prosperous and glorious to attain so desirable an end. I am ready to sacrifice my all. . . .
>
> If as I expect every citizen of the country and our colabrators from the United States are animated by the same spirit, Destiny will be compeled to acknowlege us as her favorites, from the time of my taking the field in the defense of Texas liberties up to the present moment, my labours and watchfulness have been unremitting and they shall continue to be so until I see the land of my adoption free.

Neill explained to government officials that he would consult with some of the influential Mexicans living in Bexar, believing that ⁴/₅ of them would "join us if they entertained reasonable expectations of reinforcements." Meanwhile, he advised the council to concentrate efforts in supporting Bexar and in forwarding "supplies of beef, pork, hogs, salt, $c."[54]

Henry Smith, still performing some duties, ordered William B. Travis to cease recruiting in San Felipe and march to San Antonio. Travis pleaded with the governor to rescind the order that would send him to Bexar "with such little means, so few men, and them so badly equipped."[55] Reluctantly he headed west, believing that the order put him in direct command of the fortress. From Burnham's Crossing on the Colorado, he notified Governor Smith he had experienced difficulty in rounding up horses and provisions and that he had only thirty men in his command.[56]

The Travis squadron arrived in Bexar on February 3.

11

MARCH TO INDEPENDENCE

"With these soldiers, we must achieve our independence."
Sam Houston to George W. Hockley
March 1836

The Tennessee Volunteers clamored behind Davy Crockett into Bexar, and the plaza soon swarmed with citizens and soldiers. Davy's coonskin cap bobbed as he told the group how he had been defeated for a fourth term in Congress.

"You can all go to hell," he had told his former constituents. "I'm going to Texas."

And here he was. His Texian audience wildly cheered him and his men. Crockett gestured for the Texians to be quiet. "Fellow citizens," he said when there was a lull. "I am among you. I have come to your country, though not I hope, through any selfish motive whatever. I have come to aid you all I can in your noble cause."

Again, the Texians yelled their approval.

The arrival of Crockett and the Tennessee Volunteers called for a celebration, so San Antonio staged a fandango. When the residents and soldiers were not whirling on the dance floor or toasting each other, they talked about old times in Tennessee and speculated on why Col. J. C. Neill had left the garrison.[1]

On February 11, 1836, Colonel Neill, "a patriot and a brave gentleman soldier,"[2] mounted his Tennessee Walker, an official leave of absence tucked inside one of the saddlebags. Neill rode east from the Alamo.

Questions continue to arise over why the commander of the

Bexar garrison left his post at this time. Green B. Jameson, a man close to Neill through the work in repairing and designing the fortifications of the Alamo, wrote Gov. Henry Smith that Neill had gone "home on account of express from his family informing him of their ill health."[3]

William B. Travis informed the chief executive from the Alamo on February 12, 1836, that "in consequence of the sickness of his family, Lt. Col. Neill has left this Post, to visit home for a short time, and has requested me to take the Command." Travis, feeling "delicately and awkwardly situated," asked the governor to supply him with "some definite orders, and . . . immediately!"[4]

John J. Baugh,[5] adjutant of the post, also wrote the governor:

> Lt. Col. J. C. Neill being suddenly called home, on consequence of the illness of some of his family, requested Col. Travis, as the Senior officer, to assume the command of the Post during his absence.

Travis informed the volunteers in the garrison that if they were dissatisfied with his appointment as commander, they were at liberty to elect "one of their own body." The volunteers had objected that Travis was a regular officer, so they immediately supported Colonel Bowie. The result was a split in the garrison. Travis would not submit to the command of Bowie, and Bowie, "availing himself of his popularity among the men seemed eager to arrogate himself the entire control."[6]

Colonel Travis addressed the governor on the matter February 13:

> Dear Sir, I wrote you an official letter last night as Comdt of this Post in the absence of Col. Neill; & if you had taken the trouble to answer my letter from Burnham's, I should not now have been under the necessity of troubling you—My situation is truly awkward & delicate—Col. Neill left me in command—but wishing to give satisfaction to the volunteers here & not wishing to assume any command over them I issued an order for the election of an officer to command them with the exception of one company of volunteers that had previously engaged to serve under me. Bowie was elected by two small company's; & since his election he has

March to Independence 99

been roaring drunk all the time; has assumed all command—& is proceeding in a most disorderly and irregular manner. . . ."[7]

The day after Travis penned the letter, he and Colonel Bowie signed a joint letter to Smith indicating that until Neill returned to the fortress, both would sign all general orders. With the question of command settled, soldiers began preparing for an attack—digging a well, rounding-up beeves, rustling corn.[8]

Was illness at home the reason Neill rode from the Alamo? Dr. John Sutherland,[9] who lodged in the home of Lt. and Mrs. Almeron Dickinson, wrote that Colonel Neill "readily forsaw that something must be done and that, too, without delay, or his position would be abandoned and subject to be retaken by the enemy." Neill was "determined to procure if possible a portion of a $5,000 donation which had been made to the cause of Texas by Harry Hill of Nashville."[10]

If true, details of Neill's work—where he visited and with whom he conferred—were not recorded. The Hill contribution, however, is well documented in Texas history. Hill, who had been a stockholder in the Bank of Tennessee, founded in December, 1831,[11] and in the toll road operated by the Franklin Turnpike Company, established in August 1830,[12] also invested in Louisiana railroads.[13] One writer has labeled him "the merchant prince of New Orleans." His stepfather, William Parkham, resided in Spring Hill, Tennessee.[14]

On November 19, 1835, Hill had sent George C. Childress a bill of exchange on N. & J. Dick & Co. of New Orleans for $5,000, requesting him "to place the above sums in the hands of those in authority, with my prayers for their success." He indicated that he would "leave it with the government to set apart a piece of land, equal to the amount furnished, provided a republican form of government is established. If a tyranical or dictatorial government is formed I do not wish my children to inherit any part of the soil."[16]

Gov. Henry Smith reported to the Convention, assembled in Washington-on-the-Brazos, that he had received the donation "to aid Texas in her struggle for liberty." Sent to Brazoria for negotiation, the draft allowed him to withdraw $3,000 Applied to the use of the army," the balance to remain on deposit.[17]

Hill, in February of 1836, directed "all the steamboats to charge to him the passages of all the volunteers for Texas, and has bound himself to advance everything here to facilitate the removal of volunteers."[18] Hill's offer came after the women of Nashville pledged to "arm and equip a company of 200." William Wharton, acting as a Texas commissioner, wrote the governor that by February 12, the Tennessee women had enrolled thirty young men; by five or six weeks they believed they would be able to "dispatch a company of 100."[19]

Wharton also reported to the chief executive of Texas that Hill had offered "to take $50,000 of . . . treasury notes." Optimistically, Wharton mentioned that "the ablest financiers here" believed Texas could "raise the money we want." He proposed issuing scrip for 160 to 640 acres of land at $1 per acre. The second proposal, one he thought would interest Hill, would be to print treasury notes bearing 5 per cent interest and to be redeemed in five, ten, or fifteen years.[20]

John W. Smith, public store keeper for the garrison, took an inventory on December 31 and reported 102 pairs of shoes. When he took another inventory February 3, he counted only 97.

On March 5, although away from the post, Neill signed a document to Smith, requesting him to issue five pairs of shoes and place them at the disposal of a man named Fitch, to be sold for the use of the garrison.

A number of Texians assembled at Gonzales and placed themselves under the command of Colonel Neill, who planned to return to Bexar. Anxiously, the men awaited enough reinforcements "to justify an attempt to cut their way into the Alamo."[22]

Before leaving the Alamo, Colonel Neill had promised the men he would rejoin them before twenty days passed. He was true to his word—not in returning to the Bexar garrison, as he, no doubt, intended to do, but in taking over the Texas forces at Gonzales, where on March 6, 1836, as "col. comdt. of the Post of Bexar," he signed a receipt. He paid Horace Eggleston[23] $90 for a "set of medicines for the use of the Post of Bexar." He bought from William Newland[24] for "use of Volunteer Army 104 lbs of coffee," paying $26 for the beans.

On the same day, he purchased from Stephen Smith[25] clothing "for the use of the army of Texas." He paid $2.50 for a pair of shoes and $2 for a shirt for J. B. Crawford.[26] For $2.50 he bought a pair of shoes, for $4 a Rounabout coat[27] and for $2 a shirt for D. W. Smith.[28] Neill must have been delighted and surprised that he was able to fit Jennings O'Banion[29] with shoes and suspenders. O'Banion, weighing more than 300 pounds, was not easily fitted in a majority of the Texas mercantile houses. Neill paid Stephen Smith $15.87 for these items of clothing.[30]

On the same day, while his former associates were drawing their final gasps of life in the Alamo, Neill made a second trip to Stephen Smith's Gonzales store. He bought nine pair of shoes, two pair of boots, twelve shirts, and twelve plugs of tobacco. The bill totaled $69.50. In the statement, Smith listed the soldier for whom the boots and shoes were purchased, but each may have received a shirt and a ration of tobacco.[31]

How did Neill plan to get the supplies and medicine back to the Alamo? Certainly, when he joined the men at Gonzales, he believed he could carry these supplies himself, or dispatch them by some of the troops.

While calling on merchants Smith and Eggleston, Neill had time to notice that Gonzales was laid out in the form of a huge Spanish cross with wide avenues, cobblestoned plazas, or soil worn hard through hundreds of feet, and seven wide squares—dull brown this time of year but promising to burst into greenery.[32] No doubt, Neill remembered the days in October. Trees along the Guadalupe River were like newly minted copper when Gonzales residents adamantly refused to turn over their cannon to Mexican authorities. Neill remembered helping dig the cannon from the orchard; he could never forget the struggle to move that "Come and Take It" artillery piece toward Bexar. How long ago was that? Less than six months, but to Neill the time seemed measured in years, not months.

On March 6, Gen. Sam Houston listened to a letter William B. Travis had penned from the Alamo. Besieged by a thousand Mexican soldiers under Santa Anna, Travis promised:

> I shall have to fight the enemy on his own terms. I will, however, do the best I can under the circumstances; and I feel confident that the determined valor, and desperate courage, heretofore, evinced by my men, will not fail them in the last struggle; and although they may be sacrificed to the vengeance of a gothic enemy, the victory will cost the enemy so dear, that it will be worse for him then a defeat.[33]

Earlier Travis had written that so long as the Alamo held out against the enemy, signal guns would fire at sunrise. For several days, roaring cannon shots, like cathedral bells, wafted across the prairie in the still morning. As he and his two aides rode toward Gonzales, the southernmost Anglo settlement, General Houston listened.

"I listened with acuteness of sense which no man can understand whose hearing has not been sharpened by the teachings of the dwellers of the forest," the commanding general recalled, "and who is waiting a signal of life or death from brave men. I listened in vain. Not the faintest murmur came floating on the calm morning air. I knew the Alamo had fallen . . ."[34]

With hope gossamer thin, Houston galloped into Gonzales, where 374 men awaited him. He looked over the troops. "Without organization and destitute of supplies, the men needed clothing and arms if they were to participate in a military campaign."[35]

Sources are conflicting as to where Colonel Neill was when General Houston arrived at Gonzales.

William Physick Zuber wrote in *My Eighty Years in Texas* that Colonel Neill was returning to the Alamo on March 8 and was on the Cibolo, halfway between Gonzales and Bexar, when he met Susanna Dickinson, her babe, and the two black servants.[36] Recognizing Neill immediately, Susanna sobbed out the story of the fall of the fortress telling him that her husband, Lt. Almeron Dickinson, who had worked in attempting to move the Come and Take It cannon to Bexar and who had been shoulder to shoulder with Green Jameson in rearranging the fortification of the mission, had been slain. All Texians defending the Alamo were dead. Certainly the account gave Neill cause to think. Lieutenant Dickinson, "a brave noble man, well worthy of the distinction shown him in electing him to the command of the Artillery in the absence of Colonel Neill, who had been the principal officer in that department,"[37] slain. Neill brooded over the fate of Dickinson and other friends.

Neill attempted to comfort the widow. He persuaded her to let him hold the baby during part of the ride into Gonzales, at least giving her arms a chance to regain some feeling.[38]

Zuber's date may be incorrect, for on March 10, Neill acknowledged a letter from General Houston. He agreed to forward the message to Col. James W. Fannin, "giving him due time to concentrate his forces with mine at the time and place I shall designate.[39]

The day before, George W. Hockley, Houston's aide, had sent an express from Burnham's on the Colorado with a message to Neill, identified as "commanding at Gonzales." Hockley explained that orders were for Colonel Fannin to march immediately "with all his effective force (except one hundred and twenty men, to be left for the protection of the post)" to cooperate with Neill in giving relief to Travis at the Alamo. Fannin was ordered to follow a route to be recommended by Neill and "to bring two light pieces of artillery, and no more; fifty muskets with thirty to fifty round ball cartridges for each."

A letter also went to Edward Burleson, requesting him to join Neill in working out the route for Fannin to follow and to help in forming the new regiment.[40] These instructions are interesting in light of the general council's action. On March 10 the council announced the appointment of regular officers—James W. Fannin as colonel of the artillery, and James C. Neill as first lieutenant colonel.[41]

General Houston had more time to look over his troops. His soldiers were youths—a majority of them boys under twenty years of age. They were farmers, herdsmen, volunteers. The older men had left the army, returning to their homes to protect their families. Houston ordered the camp moved several hundred yards, and on the edge of the prairie tents were pitched in two parallel rows.[42]

The following day, a lone Mexican rode into camp, confirming what Houston already knew in his heart—the Alamo had fallen. To insure the accuracy of the account, Houston ordered scouts "Deaf" Smith, Henry Karnes, and R. E. Handy to comb the area for news, and on March 13 they returned with Mrs. Dickinson's party.[43] Houston was appalled at the story Susanna related between sobs. Santa Anna had sent her to tell the Texians about the fate of the Alamo fortress. She told Houston the Mexican general must have lost approximately 600 soldiers. At least another 500 wounded were sprawled around San Antonio. A total of 182 Texians had given up their lives.[44]

Running through camp was the rumor that a Mexican force of 2,000 men was approaching Gonzales. In the community, families became distraught. Some persons who had lost loved ones in the Alamo now feared their own lives were in danger from the same enemy. Houston ordered some of the soldiers to turn over baggage wagons to the civilians, but when the men tried to locate the teams, they were grazing on the prairies. Houston commanded his men to prepare as quickly as possible to move. Some troops who had relied on their baggage wagons began tossing clothing, tents, and some provisions into the camp fires. Spires of flames shot up, lighting the flatlands.

"General, my company is ready to march," one leader reported.

"In the name of God, sir, don't be in haste. Wait till all are ready and let us retreat in good order."

All were ready by 11:00 P.M., and columns four deep cut into the warm darkness. Almost silently, the Texians marched through the streets of Gonzales, observing the lamps in the windows that revealed families hastily packing household goods. One man stepped onto the gallery of his home and called, "In the name of God, gentlemen, I hope you are not going to leave the families behind."

The march continued approximately a mile east of Gonzales. The troops followed the road into a post oak forest. They became tired trying to pull their feet through the deep sand.

In the darkness just before dawn, the Texian Army arrived at McClure's place on the east side of Peach Creek, approximately ten miles east from Gonzales. "Lay down your arms," came the order, and as quickly as they had stacked arms, soldiers fell on the ground, too tired to spread their blankets.[45]

Sleep was disturbed by explosions from the direction of Gonzales. Enemy cannon? Was Santa Anna this close in pursuit? Some soldiers spread the story that barrels of gin and wine, which had been spiked with arsenic, had been destroyed.[46]

A wagon train of civilians caught up with the army, and the women helped prepare breakfast. Houston, when he saw how eagerly the men consumed the pancakes and coffee, sent Juan Seguin and a detachment to roundup and slaughter beeves on his proposed line of march.[47] Neill devoured the pancakes, remembering too well the days in the Alamo when his diet consisted of beef and cornbread.[48]

Following a brief rest, the troops began marching again. A dispatcher brought Houston a message that James W. Fannin was determined to defend Goliad, which he and his men now called Fort Defiance.[49] He was willing to suffer the consequences of disobeying orders from his commander in chief. He would not join his forces with the main army.[50]

Hockley watched Houston accept the news. The aide remembered when he had first met Houston. Hockley was a clerk in the war department in Washington, D.C., and Houston persuaded him to move to Tennessee. Houston was governor. Then Hockley had followed Houston into Texas. He revived memories as he watched his commander. Silent for a time, obviously deep in his own thoughts, Houston took a long look at the parade of men. Eventually, he broke the silence. "Hockley, there is the last hope of Texas." Houston's army swept over the scene of troops. "We shall never see Fannin nor his men—with these soldiers we must achieve our independence or perish in the attempt."[50]

Its ranks swollen to 600, the Texian Army, commanded by Gen. Sam Houston, began its retreat to San Jacinto.[52]

William Zuber, with a group of men, reached Col. John H. Moore's ferry on the Colorado, where LaGrange now stands. On March 13 the men camped along the ruins of log cabins. Sometime after nightfall, Zuber wrote, J. C. Neill "rode into our camp but did not dismount. Sitting in the saddle on his horse, he, in my presence confirmed the report we had heard on that day of the fall of the Alamo."[53]

Zuber recalled that on the same day, four young men—claiming to have come from Bastrop—also joined the force. The unit soon joined General Houston's retreating army.

12

THE TWIN SISTERS

". . . to concentrate, retreat and conquer. . . ."
                                        Sam Houston

Sam Houston did not retreat. In his own words, he "fell back, but fell back in good order."[1]

Early in April, when General Houston and his forces were not advancing, the commander in chief of the Texas Army shared the contents of two letters with Colonel Neill. Predicting that Neill's days of inactivity were numbered, that soon he would have his work cut out for him as commander of the Texas artillery, Houston pressed into Neill's hands a letter from J. M. Allen.[2] From Brazoria, Allen had written that he had approximately forty men, two fine field pieces with shells and 880 round shots, 400 stands of muskets with a large quantity of powder, rifles, 300 barrels of provisions, 200 knapsacks, and a quantity of tents. But, he was puzzled. Col. A. Huston[3] had told him to return everything "in shape of arms or provisions."[4]

When Neill had finished reading the message—his face wrinkled questioningly—Sam Houston pulled from his pocket a crumpled note from William Bryan.[5] The New Orleans merchant, who had sent men and supplies on other occasions, informed Houston that the Texas Army soon would receive two artillery pieces "complete excepting harness."[6]

Neill and Houston fully appreciated the increase in firing power the two artillery pieces would bring to the Texas Army.

Each day he "fell back," Houston subjected himself to criticism. President David G. Burnet began speaking. "The government looks to you for action," the chief executive chided Houston. "The time has NOW arrived to determine whether we are to give up the Country and make the best of our way out of it or to meet the enemy and make at least one struggle for our boasted Independence. . . ."[7]

The main body of the Texas Army was camped at Groce's Retreat, east of the Brazos, on April 13, when the general dusted off his lap desk, dipped his quill into the small ink bottle, and began answering some of the "taunts and suggestions . . . gratuitously tendered." He wrote:

> At ten A.M. yesterday I commenced crossing the river, and from then until now 12 Oclock M., the Steam boat and yawl (having no ferry boat) have been engaged. We have 8 to 10 Wagons, ox teams and about 200 Horses in the Army, and these have to pass on board the Steamboat, besides the Troops, baggage &c. This requires time. . . .[8]

When General Houston stepped from the *Yellowstone* to the east bank of the Brazos, he and Colonel Neill expressed pleasure at what they saw. John A. Wharton greeted them warmly. He nodded rather than extend his hand, reminding his fellow former Tennesseans that his right hand had not healed completely since his duel with William T. Austin two years earlier.[9] A smile covered his young face as Wharton watched Neill and Houston examine the artillery pieces.

Attentively, Houston and Neill listened as Wharton told what he knew about the Twin Sisters, as the cannons were called. The two cast iron cannons were the gifts of the citizens of Cincinnati, Ohio. The "two pieces of hollow ware"[10] had been manufactured in Cincinnati after leaders of a meeting in 1835 had accepted the suggestion of Robert F. Lyttle to do something to aid the Texians in their fight for independence. A committee of William M. Corry, Dr. Daniel Drake, Nathaniel Seaman, Col. Charles Hales, and Israel Ludlow had corresponded with the New Orleans agents; later Corry, Edward Woodruff and Pulaski Smith had contracted with the Greenwood and Web foundry to manufacture, mount, and supply the pieces with shot. Committee members then dispatched the cannons to New Orleans, where they were accepted by Texas Agents who arranged to have them sent to Brazoria.

General Houston admitted he had known about the cannons in Brazoria. Twice he had sent for them, but the roads were quagmires, there had been a shortage of dray animals, and rumors of approaching enemy troops had blocked delivery. The general assured Wharton that he had known about the cannons—up to a point.

The quartermaster general, Colonel Huston, had arranged for the six-pounders to be loaded on the schooner, *Pennsylvania*, moved to Galveston Island, thence to Harrisburg. Wharton told how the horses had pulled the cannons to this side of the Brazos.[11]

Several of the men who had accompanied the twin artillery from Harrisburg joined Houston's army.[12] Soon, they, other members of the army, and Houston and Neill were caressing the twins. Houston and Neill ran their hands over the smooth glistening barrels—Houston feeling relief that the artillery finally had reached him, Neill sensing that with the cannons responsibility returned.

Neither Houston nor Neill could spend too much time admiring the Twin Sisters; too much work begged for attention. Almost immediately Neill focused his efforts on organizing a company of artillery. Each gun required a crew of nine men, but when the call went out for volunteers, forty men stepped out of rank, eager to work with the sparkling artillery pieces.[13]

Houston, wearing a frayed leather jacket, went to the blacksmith's forge to help cut up horseshoes and scraps of iron that had been collected. As Houston labored over the forge, an old man walked into camp and approached some of the soldiers. "Is there a blacksmith in camp?"

A recruit answered quickly. "Yes, sir. See that tent down yonder? The only one in camp."

The man, cradling an ancient flint lock rifle, approached. "I want you to fix my gun," he said, pressing the weapon into Houston's hands. "The lock is out of order. It won't stand cocked."

"Very well," Houston said. "Call for it in an hour, and she will be ready."

Leaving the scrap iron alone, Houston began cleaning the rifle, snapping the trigger, and making certain the weapon cocked properly.

Meantime, the owner of the rifle learned that he had talked with the commander in chief of the Texas Army and had ordered him to repair the piece. "What shall I do? They told me he was a blacksmith; I didn't know it was General Houston."

Nervously, he approached Houston to apologize. "My friend," Houston said warmly, "They told you right. I am a very good blacksmith." To demonstrate, he cocked the rifle several times, showing the owner how smoothly the rifle worked.[14]

When the owner again cradled his rifle and left the forge, Houston resumed preparing slugs for the artillery.

Colonel Neill named five men from Capt. Isaac N. Moreland's Company to care for the Twin Sisters. The detail Neill appointed appears to be one of the most stellar in military history.

Pvt. Benjamin McCulloch was born in Tennessee, and like his neighbor, Davy Crockett, moved to Texas, arriving in time to draw the Twin Sisters assignment. After the war he lived in Seguin, but when a position in the county surveyor's office opened, he entered a new profession. His reputation as a fighter grew in the Plum Creek Indian skirmishes, in the Vasquez Expedition of 1842, and through his work in John C. Hays' Ranger outfit. McCulloch was elected major general of the militia in 1846 and became a colonel in the Confederate Army in 1861. He received the surrender of Gen. D. E. Twiggs of the Federal garrison in San Antonio. He was assigned to command the troops in Arkansas and south Kansas.[15]

Pvt. Thomas Green, Virginia born, was appointed assistant adjutant general in the army soon after the Battle of San Jacinto. He served in the Congress until he entered the Confederate Army. He had gone with John H. Moore and Col. J. C. Neill on an expedition against the Indians in 1841, was a captain in the Vasquez Expedition, and served as Inspector General with the Somervell Expedition. He was a captain in John C. Hays' army in the Mexican War. During the Civil War he held the rank of colonel in Sibley's Brigade and became brigadier general, commanding the forces that captured Galveston Island.[16]

1st Sgt. Richardson A. Scurry had been a lawyer in his native Tennessee. He opened a law office in Red River County before enlisting in the Texas Army. He was discharged with the rank of first lieutenant. He served as secretary of state in the First Congress, district attorney, judge of the Sixth Judicial District, member of the House of Representatives, and in 1851 went to the U.S. Congress.[17]

Pvt. Temple O. Harris could trace his family in his native Virginia to Thomas Harris, who had settled there in 1613 and had been a member of the House of Burgesses. Private Harris had married Martha M. McGregor, whose family had founded Nashville, Tennessee. Harris took part in the war with Mexico and later became active in the shipping of sugar from New Orleans.[18]

Pvt. John M. Wade, a native of New York, had set type for Horace Greeley and George W. Kendall. He had joined Thomas J. Rusk's company at Nacagdoches, but because of illness was left at San Felipe. He joined Capt. William Ware's company at Groce's. After the Battle of San Jacinto he rejoined Ware's company, serving until June 11. Later, he was elected captain of a company stationed at Victoria. He worked as a printer on the *Telegraph and Texas Register* at Columbia and Houston and in 1845 established the Montgomery *Patriot*. He died in Travis County, October 9, 1879.[19]

While Houston's 700 to 800 men drilled at Groce's, the five-man detail attended the Twin Sisters.[20] On April 16, Texian scouts ushered a black man before the commanding general to tell about his capture and release by the Mexicans.

"Tell Mr. Houston," the black man reported Santa Anna as having said, "that I know where he is, up there in the bushes; and as soon as I whip the land thieves down here, I will go up there and smoke him out."[21]

Houston smiled slightly as he heard the threat, but the grin broadened and stars appeared to dance in his eyes as he listened to the black man answer questions about the composition of the Mexican force. The Mexican general was with the advance detachment of the army marching toward Harrisburg.[22]

A confident Houston now was ready for battle with the Napoleon of the West. Houston's son explained the situation:

> ... the Texas General had a force equal in number. He felt confident that he could defeat and capture them. The two cannon, which had been sent by the patriotic citizens of Cincinnati, Ohio, were received while the army was in camp near Groce's. Horses were obtained and ammunition was prepared by cutting old horseshoes.[23]

Houston's men marched into Harrisburg, crossing prairies oozing with mud. Military wagons had to be stripped of their contents—the contents loaded on the backs of soldiers, and the empty wagons pulled by animals and men. The general frequently dismounted to put his shoulder to a stubborn wagon.[24]

Sitting on a log before a glowing campfire, Houston on April 19 wrote his official report for delivery to the secretary of war. He prepared a second copy for a friend. Houston wrote, "This morning we are in preparation to meet Santa Anna. It is the only chance of saving Texas." His men were in fine spirits. "Now is the time for action . . . ." Before dispatching the message, Houston handed it to his aide, George Hockley. Hockley read carefully, seeing in the material a new key to his commander:

> We will use our best efforts to fight the enemy, to such advantage as will insure victory, though the odds are greatly against us. I leave the result in the hands of a wise God, and rely upon his providence.[25]

Described as "the proudest bunch in the Texas Army," the thirty soldiers in Colonel Neill's newly organized artillery corps had not been able to fire even one practice round, shortage of ammunition and scrap metal having prevented the cannoneers from experiencing this pleasure. They ignored the chill of the early morning on Wednesday, April 20, in order to caress the Twin Sisters. They watched as Colonel Sherman and his second regiment rode out to New Washington on a scouting expedition. Near the James Routh plantation, the Texians met Marcus Barragan and his Mexican troops. Barragan wheeled his mount and sped to tell Santa Anna what he had seen, mistakenly believing that he had ridden upon the main Texas force.[26]

Texas soldiers in the camp were still fanning their fires when scouts returned screaming they had sighted the enemy.

Years later, Dr. N. D. Labadie remembered when orders came to halt for breakfast that morning. The Texians stacked their rifles. Three cows grazing near were slaughtered, and many soldiers began gathering wood. The surgeon, Dr. Shields Booker,[27] delivered a dozen eggs, soon dropped into a pot of brackish water with a half pound of coffee. The water had begun to boil when the scouts appeared. "To arms. To your arms!"

Hungry soldiers hastened to grab their share of the eggs from the coffee. When Labadie discovered his eggs contained chickens, he gave up his ration to others. His associates, finding the eggs well cooked, devoured them before grabbing their firearms.

Deaf Smith rode into camp, calming the Texians by reporting there was no emergency, that only the advanced guard had been sighted. The army assembled, however, and began a march. The men ferried over on Lynch's ferry, covered half a mile, then tossed their knapsacks on the ground under a grove of live oaks on the banks of Buffalo Bayou. From this grassy crest, they could see Lynch's Ferry at the point Buffalo Bayou emptied into San Jacinto River. Beyond the river was Lynchburg, a clutter of unpainted houses. When the Texians saw the plump cows grazing placidly near the village, they curbed their eagerness to fight the Mexicans, turning their attentions instead to butchering, igniting campfires, and threading steaks on spits.[28]

Here on the east side of Buffalo Bayou, the Texians felt curtained by the oak trees heavy with Spanish moss, hanging like veterans' beards from the bud-ripe branches. The mud-colored bayou was almost a right angle with the San Jacinto River. A prairie rolled approximately thirty feet above the bayou, bounded on two sides by marsh lands. To the troops' left was a mile of low ground gently sloping into a hill, on top of which was an "island of timber." The Texians also were in one of these islands.²⁹ The artillerymen settled into a low hollow that protected them from enemy cannon. Here, W. C. Swearingen recalled in a letter to his brother, Lemuel, "we formed our line" with the Twin Sisters.³⁰ Behind the cannoneers were two companies of infantry, backed by the cavalry. Burleson's riflemen were on the right wing; Sidney Sherman's troops guarded the left.³¹

One of the veterans described the waiting period in this version, which appeared in the *Texas Almanac, 1860;*

> Our troops, for better concealment, were prostrate in the grass, within the shelter of timber, and like eagles hovering over the stray lambs, impatient to pounce on the foe still beyond the reach of the rifles, when the Twin Sisters belched forth the secret. The astonished enemy halted, paused a moment, then wheeled, and calmly retired to his encampment at the bluff. Here he commenced fortifying by throwing up an embankment and surmounting it with saddles, *aparajos,* and such other material as he had. The disappointed army was grieved, mortified, and indignant Col. Neill, an old veteran, on being inquired of, said, "You know I am too old a soldier to fire without orders."

Santa Anna, another version explains, looked over the situation. In front of the moss-draped trees were no more than thirty artillerymen. The Mexican general snarled at the puny force and called for his musicians to strike up "Deugello," the same sign of no quarter he had given during the siege of the Alamo. Earlier in the morning, the general had placed his aide, Col. Antonio Delgado, in charge of the cannon, and told him to move the brass twelve-pounder to an island of trees between the armies. Santa Anna, his uniform glistening with medals, joined his former aide.

"Your Excellency," one of the officers shouted. "This is a good way to lose a war that we've already won."

Santa Anna paid no attention but commanded Delgado to fire on the Texian camp. From its position approximately 300 yards from the enemy camp, the Mexican gun roared.

Colonel Neill ordered his men to answer. As the smoke settled, Texians could see Mexican horses falling and men hitting the ground, obviously in agony. William A. Park[32] slumped and some of his associates hovered over him. The carriage of one of the Sisters was disabled.[33]

The second Twin spewed its load of grape, canister, and horseshoe pieces. The Mexican gun answered, snipping branches of oak and strands of Spanish moss.

Colonel Neill crumpled to the soft loam, his hip broken by enemy fire. The old veteran needed medical attention.

On August 8, 1855, area residents assembled at Lynch's Ferry[34] to discuss the political situation. They invited Lorenzo de Zavala to speak, but the forty-seven-year-old former governor of the state of Mexico only recently had returned from Paris, where he had been Santa Anna's minister to France.[35] The newcomer to Texas sent his regrets; he was too sick to deliver an address. In his letter, however, Zavala gave a sketch of current affairs in Texas and Mexico as he viewed them. Leaders of the meeting shared Zavala's correspondence with the crowd.[36]

Four days later, Zavala was well enough to confer with Philip Singleton[37] about his homestead, which overlooked the confluence of the San Jacinto and the Bayou. Zavala fell in love with the property upon sight. The well-drained plain overlooked a lane that ribboned through majestic oak trees and served as the main route linking Austin's colony on the west with the settlements that hugged the Trinity River on the east.[38] Colonel Lynch's ferry was in operation. Zavala also liked the log house facing south on a bluff and the barns, cribs, and sheds that Singleton had erected on the property.[39]

Zavala moved into the house immediately after making a deal, but it was December 1835 before his wife and six children arrived with their belongings.[40]

Had the Zavala family in less than five months begun to feel at home on the plantation? Certainly, Mrs. Zavala's work was visible in the rose garden, where Lady Banksia and Marechel Neil were in bloom and where beds had been prepared and planted with annuals and perennials.

Zavala, with birdlike movement, scurried about the cottage

on April 20, when the Texian soldiers approached bearing a litter. Zavala, short and chubby, opened the door, and when he learned that two Texians had been wounded, pointed to the majestic four-poster bed. Emily Zavala hastened to throw back the coverlet on one bed, fluffing the feather mattress as she did.[41]

"It's Col. Neill. Leader of our artillery." The information came from one of the litter bearers, John D. Morris,[42] as he gently helped roll the colonel onto the soft bed. "Hit in the thigh."

The following day, William A. Park, another member of the artillery company, was brought to the Zavala home. The De Zavalas began preparing their residence to serve as a hospital, and before long the buildings and grounds smelled of ether and echoed with the groans of men in pain. Approximately 200 to 300 Mexican prisoner-patients remained a month after the Battle of San Jacinto.[43]

When Colonel Neill left the Zavala home is not known, nor is it known whether he went to a home in the area or was transported to Galveston. On March 17, 1839, Neill, with John Shea as witness, signed a document that he "held the rank of Lt. Col. of artillery and was severely wounded on the 20th day of April 1836 and was left adjacent to the Battle Ground of San Jacinto by the army which took up the line of March in pursuit of the Enemy."[44] He declared that:

> "the govt. not having provided me with suitable quarters as is usually done in such cases, but leaving me near the Battle Ground when I was compelled to procure quarters & at a considerable expense. I was then promoted to a colonelcy in the artillery altho not having recovered from the wound which I received and—still continue to furnish my qurters &c at my own expense."[45]

Papers in the Archives of the Texas State Library show that quarters for Neill from June 1, 1835, to February 12, 1836, were paid. Holding the rank of lieutenant colonel, he drew $80 allowance for this two-month period of service. For housing from

February 16, 1836, to June 22, 1836, he drew $173, and for the period from June 22 to October 22, 1836, he was allowed $200. His fuel allowances for the periods were for $54, $79.50, and $27. On December 12, 1838, he received $613.50 in housing and fuel allotments. His time in service was verified by Charles Mason,[46] acting secretary of war, in a document indicating that Neill was promoted to colonel in July 1836.

The board examining Neill's request for reimbursement for uarters and fuel found:

> his right is purely a legal one over which this Board has no jurisdiction. The right to Fuel & Quarters should be settled with the Quartermaster Genl. and depends whether he was in Garrison or at a Post and not in the field. The certificate of officers on honor is the usual evidence required when in service when not his affidavit.

Henry A. Cobb signed the document on March 19, 1839, as chairman of the Board of Examiners.

Neill appeared in Columbia,[47] recently established as capital of the Republic of Texas. Here the first Congress had been called into session, and under a live oak tree Sam Houston had taken the oath as president. The torn jacket Houston had worn as commander in chief of the Texas Army had been replaced by a brocaded maroon waistcoat, his beard had been shaved, and he had put aside his crutches but continued to limp. During the inaugural services, Houston removed the sword he had carried at San Jacinto.

"Should the danger of my country again call for my services, I expect to resume it." He pointed to the sword.

In less dramatic manner, Neill went about clearing the paper work that would end his career as a soldier and launch him into civilian life again. On October 12, 1836, he submitted a claim for $1,456.50, and on another occasion he certified that a statement for $155.37 was correct.

Neill appeared in the office of the auditor, Asa Brigham,[48] on December 14. In Brigham's presence, he signed a document saying he had been commander of the artillery and as such had authorized discharges for John Marsh, Alexander Franklin, Landey Jones, Samuel Fry, Joel Hegns, and John Stanley, who were due $297.33 for their services.

Two months passed, and Neill, still in Columbia, called on government officials concerning paper work. On February 13, 1837, he certified before J. W. Moody, first auditor, that he owed "the government nothing on his own account, or on the account of any other person, nor has he retained, sold, or embezzled any armes or munitions of war or any kind of property whatever, belonging to the Republic of Texas, nor has he caused it to be done."[49]

13

SAN AUGUSTINE

"Peace and harmony prevailed . . . ."

James Gaines[1] was operating a ferry on the Sabine River as early as 1824, probably spending as much time fishing as he did floating persons and animals across the water. Certainly, he enjoyed staring as the towering pines above the redlands stirred under the slightest whisp of breeze. By 1824, however, he was noticing the changes. Wagons delivered large families into the area, and before long the newcomers had put their slaves and southern heritage to work establishing cotton plantations. John A. Williams[2] opened a cotton gin and at the end of the first year could boast that he had processed twenty-six bales.

The town of San Augustine, likewise, began to spread along the east bank of Ayish Bayou and on both sides of the road that beckoned into the interior of Texas. The village was laid out into forty-eight blocks and divided into 356 lots with 80-foot wide streets pointing to the cardinal points of the compass. In anticipation that principal business houses would rise along the road, town fathers named it Main Street. The earliest homes were built south of the public square. In the center of the block of buildings, surly Ephraim Tally erected a two-story building for a saloon and gambling house, and his overbearing temper often filled the four walls and echoed onto the second floor, where ink-stained men cranked out issues of the *Redlander* newspaper.

Sometime in 1837 Almanzon Huston,[3] Harris E. Watson, and Alexander Horton,[4] brothers-in-law, built a hotel, and here Judge R. M. Williamson gaveled the first District Court to order in one of the large rooms facing the street.

The most important public building in San Augustine for years was the customhouse, a plain rectangular building on Montgomery Street, where duties were collected on goods coming in from the United States of the north. San Augustine ranked third in importance of ports of entry, only Galveston and Matagorda outranking her.[5]

Into San Augustine village came John Gillespie, a native of Ireland who captivated residents with his cheerful idealism and goodness of heart, but whose feet itched to travel and whose eyes enjoyed feasting on new sights. While he had been in Mexico, he "incurred the displeasure or excited the cupidity of the Government officials" and was thrown into jail. A Mexican court sentenced him to die. Blindfolded and kneeling before the firing squad, he gave the Mason distress signal. The officer in charge recognized the sign, dismissed the soldiers, and conferred briefly with Gillespie, then slipped $30 into Gillespie's hands and helped him escape.

From that day forward, Gillespie, with typical Irish zeal and enthusiasm, devoted himself to Masonry. Naturally, when he settled in San Augustine, he hastened to organize a lodge. When he had the requisite number of Masons, he applied for a dispensation from the Grand Master of the State of Louisiana while in New Orleans on private business. Upon returning from his trip, he, as a special deputy for the Grand Master of Louisiana, organized a lodge.

Named McFarland Lodge in honor of William McFarland, the first Worshful Master, the body held its session on August 13, 1837, with Gillespie investing the officers with regalia, jewels, and insignia.[6]

Only two months after its organizational session, McFarland Lodge[7] approved the petition of J. B. Denton[8] to receive the first degree. The ballot box was prepared, "it being a case of emergency," and after a favorable vote, Denton was prepared to receive the entered apprentice degree.[9]

On November 4, 1837, the lodge was opened in the upper

room of Dr. Samuel Stivers' residence[10] "in Case of Emergency in the Fellow Crafts (*sic*) Degree." James C. Neill served as tiler, pro tempore.[11]

Attending was John Gillespie, representing the Grand Lodge of the State of Louisiana. During the session, Denton was approved for the second degree, and Wyatt Hanks[12] was "duly elected to be passed to the Second Degree." Minutes record that "Brothers Denton & Hanks being duly prepared were admitted and the degree of a Fellow Craft Mason was conferred on each of them in due and ancient form." [13]

In an emergency meeting later in the year, the petition of R. B. Irvine[14] was read, and he was prepared for the first degree. The petition of D. McDonald[15] was read, and he, likewise, was elected. The entered apprentice degree was "conferred on each of them in due and ancient form."

The lodge approved Neill's account for tiling ten nights at two dollars a night, and the sum of $20 was ordered paid.[16]

14

SAM HOUSTON, PRESIDENT

"We wish to bury the tomahawk...."
Sam Houston to Zachary Taylor
December 9, 1842

Wind whipped through Austin on December 14, 1841, and cold nipped the faces of approximately 1,000 persons who had gathered at the capitol. Members of Congress hovered at the rear of the new government building, where a canopy had been erected to protect dignitaries. Behind the platform and above it fluttered the flags of battalions taken at San Jacinto. In the center was the portrait of Stephen F. Austin that had been hauled overland to the new capital. On the platform were chairs to accommodate congressional leaders and the men who would take their oaths of office.

Secretaries of both houses of Congress called the rolls, and committees assigned the duties invited incoming officers to take their seats under the awning. The Travis Guards, after escorting officials, retired from the stage. Judge R.E.B. Baylor asked the "divine blessing upon the solemn ceremonies" and in a lengthy supplication sought "the well being of the country."

The speaker informed Sam Houston it was time to take the oath of office, and representatives of the people of the Republic then would welcome any remarks he wished to make. From the moment that Houston appeared, wearing a hunting shirt, a pair of old pantaloons, and a wide-brimmed fur hat, he made it clear he objected to the life style of the retiring president, Mirabeau B. Lamar, whose retinue Houston termed "The Court of Witumpka." Houston read the oath himself then launched into his inaugural address. He emphasized that the nation's salvation would be in economy and in industry. He frequently used a bandana "with fine stage effect," and the ladies in the audience promptly adapted the mannerism.

When the president had finished talking, the artillery began firing, using a system that had been worked out so there would be no waste of time "between the oath and the booming of the first gun."

After the vice-president, Edward Burleson—also wearing a hunting shirt—took his oath and made a few remarks, another volley of artillery fire rent the air. New officers and lawmakers then marched down Congress Avenue to the Eberly House, where Houston, Burleson, and Lamar were called upon for toasts.

Houston later revealed he would not occupy the residence in which Lamar had lived, but would take a room in the Eberly House. He mentioned that the roof of the mansion was in need of repair, and in obvious reference to the fact that Lamar was a bachelor, Houston said, "Texas will have a Lady Presidente." Mrs. Houston, however, did not appear in Austin. Whether because of ill health or the primitive conditions in the new community, she remained in the town of Houston while the chief executive was in the new seat of government. Sixty days after taking office, Houston rode a mule from town, late setting up government offices in the town of Washington that was located on the banks of the Brazos river.[1]

The president's office in Washington was a one-room affair which had served as W. Z. McFarlain's law office. A fireplace centered the wall on the east and the door was on the west. The south and north walls had windows, and a couch had been placed under the opening on the north. In the center of the room was a table, at which Houston's secretary sat to take dictation. Eventually, President Houston ordered half a dozen chairs—of white ash and with white cowhide bottoms—made in the area.

For his routine office work, Houston wore a "hunting shirt of linsey woolsey checks, a common pair of pants, I think of osnaburg[2]—a broad-brimmed hat of smoky color, with fur nap half an inch long," recalled John Washington Lockhart. The "hat was a very fine one," and Houston wore russet shoes without string.[3]

An observer remembered that there was some relief in the presidential costume after the Sultan of Turkey sent Houston "a long flowing red robe of beautiful silk which came to near his ankles, pants of the regular Turkish fashion, large and baggy; around the waist they would measure several yards." Yellow shoes were attached to the pants. Houston wore the robe while attending office chores.[4]

For his second term, Houston set up a plan of dealing with the Indians. He pushed through Congress approval for the establishment of a Bureau of Indian Affairs in the Department of War and Marine, whose chief clerk would assume leadership of the bureau at no extra cost to the Republic.[5] For a time this position was occupied by Joseph C. Eldridge.[6]

Also as a means of bringing about peace with the Indians, Houston called for the establishment of a string of trading posts[7] conveniently located for the tribes, and he received authority to appoint resident agents at these posts. He also planned to sponsor councils, from which he hoped to get treaties with the various tribes.

Houston dispatched agents to ride into Indian territory to invite the chiefs to meet with him in Washington City. Moses Evans was one of these riders. His copper-colored hair was divided into two plaits, the ends tied with narrow red or blue ribbon, and his beard was fiery red. He moved among the Indians with a step that could be regarded only as vain.[8]

When George Whitfield Terrell's[9] health failed, Houston proposed that the attorney general travel as an Indian commissioner. He and the General Superintendent of Indian Affairs went into the frontier, presenting the head chiefs with plugs of tobacco and shawls for distribution to the lesser chiefs.[10] A mule train carried the president's gifts and the agents' supplies.[11]

Some Indians and Republic of Texas commissioners assembled at Tehuacana Creek to open a council on Tuesday, March 28, 1843. Representing Texas were George W. Terrell, John S. Black, and Thomas I. Smith. Present as commissioner of the United States was Pierce M. Butler, escorted into camp by Captain Blake and fifteen soldiers.

Houston, unable to attend, had addressed a letter to Linney, the Shawnee chief, and it was read and translated before General Terrell began his opening address. Terrell explained:

> We will give our red brothers a country to live in, in Texas. We have a great abundance of buffalo and other wild game to feed the red men who come to live in Texas. But the red men ought to recollect that the game in the woods and the prairies will not last always. For this reason they ought to settle themselves, make them farms and raise something to live on when the game is all gone. We will establish trading houses in their country to sell to the Indians all the goods they may need. Our traders will buy from them all their horses, mules, skins and other things they may want to sell. We will also send Agents to live amongst them, who will always send the talks of the red man to the President, and carry back his talk to them.

He announced that "the President has sent across the great waters for three hundred fine lances to present to the chiefs and big warriors amongst the red men; they will be here in seven moons . . . ."

He mentioned that the president wanted the chiefs who were in council to visit him in Washington City, where they would receive "handsome presents." Once he had determined the chiefs intended to keep the peace, the president would give them powder and lead.

"Texas is now like a child; it has to crawl, but will grow up bye and bye to be a man. We will then protect and take care of our red brothers . . . ," Terrell said.[12]

Governor Butler echoed Terrell's statements:

> The time is fast coming when the Red man can no longer rely on the Game in the Woods and on the prairie for his subsistance; the wallowing places of the Buffalo are fast growing up with grass. Like my Red friends the Muskogee and the Cherokee, should learn to cultivate the soil, then the white and Red man might visit, eat each others Corn and exchange their labour.[13]

Butler concluded his talk with, "if you meet me with a forked tongue, I will be angry and growl like a dog. But if you meet me with truth, I will be pleased and meet you with embraces and presents."

Roasting Ear, muscular chief of the Delaware, stood straight as a lance to address the conclave. The white men were impressed that he was cleaner, better clothed than the other Indians. He rejoiced over a treaty prospect.[14]

The Shawnee leader, Linney, promised that he and Roasting Ear would assist and stand by the white men in preparing a treaty. "Let not our meeting here in council be in vain," he said, "but let us endeavor to carry out our intentions . . . ."[15]

Bintah, whose ears had been split, each section wrapped in lead and tin, and whose nose contained a silver ornament, spoke for his Caddo braves. "I will follow like a child. I have only one thought in my heart. I have heard your talk and hold fast to it. Your talk is good."[16]

The Anadarko, José María, had little to say. Wirey, of medium height, and weighing approximately 145 pounds, he commented he had heard all.[17]

Acaquash, the Waco chief, however, spoke sadly. "Where I and my people now live appears like a Cloud of smoke caused by warfare—on my return I will endeavor to put out the war fires."[18]

When the council was preparing to wind up business, Terrell addressed the gathering:

> Our Council is now concluded. This day, like the one on which we first met, is bright and beautiful. This we look upon as an evidence that the Great Spirit smiles upon our proceedings. The winter has just passed off, and Spring is breaking upon us.
>
> War is like Winter; its face is surly and dark. We must let all thoughts of war pass from our minds with the winter. The grass is springing up from the earth; the leaves are putting forth on the trees; the birds begin to sing in the forest. All nature seems to be smiling around us. So when we return to our homes our hearts and the hearts of our people will be glad and joyful. They will rejoice in the prospect of a lasting peace between the white and the Red man.[19]

Certain that the great chief did not speak with a forked tongue—that when he invited them to call on him in the Town of Washington, he meant "Y'all come"—a number of Indians rode into the temporary Texas capital. The women set up a camp in a grove of trees—erecting tents, hanging pots, gathering wood. Their braves stretched out on buffalo hides, leisurely smoking tomahawk pipes. At night, men and women were ready for dancing. They formed two circles—the braves in one and the squaws making up the other. As one old woman pounded the skin that had been stretched over a hollow log and several other women rattled dried gourds, the two circles, participants elbow to elbow, began to move.[20]

The braves were dressed in beech clouts with strings of gray moss draped around their arms and necks. The squaws, wearing full calico skirts tied around the waists and with blankets hanging over their heads so that they fell loosely behind, kept to themselves for their dance.[21]

William Nangle, a Philadelphia lapidary who after becoming involved in "an imprudent enterprise" had moved to Texas, where he began selling mementos fashioned of stones from the Alamo—vases, candlesticks, seals. He had prepared a miniature of an Alamo monument he wished to sell to the Texas government.[22] In Washington to display the model, he had called upon Houston, who immediately commissioned him to prepare a calumet with a long stem of cane.[23]

The president remained aloof from his red visitors, and they began to grow restless. Even the dancing at night and the rations of corn and beef that Luis Sanchez[24] and Jesse Chisholm[25] made available did not ameliorate the apparent neglect of visitors.[26]

Then one day the president and his staff galloped to the grove where the Indians had raised their teepees. Without warning, the horsemen appeared. What happened is described by Herbert Gambrell:

> When the procession reached the campgrounds the horses were slowed to a canter and the riders circumscribed the camp, their eyes fixed straight ahead, as if passing in review. The chiefs hurriedly formed an aisle through the middle of the tents down which the official party walked. His Excellency ceremoniously greeted each chief, then embraced him Indian-fashion. . . .[27]

Houston, his aides, and guests seated themselves around the stone peacepipe Nangle had fashioned. The pipe was filled with tobacco and sumac, and the long stem was passed from Houston to the eldest chief to the next. After all men in the council had puffed on the pipe, Houston—as physically fit as a young brave and as impressive as a brass statue—stood. He was silent a moment, long enough to draw all eyes to him.

As he had promised, Houston presented Red Bear and Acaquash gifts of rifles. To Acaquash he handed a flint and steel gun, and the chief accepted it joyfully, but Red Bear drew back from his gift. In a huff, he withdrew from the circle. Undaunted, Houston handed the gun to an aide. Half an hour later, Houston entered the house where Red Bear was quartered. The chief sulked in bed, his head and ears covered with a blanket. Houston joined the several braves sitting around the room, and when Houston saw the figure under the blanket move, he asked if it were a squaw. The insult aroused Red Bear, who made his way to the general and embraced him, "as humble as a whipped dog."

Houston listened to an explanation. Red Bear did not want the percussion lock gun because caps for it were too difficult to acquire.[28] Houston, however, already recognized the petulant chief as "a talking man," a treacherous shyster.[29]

Joseph Eldridge, as general superintendent of Indian Affairs and as commissioner to the Comanche nation, signed a pact with Pah-hah-yuco, calling for a council on the Clear Fork of the Brazos "at the full of the moon in December . . . to enter into and conclude a firm and lasting treaty."[30]

Eldridge must have regarded the pact an accomplishment. He wrote Houston that the Comanches were "like mustangs hard to catch and bring into the settlements." He found that the warriors recalled the San Antonio incident and feared treachery. They wanted to talk with the chief himself—not with his commissioners. "We want to talk with him, take him by the hand and hear the words of his own mouth, then there can be no mistake but all will be understood," he stressed in his letter to the president. The letter was sent from a Tawakoni village on the Trinity River and dated June 11, 1843.[31] Eldridge stressed:

> The Indians all say they want to see you in person—Nothing else it seems will satisfy them, and I take the liberty to suggest to your Excellency the beneficial effect your presence at the Council would have, I am confident that more could be effected by yourself, than all the commissioners that could be sent. . . .[32]

Joseph Eldridge was dismissed from office after a misunderstanding. He and Hamilton Bee had ridden into Warren's Trading Post one day. Jim Second Eye rushed to welcome them. "How are you? How are you? Glad to see you," he greeted the two men.

Usually courteous, Eldridge jumped from his pony, and before a group of Indians and whites tongue-lashed the Indian—who once had left Eldridge and Bee with only their pistols for protection.

Eldridge and Bee left Warren's for Washington, but Bee became ill with chills and fever, and Eldridge met with another delay. Before Eldridge reached the temporary capitol, Jim Shaw and John Conner had described the trading house incident to Houston. Eldridge reported to the president, was cooly received, and soon dismissed as superintendent. Later, when Houston learned complete details of the incident, he suggested to President Anson Jones that Eldridge be appointed chief clerk of the state department.[33]

15

PEACE COUNCIL

*"Here is the pipe and tobacco . . .
come and receive them . . ."*
Luis Sanchez
May 11, 1844

Thomas G. Western,[1] superintendent of Indian Affairs, was a man who overlooked few details in organizing a meeting of white settlers and Indians. When plans were formed for a pow-wow on the council grounds at the Falls of the Brazos in the spring, 1844, Western suggested to the Torrey brothers[2] that they make available in their trading post tomahawks, 100 hoes, 100 small hatchets, 500 pounds of lead, tin cups, tin pans, buckets, blankets, beads, sets of shells, a sample of shrouding—the coarse woolen cloth which had proved popular in trading with the Indians—and any other items the merchant brothers deemed would be useful.[3] A week after offering this suggestion, Western from his desk in Washington City,[4] was writing the trading post agent his concern over preparations for the caucus. The Indian Bureau had deposited at J.T. Whitesides'[5]—on the east side of the river—approximately 500 pounds of freight, and Western requested that the Torreys arrange drayage to the treaty grounds.[6]

By early April, commissioners James C. Neill and Leonard H. Williams; Dr. Benjamin Washington Hill, secretary of war and marine; and Benjamin Sloat were in camp. They must have felt surprise when they learned that Sam Houston had appointed Thomas G. Western as general superintendent of Indian Affairs. True, Western had provided meritorious service during the

Revolution, raising a company of forty-eight men after he had lost his home and mercantile establishment at Goliad. But, the commissioners could not erase another incident from their minds. They remembered when Western, commanding the cavalry at San Antonio, had fallen a victim of the propaganda of Dr. James Grant and Gen. Felix Huston, who were planning a raid on Matamoros. Western began hinting for his troops to demand military action and to plant seeds for overthrowing the Houston administration.

With enough evidence for a court-martial, Houston decided instead to handle the problem through diplomacy. Learning that his old San Jacinto aide-de-camp, William H. Patton, had plans to visit San Antonio on business, Houston revealed his thoughts of sending an envoy to London or Versailles. He was considering Major Western for that post. Was he qualified in the opinion of Patton?

As soon as Patton had time to reach San Antonio, Houston sent orders for Western to report to him in Houston. The president met with Western but said nothing about the appointment, and Western said nothing about having learned of the matter through Patton. Time passed, and Western asked Surgeon General Ashbel Smith, close associate to the president, if he had heard Houston mention such an appointment. Dr. Smith could only shake his head.

President Houston then announced the appointment of J. Pinckney Henderson. Western returned to San Antonio to pick up orders placing him in another military post. He began denouncing Houston for a dirty trick and commenting upon the lack of sobriety of the chief executive.[7]

The Texian leaders at the camp grounds may have talked of the matter among themselves, but they also were occupied with an inspection of new facilities. They commented on the 32 x 20 building Sloat had prepared for the conclave. The roof was covered with two-foot boards, and the half-log pickets forming the walls were fastened together in such a way as to provide a substantial building. Out buildings had been provided for comfort and necessity.[8]

The commissioners watched the Delaware, Caddo, and Shawnee Indians arrive upon the site. Caravans appeared. The

Indians rode single file. The men—dignified and brave, but dressed in their best—led the procession. They were followed by the squaws—many with black-eyed papooses strapped to their backs and with another child in front of the saddle—who also rode astride. The women kept their eyes on the pack horses loaded with household goods and pelts. As soon as the caravan halted on camp grounds, the squaws dismounted to begin chopping branches of mesquite and oak upon which to erect their tents. With each arrival, the scene was the same, but fascinated commissioners continued to watch.[9]

A slight rain—not enough to swell the creek—fell, and the sky was dove gray when Western, still feeling effects of a recent illness, rode onto the Tehaucana Creek Council Grounds. When he dismounted, Neill, Williams, Dr. Hill, and Sloat were around to inquire of his trip and health.[10]

"How many Indians are here?" Western, even before he dismounted, asked immediately upon arriving among the officials.

"About 200," Neill told him. "Caddo, Delaware, and Shawnee. Acaquash sent one man to return a stolen horse to its owner."[11]

"What about the Comanche? Any word from them?" Western asked, continuing to scan the grounds for members of that tribe.

Neill shook his head. "Nothing definite. Don't know whether they will be here or not. Acaquash, astride his bob-tail nag, has gone among them to round 'em up, if possible."[12]

"Acaquash? The president has mighty high regard for that Indian. Says he's a true friend. Thinks he can make the bad men of the forest—as Houston puts it—behave." There was no way of knowing whether Western was stating a fact or expressing a sarcastic opinion.[13]

The commissioners shared with the superintendent some of the rumors they had received concerning the Comanches. One messenger had said the Indians definitely would not attend. Other messengers, however, had stories that the Comanches were on the Little River, heading—slowly to be sure—toward Council Grounds.[14]

Western had not been on the grounds long before he decided to take an inventory of the foods and presents, so he and the commissioners rode to the Torrey Trading Post four miles away. They left the oak, elm, ash, pecan, and hackberry bottom[15] of Tehaucana Creek and climbed the hill on which the post had been erected. Half a dozen buildings of "rough, unhewn logs" crowned the rise of land, unprotected by palisades or enclosures. The largest building contained pelts the Torrey staff had accepted in trade. Ferdinand Roemer, who visited the post, described it in this manner:

> Buffalo robes or buffalo rugs and the hides of the common American deer formed by far the greatest number of hides. Some of the buffalo skins are brought to the trading post entirely raw, some are tanned inside only, and very often they are painted more or less artistically. Their value depends upon the artistic paintings on the inside. The hides of average quality were sold in Houston for three dollars, and the fancy ones for from eight to ten dollars.

Another log house contained the goods the Indians would receive in exchange for their pelts—bolts of shrouding, printed calico for shirts, thick copper wire from which the natives would fashion ornaments for legs and arms, knives, glass beads, blankets, and similar items.

The remaining houses contained dwellings for those persons who resided at the post—an agent, a gunsmith hired by the government to repair guns belonging to Indians, and an old trapper or fur hunter. On duty was an elderly Indian who "beat the pelts in order to rid them of insects. To watch this one at work always furnished entertaining amusement, for his face betrayed with each lick how the performing of such menial work for the pale faces was repulsive to his national inclination for laziness and his consciousness of Indian digity."[16] The Mexican woman who cooked for the post had a reputation for her strong hand with jalapeño pepper.[17]

When they approached the post, the commissioners saw a number of Delaware Indians who had received bids on their pelts and were selecting items in exchange. The pelts had been weighed, and soon would be baled; but the value had been determined, and the Indians were fingering the red and blue shrouding, running their hands along the copper wire, or holding the beads so the sun could send dancing light beams through them.[18]

Western estimated there were 200 bushels of corn on hand, and Torrey assured him more had been ordered, and more would arrive. Arrangements had been made for twenty to thirty beeves, and hunting parties were out scouting for more meat.[19]

If necessary, the hunters could rely on the thousands of buffalo feeding on the rye grass nearby.[20]

Commissioners Neill and Williams and Superintendent Western were directed through the post by the resident agent, George Barnard.[21] In his mid-twenties, he impressed the commissioners as expensively dressed[22] and unable to hide the pride he felt in having helped Thomas Torrey select the site on the bluff overlooking a tributary of Tehaucana Creek.[23] The site had been a meeting place for years, and now, with the arrival of the ox-drawn carts from Houston, he was aware it was a "meeting place of east and west."[24] Neill and Williams were shown through a well-stocked store. For the Indians, Torrey was supplied with 45 pounds of glistening beads, 195 blankets, 13,000 yards of calico and domestick, 49 kegs of powder, 484 pounds of brass wire, 108 dozen butcher knives, and 286 looking glasses. For the white customers were 141 pairs of shoes and boots, 51 dozen hats and bonnets, four kegs of nails, 3,500 pounds of sugar, stationery, and similar items. As well stocked as any other general store in the Republic![25]

Satisfied, the Indian affairs officials rode across Tehaucana Creek and galloped onto council grounds.

On April 19, Western called the council to investigate reports of the murder of some Creek Indians living near the Falls. They had been asleep in their homes when the murder took place. Western assured commissioners that such a meeting was essential in order to bring peace to the minds of the braves and squaws already assembled. Interpreters learned that the woman who reported the deaths was named Samamigey, a member of the Muskogee or Creek tribe.

Western faced the woman. "What do you know in relation to a murder committed below here upon some Creek Indians a few nights since? The Great Spirit is looking down upon us now and knows all we say, if you tell us the truth nobody will trouble you; if you tell a lie the Great Spirit will punish you."

"In the middle of the night," the woman explained, "my husband, a white man, got up as he said to obey a call of nature, and went off; in a short time he returned and then again went out and returned again with a tomahawk, with which he killed the people who were in the house."

"What was the size of the tomahawk?"

The woman measured with her hands as she spoke. "Large. Such as we use to cut down trees."

"What did you do?"

"I ran and caught hold of him and got his axe away. He said the wild Indians had killed my people."

"What is his name?"

"Dave Barton." Barton, Western learned, was a young man and the father of an infant. He resided twenty miles from the Falls.

"Was he white, Indian, or Negro?"

"Full-blooded white American."

"Who were the people killed? Their names?"

The woman answered almost inaudibly. "The old woman's name was Solygay, and the boy's name was Friday, and the little girl that was wounded—since dead—was named Harney."

Questioning continued briefly before Western assured the woman she would be protected, and she might remain at the council site in safety, if she wished. "The whole white nation will, if necessary, protect you from harm."

Western addressed the Indians who had sat through the questioning, assuring them the white offender would be punished. Already in custody, the man would undergo a trial.[26] The nodding of heads and grunts suggested to Western the Indians were satisfied; the friendship between white men and Indians would not be impaired by the incident.

For several days following the investigation, the camp was unsettlingly calm, almost boring. Western and the commissioners again inspected the area to make sure it was ready for the Comanches—if and when they should arrive. They read again the instructions Houston had sent concerning treatment of the guests:

> If peace is made, you will make such presents to the Comanches and other chiefs of the tribes as may be necessary; say, to the Comanches five kegs of powder, and such other arti-

cles of paint, domestics, &c., as will amount to five hundred dollars in par funds. To the other tribes in all you will present five hundred dollars, besides the tobacco, hoes, axes, &c., as are especially sent as presents.

Deeper in the letter addressed to commissioners, Houston had warned:

> Give to the Comanches twenty spears, after the treaty is made and say to them that every year I will make them presents, when the leaves of the trees fall, that they may have them in the winter, and when the Spring comes they will have hoes to make corn for their hunters and their children—the men will have powder and lead to kill the game and have meat for their women and children.[27]

Because of the inactivity, Dr. Hill left for Franklin, and Colonel Williams considered making a brief trip to the Ioni villages.[28] Commissioners questioned Western to learn whether he had ordered enough beef for the meeting.

"I'm puzzled about what to do," Western admitted, "until I get some instructions from Sam Houston."[29]

"And what about tobacco?" Neill asked. "Any on hand?"

"Not a pound at this place," Western admitted regretfully. "Don't know what we will do if the Indians arrive while the Torrey wagons are still stalled at Big Creek."

"We'll be in an ugly fix—hundreds of red folk on our hands and no tobacco or beef," Neill agreed.

"Well," Williams said, "there are herds of buffalo within a short distance."[30]

"Guess we could make do—with the corn we have and that we're expecting shortly." Western mentioned that only a little had been rationed to the women and children in camp, but again explained that his responsibilities in such matters had not been defined fully by President Houston.

Because the camp continued so quietly, the Indians became restless. When would the white men call the council? When would they get down to the business of talking? On the evening of April 27, 1844, the commissioners and the superintendent called the chiefs together. Neill looked around the council fire. He recognized St. Louis, chief of the Delaware. He saw José María, the Anadarko chief with his orderly. Neill remembered the day in October 1838, when he had faced that chief in battle. José María and his braves had fought like razorbacks then fled, leaving the ground littered with the bodies of braves. Neill could not forget José María.

Bintah and Red Bear, chiefs of the Caddo, were backed by Had-dah-bah, a captain, and Ne-est-choo, an orderly servant.

Behind the circle of chieftains and aides were their warriors. Western began the ceremony, lighting the peace pipe and passing it before introducing his interpreter, Luis Sanchez, a Mexican who had been kidnapped as a boy, reared by the Indians, and had become chief of the Keechi. He spoke English, Spanish, and numerous Indian dialects.[31] The ritual and introduction completed, Western stood before the assembly and began speaking:

> Sam Houston sent me here; Sam Houston is the father of all Texas; the father of the white folks, the father of the red folks. Sam Houston told me the path was white between him and his red brothers; he told me, when I should see the red men I must embrace them all for him, that he loved them very much. He told me, no red man would steal from the white man; no white man would steal from the red man. He told me I must come here and be a father to the red men until he should come here.[32]

Western looked over his audience, attempting to evaluate the response. The men before him appeared emotionless, like wax figures in a museum. "He did not send me to make a Treaty with the Comanche and other Indians; he sent this man." Western put his hand on Colonel Neill's shoulder, then pointed to Williams and Hill, "and two others as commissioners." Western said for two weeks he had looked for the Comanches, but they had not appeared. He continued:

> Sam Houston intended to come here to meet the Comanche and all his red brothers two weeks ago. Now the Comanche did not come; Sam Houston did not come, because he

has a big talk with the English, and the United States, the American and other people. When we understood the Comanche were not coming we wrote Sam Houston about it—the man that took the letter has not come back, that man may come in four days; he may come in eight days; it may be Sam Houston will come back with him. It may be he will not come.[33]

Obviously dejected by the announcement, the Indians groaned and began talking among themselves. Neill and Williams could only shrug their shoulders, for on April 6 Houston had written commissioners he had been "necessarily detained . . . on official business."[34] Dr. Hill also had received a letter from the president saying he had resolved to attend but had found it necessary to handle "our foreign relations."[35] He had sent Williams and Neill his ring so "those chiefs who know me can tell those who do not that you are true men and sent by me to make peace."[36]

Western hastened to explain the disappointment:

If the Comanche had come and we had had a big talk and peace with all, Sam Houston had sent many presents. Now on the road, coming from Houston, are some things. Houston knows the people want hoes for corn, and axes for the women to cut wood; when they are here, they, and some small things shall be given. Until the wagons arrive with the hoes and axes, and the letter arrives, the people must be quiet and remain content. We have got plenty to eat; corn plenty; tomorrow, or next day, plenty of meat. We now have nothing to do but sleep, drink, and eat.

I must now close this talk by doing what Sam Houston told me: to embrace all for him. All. Everyone of you.[37]

Taking his instructions literally, Major Western went around the circle, throwing his arms around each chief. After he had completed the circle and was taking his seat, Western saw St. Louis arise slowly. The Delaware began to speak:

I want all to hear what I say. Now, I have heard all this talk; now you have heard a good white talk, just about such as Houston would give. It is good as brothers. The white and red meet here together. Sam Houston has sent his word to us; we are all very glad of it. Now they listen to the words Houston sends; all the nations will be glad to hear it. What has been told here today gives us great spirits, as by looking around we can witness. When we meet in Council we are now, once more, as we were in olden times. I hope every one will listen and take hold of the words of Houston.[38]

St. Louis acknowledged that Red Bear showed an eagerness to leave the meeting but urged him to remain. "You know what has been told you—to wait three, four or eight days. Be satisfied all to wait. Now we are all together, we must stay all together until we hear the best of the Council. And the men must listen to the captains."

St. Louis continued, "This is no council. In a few days it will take place, and the Commissioners will tell us where to make our homes, and when it is over our young men can go and hunt the buffalo and deer with a good heart. Now the Chiefs and captains are all here, I want them to remain with their young men until the Council takes place. We have nothing to do but eat, drink, and dance all the time."

The silence which followed was broken with mumbling as the chief draped his blanket around his bronzed body and took a seat. Bintah, chief of the Caddo, stood. "I have waited many days," he said, "But am not in a hurry, as I want to hear good talk and counsel, and because I have plenty to eat and am satisfied; if I get beef or fat hogs, it will be much better; all my people will hear and be satisfied." [39]

Before secretary Walter Winn got around to writing his report of the meeting—transcribing the careful notes into a letter to Houston—a Keechi ran into camp with the message that Acaquash and the Waco tribe were on the way. Jesse Chisholm and a number of the Cherokee single filed into the area until approximately 350 Indians were milling under the mesquite and live oak trees.

Acaquash later received a warm welcome into the circle, and he offered praise for Houston, saying the man had made the path white and clean. "If Houston will come, all will be right," he declared. "But, Houston often has said he will meet with us, yet it never occurs."

The Indians gasped at the statement. So did the white settlers.

Acaquash continued, "We think it strange. We do not wish to do anything until Houston comes. The young men, women, and children are coming to see Houston and to get the presents he has promised. Last winter the Comanche told him to come down and make peace; they were weary of living so. They will be at the council grounds in three or four days."

The Waco and Tehaucanna, he said, were planting corn but would be represented at the talk.

"Send Dr. Hill to take Houston's place," the Waco chief suggested to commissioners. "I know Houston is not ill. I know he is nearly at peace with the Mexicans and I cannot see what could prevent him from coming."

Western reported the incident to Houston.

Another session got underway, and the Delaware and Shawnee presented wampum beads to the Keechi. For a time, Neill and Williams considered distributing gifts to the chiefs, but St. Louis indicated he wanted to give the Waco and Tawakoni another talk. Some of the chiefs had left the grounds, saying they had crops to tend. Some indicated they wanted to see that stolen horses were returned to their owners.

Western, always a prompt correspondent, wrote Houston of the progress—or lack of it—and on the back of the letter penned a question of whether he should remain on the site after the treaty was signed, or "retire with the Commissioners."

Word came that the Waco and Tawakoni had been sighted, and commissioners and some Indian dignitaries hiked to the prairie approximately four miles from camp. Once there, each group formed a line, and Luis Sanchez instructed the principal men on each side to advance for an introduction.

"Brothers, you have met here today your white brothers in this prairie. You see them here now all present before you," Sanchez said.

The interpreter pointed to Colonel Neill. "This chief is one, who, when you embrace, calculate you are embracing Gen. Houston, and the same when you embrace this chief." He pointed to Thomas I. Smith. "Or this." His finger directed the Indians to Williams. "And the same when you embrace any of the whites now here."

He continued:

> You see, at the same time, how many red brothers have united with the whites, to come out and meet you. At this time they all look upon you as the children of Gen. Houston. They are all glad to meet you here, and expect you to feel the same way. Look around and see how many tribes are here to meet you; and what you see don't forget.

The Indians and white settlers embraced, then one of the commissioners proposed that they retire to the grove for a smoke. "Here is tobacco, by the Big Spirit sent," Sanchez said. "I want you to take this tobacco that was brought you at the first meeting, by Jim Shaw and Jesse Chisholm, to smoke. I want you to turn it over on every side, and see if it is bloody; or if it still is white tobacco, as it was when first sent to you. I want you also, to see the pipe, which like the tobacco is all white."

Sanchez invited the Indians to join him in smoking. Acaquash took a deep draw then asked if the commissioners had anything to say. Neill spoke. "We meet once more in peace, and we are glad of it. We will always be glad to meet you as we now do, and hear from your lips the words of peace. We have no more to say until we meet in council."

Acaquash spoke. "I alone have been among you and for my people spoken; but now you see here other chiefs belonging to my race. They have come and you can hear them talk. I am glad to meet and smoke with you, and sitting as we now do, all together in this manner, makes me feel happy."

When no other Indian expressed a desire to speak, the members of the group mounted their horses and escorted the Waco and Tawakoni to the higher council grounds.[40]

On May 13, Indians and white settlers discussed regaining horses that had been stolen from the settlements and distributing gifts. Sanchez filled the pipe with tobacco and ceremoniously tamped it. Then he lighted the pipe. "My white and red brothers, each and all of you sitting here. Chiefs and young men. I want you all to hear . . . .Now this day, Houston, our father, will speak through our white brothers, of the big white path which he has made. He is a father who loves you all as a father loves his children . . ."

He began passing the pipe.

"My Red brothers," Colonel Neill said, standing as Houston's spokesman. "We meet you here together once more in council. We intended to meet you often from the time we first talked of peace. The Great Spirit looks upon the white and red brothers when they meet as friends, and is glad. The Great Spirit smiles upon us now, and all around us is clear and white. Many of our red brothers who were not present at Councils before are now here. It is good for chiefs and brave men to meet in council, and we are glad to see them.

"To meet together and talk as friends make peace strong and lasting as the ground we are upon. To keep and walk after the words of good men in council keeps harm from all people, and makes the women and children always happy," he continued.

He expressed his belief the whites should be able to buy "all the things their red brothers have to see, and can sell to their red brothers, all the things they want for their women and children; and for themselves they can make corn, potatoes, and all other things they want to raise, and be happy."[41]

Recognizing that there "are some bad white men, and there are some bad red men," Neill called on both peoples to "watch these bad men, and make them follow their good counsel."

Neill pulled a sheet of paper from his leather jacket. "I will now read to you the words of Sam Houston, the great chief of Texas. These are the words of his own mouth, spoken by him and sent to us to deliver to his red brothers." He explained Houston's proposal to "draw a line, and until peace is made with the Comanches, it would be wise for no Indians to come below that line, unless they come by Torrey's trading post, where they could get a letter from Agent Sloat, permission to hunt or trade."

Neill read,

> When the line is marked I want chief of each tribe to go with the men who mark it. When the leaves fall and I meet the chiefs in council I will have medals and such presents for my brother

chiefs as they will be happy to receive. This will be four moons and a half from the present time.

Tell them all to keep blood out of our path, and to let no horses be stolen; tell them this year to raise corn anywhere they please above the trading house on the Brazos, Nolan's River, Clear Fork or any of their old villages. They shall not be disturbed at their camp fires by good men or by those who obey my orders; and if bad men go to them to disturb their women and children they must treat them as enemies. If good men go to them they will meet them as brothers and must feed them. If they are lost they must point to them the road that will lead them to their homes, and see that they are not injured. If the Comanche Chiefs who intended visiting the Ioni during the roasting ear season should conclude to come down to Washington to see me, I will be very happy to see them, and Mr. Sloat will give them a safe and trusty guide, or accompany them himself.

Neill folded the paper and returned it to his pocket. "I have done now, but will talk again about the trouble which has come upon the white people by bad men after I have heard my red brothers talk."[42]

Acaquash recalled other meetings with Houston. "I have brought along my young captains, not for myself, but as presents to Houston, to make their hearts good for peace. All my white and red brothers feel as I do; all want peace. I want to eat of the same dish, drink of the same water, smoke the same pipe with Houston and my white brothers in peace."[43]

The Tawakoni chief, Ke-chi-ka-roqua, admitted he had studied Houston's words and had found what he said straight. "Yet, I am not satisfied. I do not see Houston here. I want to see and hear him talk and talk with him myself. The Delaware captains say they met him at Bird's Fort, and made peace; they have shaken hands and hold firm to it. We will do so too. I am strong for making a firm peace. War is like an arrow sticking in the side; I have plucked it out and now I am for peace. . . . It matters not if Houston is not here; I have his words, and the talk is straight." He stuttered, "Yet, I would rather see him."

Sah-sah-roque, Keechi leader, was also disappointed Houston had not attended. "You hear it and the blowing winds will hear it too; the Big Spirit will hear it, and he, my white brother, will hear it also. It is hard that Houston is not here. I have listened to my white brothers talk and am glad to hear it; my heart is happy. When I want to see Houston I found a big road and a white path. I had plenty to eat, and at the same time Houston gave me this paper which I hold in my hand. He told me that this was the council ground, and that here he would be; the Great Spirit heard it, and the mother, earth, and was glad, and he told me presents should be here. Yet Houston comes not here himself. He told me I should keep my path white going home and ever to keep it in the same fair way. My young men wanted to go to war, but I forbade and kept them all at home. You have come for Houston, and I am glad. When you go back you will take my talk to him; he will be glad to hear it."

"I do not like to see guns firing and blood spilled, for I am a friend of peace," said Red Bear, the Caddo chief. He talked but little, and left his associates with a smile. "I fear if the Tawehash or other Indians take horses from the whites and I try to get them away, that they will kill me. This is all I have to say. My hands are bloody only from killing deer."

The Indians laughed heartily, saying that they never had known Red Bear to kill any kind of game.[44]

St. Louis opened the May 14 session, expressing a desire for peace. He presented Narhashtowey tobacco and a string of wampum beads. "When you look upon them think of what I have said."

Had-dah-bah, the Caddo captain, reminded the men they had listened to the older chiefs, but he was a young man with the same words. He presented a string of beads to Sah-sah-rogue. "I want you to hold fast to it. Now you have got the road I want you all to hold to it, as these, my older brothers, you see do."

"I am myself small in size," said José María, the Anadarko leader. "My words to fit me, shall be few. Long talks admit of lies; my talk shall be short but true." He held up a string of beads. "I hold the white path in my hands, given by our white brothers. Look at it. See it is all fair. To you, Waco and Tawakoni captains and warriors I give it. Stop going to war with the white people. They, the white people, gave it unto me; I give it now to you. Use it as I have done and your women and children will be happy and sleep free of danger. I give this piece of tobacco to smoke and consider the white path. When you return to your village, then smoke this tobacco, think of my words and obey them."

The commissioners requested the Kiowa Good Shirt come forward.

"Where do you live, and when do you intend to return to your people?"

"My people now live far away, but when the leaves fall they will be near, and I shall go to them. They fear your race and do not come here, yet would be glad of peace."

"Say to them we do not wish to make war upon them but be friendly to all nations. We want you to listen and attend, and what you here see and hear carry and report to your people. Before you leave we will give you a present as a token of our respect," one of the commissioners said.

Ke-chi-ka-roqua, chief of the Tawakoni, spoke at length. Then he said, "We have come with all our strength to see Houston and get presents. Why should they steal from the whites? They shall not do it. My young men and women come to see Houston. We are very poor. If Houston gives us presents we shall be glad, very glad. The white people are good and give us many presents."

When the session adjourned, the commissioners could not keep from drawing conclusions. "They're like children—so interested in the presents they were promised. Almost go to the point of saying the only reason they're here is to get the gifts." The commissioners also commented on the disappointment over Houston's absence.[45]

The men assembled on Wednesday, May 15, for the third and final day of the council. Commissioners thanked the Indians for having joined them and then issued a description of horses stolen since the treaty at Bird's Fort. Neill promised, "We will give our red brothers tomorrow such presents as we have to give. In four moons and a half we will give them many more, and such as they will be happy to receive. We want the principal chief of each nation to receive such presents as we have for his people, which he will divide among them. The Great Spirit hears all I say, and they are the words of truth."

Acaquash seemed to break the line of thought when he said

he did not want the traders to take ammunition among the Comanches until the peace had been made. "They are a wild people, and by giving them what they want at home they never will come here," he warned. "Is it good to take such to them? I say no.

"I want to see Houston, but you have lost horses, and you think my people have stolen them. I will go back and I want some one to go with me and see if we have them; and get some of the other tribes to assist in bringing them back. Since we left our village they may have been taken, and carried there. Send some one, and if so, we shall have them."

The commissioners saw in Acaquash, whom Houston regarded so highly, a man whose patience was on the verge of breaking, but before they could dwell on the matter, Jim Ned, a Delaware, explained, "The Waco and Tawakoni have the horses stolen from the whites, and we all know it . . . ."

Red Bear said, "Most of the chiefs now here went to Washington to see Gen. Houston, and after passing words of peace and friendship there, we then went home. Acaquash has said none of his people are here who have stolen from the whites. The man that now stands yonder, with ten other came into my village the day after I reached home. They had eleven horses when I saw them. I asked them of what tribe they were? They replied that all of them but two, a Tawehash and a Pawnee, were Waco. Then I said to them, 'What sort of men are you? You of the tribe of Acaquash? While he, for you, is trying to make peace, you are stealing horses from his friends, the whites. He Acaquash, went with me to Washington to see Houston and make a peace, and you, to help, went stealing white men's horses!'"

Narhashtowey, the chief, grew angry, and Red Bear, observing the emotion, suggested he need not be irate. "For I am speaking the truth."

Narhashtowey then addressed the white men. "We wish you to stop, and talk no more. If the horses are in the possession of the Waco or Tawakoni you shall have them soon; if with the Tawehash 'twill take us some time longer. We will go hunt for them and bring them in."

It was obvious the Indians were becoming impatient and restless; the council was beginning to crumble like a rock wall built without mortar. On May 16 the commissioners began distribution of gifts. They did not hand presents of powder and lead to the Waco and Tawakoni, but promised the tribes would receive such items when they returned the stolen horses to the agent at the trading post. They remembered Houston's instructions: "Give to the Comanches twenty spears, after the treaty is made and say to them that every year I will make them presents, when leaves of the trees fall, that they may have them in the winter and when Spring comes they will have hoes to make corn for their hunters and children—the men will have powder and lead to kill game and have meat for their women and children." [46]

As the council drew to a close, agents at the trading post began figuring up the government's account. Brass wire—thirty-one pounds of it. Domestic bed ticking. Blue calico. Tin cups and pans. Frying pans. Brass kettles. Axes. Hatchets. Combs. In neat columns the clerk listed the items and costs, and his eyes glistened as he arrived at the total figure. The Texian government owed $822.19. Added to that figure was the amount given to Acaquash on order of Benjamin Sloat plus the freight on the hoes and tobacco—$849.69. The clerk delivered the statement to the commissioners, and Neill, Williams, and Smith certified the bill was correct and the items had been purchased for use of the Indians.[47]

On May 23 the three commissioners and the secretary, shaded by the branches of a live oak, composed a letter to President Houston of what had transpired during the sessions. Although they chronologically outlined what had taken place—omitting a number of details—the commissioners explained one problem:

> Late in the evening (Sunday the 12th) we were informed of a disaffection in the camps of the Delaware, Caddo, Anadarko, Shawnee and other Indians in consequence of an order sent by Maj. Thos. G. Western, Superintendent of Indian Affairs, to the Falls of the Brazos, countermanding an order previously given by him, for Beeves. At the time there were but two Beeves on hand; little or no dried meat in camp and the Council had not commenced. We called upon the Hon. Geo. W. Hill Sec. of War and Marine, for advice in the emergency, and after consulting with him we dispatched a messenger at midnight to Mr. Marlin at the

Falls, who was to furnish the Beeves, with a note, of which the following is a copy.

Attached was a request that Marlin deliver five or six beeves the following day, if practicable.[48]

Clearing up details occupied the minds and time of the commissioners. On May 25 Thomas I. Smith signed a statement that R.A. Barton had paid $27.12 for freight of forty kegs of powder and one keg of cartridges from Washington to the Falls.[49]

J.C. Neill and Edwin Morehouse verified that Jesse Chisholm had been paid $250 in specie for four months' service with Williams for duties required by the Department of Indian Affairs.[50]

Western rode back to his office in Washington and on June 6 composed a letter to Benjamin Sloat. Aware that Sloat desired "to perform all the duties assigned . . . as an agent with promptness and precision," Western reminded him that Colonel Smith had been furnished with funds to pay Barton on the transportation of powder. Western requested Sloat to see that the matter had been handled. The Waco and Tawakoni promised to return horses and mules recently stolen from citizens of the Colorado and Little River areas. Would Sloat receive the animals and deliver them to their owners, "free of all or any charge or expense whatsoever?" If he needed assistance, he should employ a person "on account of the Government." He also reminded Sloat to take care of any Comanches within the limits of his agency, seeing they were treated with "kindness and humanity" and to report their situation.

Western also warned Sloat against permitting any Indian to pass into the settlements except on government business—and then when accompanied by an agent.[51]

Sloat, meanwhile, wrote Sam Houston from Tehaucana Creek that before the council broke up, he had given Western his accounts for the corn and for building the council house. He had promised men handling the corn they would have their money as soon as the council concluded. "Now these men are very much in want of the money and are constantly annoying me about the same," he wrote. Sloat's bill for corn, $75; for hauling, $83.50, and for building, $83.

On another subject, Sloat confided in the president that "the Indians so far as I can learn are uniformly well behaved and we commit ourselves to the arms of Morpheus at this place with as little fear of the Tomahawk and Scalping Knife as Queen Victoria can possibly do with her Maids of honor." [52]

16

FALLS TREATY

"When the Leaves Fall...."
Minutes, May 13, 1844

Some of the animals stolen from the whites were delivered to agent Benjamin Sloat to be returned to owners.[1]

As Western had ordered, Sloat inspected the government property stored at the Falls to make certain the spears and powder were "free from wet or damp."[2] Maj. R. N. Porter, however, refused to surrender the property to any person but Sam Houston.[3] He acknowledged he had at Bucksnort Falls thirty-five kegs of powder, a box of spears, a box of shafts for spears, one half keg of musket cartridges, and forty kegs of Balten powder.[4]

Western himself visited the grounds and arranged with John Marlin to transport a piece of artillery from Nashville to Tehuacana Creek.[5]

As September dawned, the area that in the spring was a quilt of bluebonnets and scarlet Indian paintbrushes was now suntanned, parched. Indians remembering the promise of presents began looking for signs in the leaves that were falling from the trees and for signs of color in the sumac. Back in his office in Washington, Western began considering details of the scheduled meeting with the Comanches. Should the Indians arrive at the Falls before the president or the commissioners, Sloat was instructed to give them a warm reception. He was reminded that he could dispatch his helper Sam if he heard news of the approach of the Comanches.

Houston, temporarily out of the capital, was scheduled to return on September 10 and planned to leave directly for the Falls.[6] Later arrangements changed the date that President Houston would set out for the pow-wow to September 15.[7] Torrey's wagons already had left Houston loaded with goods for the conclave.[8]

James C. Neill was one of the first official delegates to leave Washington for the council site. He had orders to make purchases in preparing for the council. As he galloped along the route, Neill, no doubt, mentally figured what provisions would be required—blankets, 48 yards of domestic yards of shrouding, yards of calico, 1,486 pounds of beef, 30 plugs of tobacco. . . .[9] He could not forget the problems caused by shortages in tobacco and beef when the Indians had assembled in the spring.

On the day Colonel Neill left Washington, approximately 1,000 Comanches were within miles of the council site. They were "somewhat alarmed and very impatient."[10]

Word reached the site that President Houston would leave on September 26, but the chief executive was not feeling well. Finally, on September 29, he was well enough to shut the door on his office and set out for Tehuacana. Accompanying him was Robert Wilson.[11]

On October 7 President Houston, commissioners J. C. Neill, Thomas I. Smith, and Edwin Morehouse; Dr. G. W. Hill; and G. W. Terrell and interpreters sat down with chiefs of the Comanche, Keechi, Waco, Tawakoni, Caddo, Ioni, Anadarko, Cherokee, Delaware, Shawnee. Milling around were Indian captains and some of their captives. The pipe of friendship, haloed by a silver wisp of smoke, circled, and Houston remained seated to address the Indians. "We, the Chiefs of the white people, are very glad to see you. You are welcome to our presence. We are glad that you are here. We have been very far apart, and the path that led from your village to us has been a long and bloody one; the blood hath been taken out of the path between the white people and many nations of the Red people. We have not met to take away the blood from the path of the Comanche and the white people."[12]

After calling on his Comanche brothers to join in making peace, Houston arose from his seat and stood before Acaquash. "Will the chief rise?" he questioned.

Acaquash stood before the towering Houston, who tied on the old man's brow a silk handkerchief on which was pinned a badge reading "Chief of the Waco."

The council adjourned until the following morning, when the group heard talks by Buffalo Hump, the war chief of the Comanche. He said, "The Great Spirit above is looking down and sees and hears my talk. The ground is my mother, and sees and hears that I tell the truth. When I first heard the words of your Chief I felt glad; and I was uneasy until I struck the white path and came here to see him. That is all I want to say; what I came here for was to hear the words of peace. I have heard them and all is right; peace is peace. I have no more to say."

Facing Houston, he changed his mind, and spoke again. "What you have said is good. I love your words. If there is any other chief what would wish to speak. I should like to listen."

White Feather, the war chief of the Keechi, accepted the invitation, saying:

> The Great Spirit has given me a good heart to bring here, and I have forgot all of our troubles. Before now I had a bad opinion of your people and I kept away; now I have no bad opinion. I have come to meet the big Chief of the whites and I have found a big white path.

The elderly Roasting Ear of the Delaware spoke. "The Big Spirit will look down and see that it is good. I expect that your feelings and mine are one, peace is best always for our women and children. I love my children and I know the whites love theirs, for them peace is much better. I want you and me to hang on to peace."

Lame Arm spoke for the Waco people:

> My feelings are like the other chiefs. The big spirit looks down, and our mother earth looks on and hears what I have to say. I have long wished to see your Chief. I have now seen him and my heart is glad. My heart now is big. There is not a drop of blood on it, but it is all white. All the way I have been coming here I have been in the white path and have not seen a drop of blood. I have joined with all of these chiefs to make peace and a white path and I will help to keep it.

The council took an hour recess, after which Houston held up a draft of the treaty he proposed, explaining in detail the seal and the colors of the ribbons attached to it. "The White denoted peace; the blue was like the sky, unchangeable; the green, like the grass and trees existing as long as the world stands; our hearts ought always to be pure and white and never change, and as the grass is ever green our friendship should be ever fresh." He waved the treaty so the ribbons caught the slight breeze.

Slowly, deliberately, Houston began to read. Then for pageantry he presented the two principal Comanche chiefs a blue robe. He promised presents to the others.

On Wednesday, Houston talked with Pochanaquarhip, the Comanche war chief.

"I like the treaty well enough, all but one thing. The line is too far off; too far up the country," the Comanche said.

"On which side of the Brazos do you mean?"

"I mean between the mountains and San Antonio. It is on account of the buffalo," Pochanaquarhip said. "When they come down I want the privilege to come after them. The San Saba is too high up."

"How low on the Colorado would you wish to come?"

"To begin at the timber above Austin and to go from that up."

Houston asked, "How many leaves do you think it above Austin?"

"A good day's ride, to ride fast one might get there before sun down. The distance perhaps 50 miles. It is all prairie from there on West, and I want the privilege to follow the buffalo on down. That country is full of bear, deer, wild horses and buffalo for my people to live on."

"How far do you mean this line to be above the mouth of the San Saba?"

The chief shrugged. "About four days' fast riding below the mouth."

"That cannot be," Houston said. "It would bring you below Austin and Bastrop. Do you want the line to run by the mountains above the St. Mark?"

"I want the line to run on the edge of the mountains in the prairie to San Antonio; then on the San Antonio Road to the Rio Grande, where the town is of that name."

"Will it not do as well for the line to run 25 miles above San Antonio, and to leave San Antonio 8 leagues to the left and strike the Presidio road above?"

The questioning continued.

Houston asked, "Do you want the line to start at the Comanche Peak on the Brazos?"

"No," the chief said. "I want it to start at Sandy Creek, five leagues above the Falls of the Brazos."

"I have always heard that you wanted it to start at the Comanche Peak or the mouth of Nolan's River, and then to run on above Little River and above Bryant's, through the prairies on the Rio Grande. Why do you now wish the line to come below?"

The chief answered with a question. "Who told you that was our wish?"

Houston explained. "We never said so. The paper lied. We then said what I now say. The Great Spirit sees and knows I speak the truth. I want the line to run as I have said. It is a good country and has good grass, and I want to live by the white people."

Houston explained he had plans for establishing a trading post on Nolan's River. The post would have goods and a gunsmith to repair the Indians' guns.

"I want the Trading House to remain where it is; and I want my friends, these other Indians, to settle on the line and raise corn and I can often come down among them. I am like the bird flying through the air. I can travel and am always traveling and can easily come down here. I want the Trading House to remain where it is and I will come to it."

"If the line should start at the place you speak of," Houston returned to the subject, "how would it run?"

Finally Houston said, "The line, as before agreed on, runs from the Comanche Peak, between the Cross Timbers to Red River. The line was made at a Treaty that was signed by Red Bear. When Col. Williams, Messrs. Durst and Stroud went over the Red River, then Red Bear wished the line to be high up, as he did not wish to come near the whites."

The Comanche chief objected. "Red Bear never owned lands to run lines with the white people. The lands belong to the Comanche. Red Bear lives high up and if he ever had lands he may have sold them."

"The white people have 60 counsellors to make laws," Houston explained. "I am their chief and must listen to my counsellors. My people have settled up to the Lower Cross Timbers to the Comanche Peak, thence through the prairie, over the Colorado, and above the St. Mark and above San Antonio and to the Rio Grande. I and my counsellors heard this was your wish and we believed it."

"The Comanche never understood it so. When the buffalo come below there is nothing for us to eat above."

"If the buffalo would not come down should you then want the country?" Houston inquired.

"The buffalo do come down and it is them I want."

Patiently Houston explained. "We have met here to make peace and be friends and then put our names to this paper as friends. Before we part we will sign this paper and we want it to be right. You are pleased with the treaty and call it all good but that part about the line; we will sign all but that part, which we will rub out and go on as before. If we send people among you we will give them a paper that will have a big seal, so that you may know them as good men. If any white man goes among your people and steals horses or mules and you catch him, do not harm him but bring him in and we will hang him for it and if any bad Indians should steal horses from my people and run away with them, bring them in to the Trading House and whip the men. I want the Comanche Chiefs to know that here are some poor men who depend upon their horses to make corn for their wives and children; the Waco have stolen their horses and I want to know if they are to get them back?"

Narhashtowey explained that some of the animals might be dead, but the living would be sent to Colonel Williams, as requested.

"For every horse that's dead or missing a Waco shall be hung," Houston declared. "I would say to my Comanche brethren that at the place where the ships come in there has been much sickness, for which reason a ship that has many things for them has not yet come in. We have shrouding, lead, calico, etc., but not as many presents as we expected to give them."

Houston then called for the Indians to sign the treaty. He

made it clear that the articles referring to the boundary line had been stricken.

Houston urged the red men to spread word of the treaty. He then added:

> And stop those other Indians, so that my people may not think the Comanche the aggressors. See. The sun is not setting clear, and through our Council it hath smiled kindly upon us. We have had plenty to eat both of meat and corn, and all are in good spirits. The Wagons have come and presents shall be distributed tomorrow.

José María asked, "As we are now soon to part, when shall we meet in council again?"

"The light of this moon next year, or about twelve moons. We will then have plenty of corn and the roads will be good," Houston answered.

"At any time you send to them Jim Shaw or John Conner, the Comanche will be ready to come in," the chief promised.

"If I send," Houston said, "you will know the runner by the paper and the big seal."[14]

On October 9, 1844, commissioners J. C. Neill, Thomas I. Smith, and E. Morehouse affixed their signatures. The chiefs single filed to add their marks to the document, observed by seven interpreters and nine witnesses.[15]

In small groups, the Indians left the council site, leaving the commissioners time to examine the accounts Torrey Brothers submitted. The list contained the usual shrouding, cotton handkerchiefs, butcher knives, brass nails, brass wire, calico, and squaw axes. The men carefully checked the items and approved the $1,238.81 total. Sam Houston added his signature to the document approving the statement.[16]

Commissioners began composing their report of the council, adding to it the minutes of the council, and a list of presents they had purchased for the Indians.[17]

Back in Washington, Neill and Morehouse were commenting on the success of the council when they decided to send a note to Houston. They informed the president:

> We the commissioners are of the opinion that Mr. Watson[18] and John Conner[19] have been of much service in bringing the Indians in and of all the Agints (*sic*) sent out they deserve as much if not more than any others.[20]

Little known to the commissioners, the treasury at this time was short of money in the Department of Indian Affairs account—so short that payments for hauling the meat and corn to the conference was delayed.[21]

17

ANNUAL INDIAN COUNCIL

"At peace with all men both red and white."
Thomas G. Western

Residents of the temporary capital, Washington-on-the-Brazos, already knew details about the scheduled meeting of their commissioners with the Indian chiefs, but the *Texas National Register* confirmed the event if there were skeptics. On September 4, 1845, the paper informed readers:

> The annual Indian council will be held at post No. 2, on Tahwoccaro Creek, near the Brazos, on the 15th inst. We are informed that this council will be numerously attended by the several tribes. Besides those with whom relations of peace have been established by treaty a very large number of Comanches will be present.

Edwin Morehouse, Thomas I. Smith, and J. C. Neill were reappointed commissioners for the 1845 meeting, and President Anson Jones heard the suggestion that W. G. Cooke, his secretary of war and marine, also might attend.[1] From Washington City, on September 8, Thomas G. Western, superintendent, wrote Neill, Morehouse, and Smith, presenting the president's instructions for governing the council. They were told the superintendent would place at their disposal an invoice of $2,000 in goods for "making suitable presents to such of the Indians, as you may deem worthy, and expediency may require."²

Earlier in the year, there had been tension. Buffalo Hump, war chief of the Comanches, swaggered into the gunsmith's shop at Torrey's in the spring of 1845. Noah Turney Byars³ was in charge. The Hump, wearing only a beech clout, had draped a buffalo robe around his hips. His long, coarse black hair was plaited, his fingers were heavy with brass rings, and strings of bright beads glittered around his neck.⁴

Haughtily the Indian requested a gun. Parson Byars insisted the gun to which the Hump pointed was not for sale. It was his personal rifle. The Indian drew his knife; to defend himself, Byars grabbed a hammer and drove the chief from the shop. Buffalo Hump's braves demonstrated. Byars closed the shop and refused to make repairs to the Indians' guns.

Leonard Williams, resident agent, reported the matter to superintendent Western, who asked Byars to surrender "the public blacksmithy and armorers shop, tools," and to report to Washington.⁵

Tension over the matter settled smog-like over the council grounds.

The commissioners, however, were told that Santa Anna, the chief, had expressed an interest in attending and in signing the treaty his fellow chiefs had approved at the last meeting. Commissioners were encouraged to let him read the treaty and sign if he concurred. They were reminded that last year the Indians had refused assent to a permanent line as proposed by Sam Houston, and the president did not desire the commissioners to urge this point. Instead, the president said he did not wish "to deprive the Red Man of his hunting grounds. We have no present use for that section of Country best adapted to Hunting purposes, the Buffalo range; the President is therefore of the opinion that there will be little difficulty to be apprehended in adjusting the Boundary line to suit all parties."⁶

Interest in the conclave began to mount, although the Washington newspaper carried little news until the commissioners were assembling on council grounds. By the middle of August, word reached the capital that St. Louis had promised to attend, but several of Jim Ned's Comanche party, contacted on their return from an expedition to the Wichita, said the chief was using all his influence to prevent the Delaware from attending. José María, however, was pleased with the arrangements described to him.⁷

Meanwhile, Western, as usual, focused on details. On September 3, he wrote Williams that the corn was much higher than he had anticipated, but if it could not be obtained for less, he saw no alternative. He felt all goods should be on the grounds by the 15th, so he requested Williams to make delivery by that date. He would like the corn by the 12th, if possible.

A superior gunsmith, E. B. Goswell, had been engaged as armorer to the Indians, and Williams had agreed to deliver to him "the work shop Tools etc."⁸ Torrey & Brothers were instructed to order such additional articles for Goswell as a hand saw, set of brace and bits, stock and dies, hand vices, oil stone, and an assortment of files.⁹

On Friday, September 12, commissioners Neill and Morehouse and Secretary Daniel D. Culp, accompanied by agents L. H. Williams and Benjamin Sloat and interpreter Jim Shaw left Torrey's Post. Their horses picked their way over the pebbles toward the council grounds, and they camped, and soon were met by Indians.

Mopechucope, head chief of the Comanches, with eight of his braves rode their pinto ponies into camp, and after smoking the pipe, declared they would be happy to meet the new white chief, Anson Jones, and his captains. They were told that Commissioner Smith had not yet ridden in but was scheduled to arrive in a few days; they were assured there would be great supplies of beef and corn and presents.

During that Saturday night, several white men galloped into camp bearing letters for the commissioners. The following morning, Mopechucope, greatly concerned, asked what the appearance of the riders meant. Assured that all was peaceful and there would be no treachery, he was told the papers were instructions from the president.

"My braves are getting restless," the chief said.

"Everything's all right," the commissioners assured him.

Not all was well, commissioners learned later. The presents had not arrived at Torrey's, so it was considered wise to delay sessions. When they learned the gifts were due the 21st, commissioners gambled by scheduling the first meeting of the council for 10:00 A.M. Friday, September 19.

Williams, representing Western, called on John Marlin, but he refused to deliver the corn for less than $25 per bushel. Williams, therefore, contacted all corn growers in Bucksnort before giving the contract to E. S. Wyman, who agreed to deliver it between the 10th and 20th.[10]

As usual before such events, Torrey's made special arrangements—checking the merchandise in the log warehouse and placing special orders for items that would make appropriate gifts. From New York had come handkerchief blue broadcloth, blue merrimack, beads, beef kettles and half axes. Torrey was especially proud of the Hunts squaw hatchets created especially for the trading post.[11]

On August 26, Western reminded Henry Kattenhorn the time was approaching "for the delivery of the Beeves" and by the time he received this letter, delivered by Neill, he would have "two weeks time to gather your cattle and drive your Beeves to Tehaucana Creek where the Indian Council will be held." Western had learned that some of the Indians might arrive on council grounds three days before the appointed date.[12] Kattenhorn delivered 24 beeves weighing 14,640 pounds and pocketed $292.80.[13]

Once on the scene, General Morehouse took charge. Examining the face of the several chiefs, he said, "In looking around we see that some who were here at the last Council are now absent. What keeps them away?"

The chiefs sat silently, noncommital.

"We do not know of any thing we have done that keeps them away from our councils. We now have assured you of our friendship, and if you have any thing to say, we will be happy to hear from you," the general continued.

Several of the Indians explained their reasons for attending, but could throw no light on the reasons for the absence of others.

Rain pelted the area all day Saturday, so the Indians remained on their buffalo blankets in their teepees, and the commissioners were dry in their canvas tents. A rider churned through the mud to deliver a note to Colonel Smith, mentioning that a wagon loaded with presents had broken down at Fish Creek, approximately eight miles below the falls. It would be impossible to have the wagon repaired in order to deliver the presents before Monday or Tuesday.

The sun appeared Sunday, so the Indians and white men assembled and leisurely puffed the calumet before Morehouse spoke. "One of our council captains is sick," he explained, "and unable to attend this morning but his heart is with you." Neill remained in his tent much of the time, nursing his old San Jacinto wound and feeling acute pain from arthritis. The damp ground had not helped the ache.

The air around the council grew crisp, tense. Bintah, the Caddo, spoke, "The Commissioners at the last council promised to give us presents whenever we met again, and as they do not lie, we will expect them at this council."

Smith was uneasy, knowing the wagon could not arrive for several days.

Toweash, chief of the Ioni, recalled that he had been one of those attending the first treaty council.

> The President then gave us powder, and lead, and told us to go home and shoot deer and buffalo, and raise corn, for our women and children, so that in the cold rainy weather they would not cry for bread and meat. We have done so and found that it is good. All that he told us was true, and now I can go home to my people and tell them that all is still good, that they can eat and sleep in safety and feel no more afraid.

On Tuesday the commissioners were relieved to learn that the wagon had arrived at Torrey's, so they adjourned to the post to open and distribute the presents. The Comanches received their gifts and divided them. On September 24, the commissioners distributed presents to the Comanche chiefs and they promptly left for their homes. The Caddo, Cherokee, Ioni, Anadarko and Delaware received and divided their gifts and were more leisurely in riding for their camps. On Thursday, September 25, the commissioners distributed trinkets to the Lipan and Tonkawa Indians, who left in peace and quiet at 4:00 P.M.[14]

On Friday the commissioners took an inventory of goods remaining on hand, figuring they had $1,303.87—one-half left after distributing gifts.[15]

Saturday morning the commissioners composed their report to President Anson Jones.[16] They had met with some Comanches on the 12th, greeting them near the Brazos within four miles of the post. On September 19 they held a general council and on Sunday another session. They had distributed some $2,617.93 in gifts, but being assured that other parties and tribes would meet in council in a few weeks, they had economized, spending only $1,314.06, leaving the remainder on account. The secretary made a copy of his journal for the president.[17]

During the session, the Indians had received $37.37 worth of tents and tin ware for their use during the conclave and for their retention.[18] Accounts show the commissioners distributed 10 dozen German looking glasses, 25 dozen tin cups, 20 dozen two-quart pans, 10 dozen two-quart pails, 21 dozen fine tooth combs, and vermillion paint. They also had handed out shrouding blankets, ticking, unbleached domestics, fancy shawls, cotton handkerchiefs, and coffee.[19]

Their report completed, the commissioners shook hands, mounted their horses, and headed for their homes. Neill, probably aware that as the Republic of Texas neared the end of its brief life and approached statehood they would call no more council meetings, could take pride in the evaluation Western gave: "It must be a source of congratulations that during the past year as well as at the close of our separate national existence, we have been and are at peace with all men both red and white."[20]

On October 19, 1844, Houston signed an executive order directing J. H. Raymond, acting treasurer, to pay James C. Neill $175 from the Indian fund. Such pay, $5 a day, was for service beginning on September 15.[21]

18

FOR THOSE WHO HAVE SERVED

"For those who have served the country long and well . . . ."
Sam Houston
January 29, 1844

President Houston, the hem of his scarlet Turkish robe falling to the floor around his feet, tackled the mound of official papers heaped on the table that centered his office. The Congress had approved a bill "for the relief of Jonathan Bird"[1] and passed it to his desk for approval. The executive read the measure carefully before dipping the quill into the ink well and noting that he withheld approval. He wrote:

> The total inability of the nation to pay these claims at this time and sustain its government, must be apparent to all who have examined into our present financial condition. There are numerous claims which the country would willingly discharge, were it able to do so . . .

The president thought. Many other citizens had spent time and money in erecting forts and block houses to protect themselves, their families, and their neighbors. There would be hundreds entitled to relief if the republic sent reimbursement to Bird. Houston dipped the pen into ink once again and concluded his note to the House of Representatives:

Partial legislation cannot but be considered a great evil, and in a country struggling with every difficulty, it cannot but be productive of discontent and increased embarrassment.²

Houston pulled another bill from the stack, this one granting relief to William G. Cooke.³ After he had scratched through another pile of papers, finding the published declaration of the expedition in which Cooke participated, Houston silently expressed appreciation for his private secretary Washington Miller,⁴ who had made the document convenient for the president's reference. Dated July 1842, the flier explained that the government of Texas would make no claim on the spoils of the expedition. Houston inked the quill and began writing, "The widows and orphans of the brave and the unfortunate decimated, have not petitioned Congress for pay or relief . . . ."⁵ He wrote:

> As a nation, we are yet in our infancy and have many things to do, deemed necessary for our peace, protection and prosperity, which require the use of all the available means which we can command. We have troops to support, fortifications to erect, and internal order to preserve. When we are relieved from these burthens—when we are stronger in population and our citizens are better able to pay taxes, we may consider favorably the claims of individuals for relief at the public charge. Until that period arrives, the Executive as far as he may be called on to act, must in conscience, and in view of the general good, withhold his assent from bills of this character.⁶

Houston looked over another bill requesting relief; he read it carefully. The House of Representatives on January 20 had passed a joint resolution for the relief of Col. James C. Neill.⁷ With this measure, Houston faced conflict—the welfare of a dear friend, one who had served Texas, versus the welfare of the young nation. Neill, who had commanded Bexar—who had been wounded in San Jacinto, and who had served as commissioner to the Indians—has served Texas with credit. Now he was disabled. The nation, however, could not afford such charity.

Houston wrote a draft of his letter, stating reasons for failing to approve relief. He looked over the letter, making minor changes. He substituted the word *preserve* for *sustain* in the fourth line. His second paragraph read: "For these reasons the bill for the relief of Col. J. C. Neill is returned to the House without signature." He struck the entire paragraph and composed a new one.[8] Satisfied with easing the rejection as much as possible, Houston submitted the note to the House on January 29:

> Were the Executive not so deeply impressed with the impoverished condition of the government, in regard to its finances, and were he not fully aware of the struggles which must consequently be encountered to preserve its existence, he might then permit his feelings of respect for those who had served the country long and well, and his sympathies for their sufferings, to influence his action as the Chief Magistrate of a generous people. But now our circumstances are such as to enforce upon him a course absolutely necessary, as he conceives, for maintaining even the semblance of a government. Were the numerous bills for private relief, which have already been presented to him for approval, to become laws, the aggregate sum appropriated would so much overburthen the financial ability of the nation as to cripple and embarrass its government to a very serious extent.
>
> For these reasons, aside from the want of some very important provisions to enable officers of the Treasury Department to act advisedly, both as to the object of the appropriation and authority to audit, the Executive is compelled to return the bill for the relief of Col. J. C. Neill, to the House in which it originated without his signature.
>
> If, however, the Honorable Congress should not concur in the reasons assigned for withholding his approval from this and other bills for private relief, it will only require the same majority in both houses to overrule his negative, that originally passed them, under that provision of the constitution, which declared that no appropriations shall be made for private or local purposes, unless two thirds of each House concur in such appropriations.[9]

A bill to pass the request for relief over the executive veto was read on January 29 along with the message the president had attached. The roll of the Senate was called, and the result

For Those Who Have Served   167

for overriding the veto announced—seven; against—five. The motion failed; the bill lost.[10]

He had made no campaign speeches and had not even expressed his opinion on the burning issue of annexation, yet on December 9, 1844, Anson Jones became president of the Republic of Texas. "Without talents, without political honesty, or popularity," commented a writer for the La Grange *Intelligencer*, he had had "greatness thrust upon him."

A week after the inaugural ceremonies, John H. Moffitt,[11] representative from Nacogdoches County, stood before the Congress assembled in the Court House.[12] The Speaker of the House listlessly occupied his chair while some of the lawmakers milled before him. Moffitt introduced a new bill calling for relief of Colonel Neill.[13] On December 16, 1844, the measure was read a second time, and on motion of Benjamin F. Parker,[14] representative of Anderson County, was ordered to be engrossed.[15] Later in the day, William L. Cazneau,[16] reporting for the group, addressed the Hon. John M. Lewis,[17] speaker, "The committee on Engrossed Bills have examined a joint resolution for the relief of J. C. Neill—also a bill for the establishment of a Post Office at the home of Jonathan Collard,[18] in the county of Montgomery—also a bill directing the President and Heads of Departments to return to the city of Austin—and find the same correctly engrossed."[19]

Only moments before adjourning on Wednesday, December 17, the House listened to the third reading of the bill.[20]

Before Christmas, Sam Houston, who earlier had vetoed the measure approving relief for Colonel Neill, galloped away from Washington, heading for Grand Cane to be with his family. He could think only of the improved cottage crowning the small hill, set among emerald trees and silver lakes. Behind him was public office; the worries of Texas now were those of President Anson Jones. Sam Houston, private citizen, had thoughts of ranching and dreams of importing Durham bulls to upgrade his Texas herds. No doubt, he felt relieved that the problem of signing or rejecting the pension for his old friend Neill was Anson's concern, not his.

On Wednesday, January 15, 1845, a quorum sat in the senate chamber when Timothy Pillsbury,[21] a member of the finance committee, discussed a joint resolution for the relief of Colonel Neill. He mentioned that the measure had been "referred, with instruction to report as to the practicability of allowing pensions to all persons wounded or permanently disabled in the defense of the Republic" and whether "in the present state of the finances of the country, it was inexpedient to allow them." He recommended rejection of the bill.[22]

At 3:00 P.M. the following day, the sergeant-at-arms of the senate was dispatched to round up enough members for a session. As soon as the absent members had reported, Pillsbury commented on the rejected motion. The Senate reconsidered the bill and approved submitting it for a third reading.[23]

In the 10:00 A.M. session, Saturday, January 18, the joint resolution was passed[24] and submitted to the committee on Engrossed Bills. Committee members examined it, and finding it correct, recommended it.[25]

As passed by members of the House and Senate, the bill provided a pension of "two hundred dollars per annum, to continue during his life, to be paid semi-annually, one hundred of which shall be paid on the tenth day of February."[26]

Colonel Neill was in Washington County on February 13, 1846, when he gave B. E. Tarver[27] power of attorney to receipt for the pension and to make "use of all other legal & necessary means to obtain" the pension as Tarver saw proper. The document was witnessed by Edmund Quinn and Hiraim Reach.[28]

19

THE GALLANT COLONEL NEILL

"One league of land . . ."
  Bastrop County Deed Book D

On February 22, 1841, Neill appointed James Smith[1] his attorney "to settle and arrange with William Cannon and Thomas Kinney" for payment of a debt against the estate of Charles S. Smith, who had died in the Alamo. Neill directed his attorney to "take lands from said Cannon in payment of said debt at two-thirds its appraised value," the lands to be selected by Smith. The document was witnessed by Daniel Gray[2] and Timothy McKean.[3] No doubt while the negotiations were underway, Neill reflected on the three months Smith had served under his command at the Alamo.

The matter would not be settled until after Colonel Neill's death, when his two sons, George J. Neill and Samuel Neill, both living in Guadalupe County, received $800 from Robert S. Rutherford and Richard W. Neely of Bastrop for their interest in the Smith estate.[4] Specifically, the brothers sold "one league of land situated in the County of Bastrop of said estate on the west side of the Colorado River on Walnut Creek and known on the map of said county as Survey Number seventeen." They appeared before Robert E. Porter, notary public, in Caldwell County, on December 15, 1854, to sign the document.[5]

In the summer of 1841, Neill found himself in the center of a newspaper feud between the editors of the *Gazette*[6] and the *Texas Sentinel*.[7] The *Texas Sentinel* on June 17 wrote that the editor of *Gazette* had called Sam Houston a brave man; the *Sentinel* writer questioned the statement. He wrote:

> We refer to our old veteran, the gallant Colonel Neill, who has fought more battles, five to one, than the stilted hero of the *Gazette*. Col. Neill was also in the battle of the Horse-shoe,[8] and we venture to assert, a braver man was not there. He has given, and would give again, *a very different account* of the conduct of Lieut. Sam Houston, on that occasion. The young hero was wounded, it is true, but in no desperate charge; and whatever the keen eye of Jackson may have discovered, it is said that Houston bellowed so lustily, on receiving his wound, as to extract many curses, long and loud, from the valuable tongue of his commander.[9]

The *Texas Sentinel* on August 12, 1841, contained another item on the same subject:

> It seems that some of Gen. Houston's partizans have got around our worthy and patriotic friend, Col. Neill, and involved the old gentleman into signing a political letter. Upon careful perusal of this letter, it will be found that the colonel does not deny a word of the anecdote we published. We know Col. Neill to be a too high-minded and truth telling man, to do so. We said that "when Gen. Houston was struck with an arrow at the battle of the Horseshoe, he bleated like a calf." Now we have called upon several gentlemen of high standing and unquestionable veracity of this city, to whom Col. Niell (*sic*) used to relate this anecdote and they used to say that the Colonel's expression was, that "he bleated like a young CUB." Those who are so busy denying this fact, are perfectly welcome to all the difference between the crying of a CUB and a CALF! Col. Niell (*sic*) has often told this anecdote, to hundreds in Texas and we know his regard for truth and honor too well, to believe he will ever deny it.[10]

Colonel Neill's narrative, naturally, differs from Sam Houston's account of the battle. As Houston vaulted a barricade, an arrow struck his thigh. Houston, undeterred, led his men in the fight until the Indians abandoned the barricade. He attempted to remove the barbed arrow, but had to call for help from a lieutenant. The fellow officer, afraid to tug hard enough to extract the arrow, suggested that Houston seek a surgeon.

Ordering the lieutenant to try again, Houston yelled, "Or, by God, I'll knock you flat."

As the arrow was removed, blood gushed like an artesian well. Houston sought a surgeon, and General Jackson, seeing the condition of the ensign, suggested he stay away from action the remainder of the day.

Later, when Jackson called for volunteers to knock the fortification out, Houston, still stretched on the ground, heard the call. He managed to get to his feet, grabbed a musket, and called for members of his platoon to follow. With only a few men behind him, he slid down the side of a ravine. He felt two rifle balls in his right arm and shoulder. Painfully, he made his way up the side of the ravine, but near the top, slumped unconscious.

Indians set fire to the log strongpoint, and the light of that fire afforded the surgeon light to remove one musket ball from Houston's arm. A second surgeon ruled it useless to make the young man suffer additionally to remove the other bullet; he had lost too much blood. Houston, he predicted, could not live to see the morning.

Regarded as all but dead, Houston spent the night on the wet ground, unattended. With pain shooting through his body, he felt himself deserted. When he was found to have life remaining, he was moved by litter to Fort Williams. Some Volunteer Tennessee troops looked after him in the field hospital, and when they prepared to leave, placed Houston on a litter between two horses. Because of the jolting pain, he cursed the soldiers and begged them to let him die where he was.[11]

In his own words, Houston said:

> I languished a short time, and when I had recovered a little strength went to Maryville to be near medical aid. Here my health gradually declined, and in quest of a more skilled surgeon, I was removed to Knoxville. The physician to whom I applied, found me in so low a state that he was unwilling to take charge of

me, for he declared that I could live only a few days. But at the end of this period, finding I had not only survived, but begun to improve a little, the doctor offered his services, and I slowly recovered.[12]

The presidential campaign that had spurred the memories of Horseshoe Bend and the newspaper attacks ended, and on December 13, 1841, Houston took office as the third president of the Republic of Texas.

Neill also found activity elsewhere. Because of the interest of a number of veterans or their assigns in locating bounty and donation lands, Neill set up a service to locate, survey, and register land claims. An appreciative Texas government had made headright grants to early colonists and settlers. On November 24, 1835, the General Council of Texas had established a regular army of 1,120 men. Each non-commissioned officer and private in that force would, upon honorable discharge, receive one mile square, 640 acres, of land. In December, the amount was increased, making a total of 800 acres a soldier, his heirs, or assigns could claim.[13]

In March of 1836, the Consultation amended the bounty grant policy, stating that men who continued in service would be eligible for 1,280 acres. Those who already had served or who completed six months of service would receive 540 acres, and those who were in service for three months would be eligible for 320 acres. A special bounty grant was approved awarding 320 acres to soldiers in the siege of Bexar, and additional donation grants of 640 acres were presented to those who participated in certain battles of the Revolution.[14]

Because a majority of the bounty warrants could be transferred, a number of warrants were sold before they were issued.[15]

Neill was aware the owner of these warrants selected the tract he wanted from among the vacant or unappropriated public domain. He then would deliver his bounty warrant to a surveyor, who would prepare field notes on the tract, draw a plat on a map of the county, and send the warrant, plat, and field notes to the General Land Office in Austin.[16]

Neill capitalized on the interest in locating holdings.

George Gardiner of Galveston in January 1846 paid Neill $1,000 "to locate for me and in my name my headright certificate for 640 acres." Under terms of the agreement, Neill would locate and survey the land, and when the mission was completed, Gardiner would deed him one half the property.[17]

Another record of these transactions shows that Neill, after December 18, 1847, undertook to locate 1,280 acres, called for in bounty warrant No. 1396,[18] issued to Thomas J. Church but transferred to Charles L. Harrison. Harrison, in turn, assigned the property to U. I. Ephraim, who signed it to Robert and Flora Ann Matthews.[19]

Possibly while on one of the land locating trips in April 1846, Neill came into contact with a party of surveyors locating headrights and headrights certificate lands. One of the surveyors was Buck Barry, who recorded meeting Neill:

> Our work was in Navarro, Hill, and Ellis Counties, which were then in Robertson County Land District. Buffalo hunters and land locaters were our principal associates. I carried the chain around the survey where Waxahachie now stands; carried it around the survey in which Milford and other towns that have since sprung up. I carried it around the survey where Corsicana with its oil treasure has since been developed.
>
> When we established the northwest corner there were three buffalo hunters with us. While we were in the timber resting and waiting for the surveyor to make out his field notes, a drove of buffaloes ran by within fifty steps of us. We did not shoot or kill any game except when we wanted meat. But the buffalo hunters shot down one apiece.
>
> We worked up Chambers and Brier Creeks to ten or twelve miles above where Corsicana now stands. We made a habit of shooting off signal guns every evening and morning to notify anyone wanting to locate certificates where to find us. One morning we fired our signal and who should ride into our camp but the old veteran, Colonel Nail, who was wounded by a Mexican lance thrown from the top of a house during the siege of San Antonio. While our distinguished visitor was eating his breakfast he told us the United States troops had landed in Texas, and the

Mexican Army had been surrounded near the mouth of the Rio Grande. He said that General Taylor, commanding, had appealed to the people of Texas through their governor for immediate help.

All the boys began saddling their horses to go to the rescue of General Taylor. The surveyors said, "Boys, are you going to leave me here with my pack mule and my Jacob's staff? You must help me get to the settlement." We helped him to the settlement.[20]

20

HAMPTON MCKINNEY

"... *being very sick in body, but of perfect mind and memory* ..."
J. C. Neill's will

Jubilee[1] and Jefferson McKinney[2] were insistent. Back in Illinois, after spending some time in Texas, they urged their relatives to return with them. Jubilee had filed claim on 640 acres, and Jeff had purchased land in Robertson County. Now they were trying to convince their older brother Hamp[3] to dispose of his property and join them.

A single man, Jubilee, was ready to begin the trip to the Republic of Texas immediately, and Jeff already had persuaded his wife Lucinda that the move was a wise one. Soon Hampton and his family—a wife, three sons, and four daughters[4]—showed signs of Texas fever, and a wagon train was formed. Hamp's daughter Nancy and her husband, John A. Harlin—some said he was a professional gambler[5] but when he became a Texian, he was listed in the census as a carpenter—were eager for a new start.[6]

Nancy McKinney Kendall, hearing wondrous tales her brothers spun about the new frontier, looked pleadingly into her husband's eyes, and Fenwick Robert Kendall soon found himself loading heavy trunks on a wagon for the trip south of the Red River. Their children, Eleanor Catherine, Mary, Martha, Joseph, Susan, and baby Elizabeth Diadem chatted excitedly about what they anticipated they would find in their new home.[7] Two "nephews," Jim Moore and John Gilliam, also joined the train.

The overland trip completed, the McKinney men reined their teams into the Mercer Colony. Hampton had applied for a 640-acre patent of land in the area, and colony officials had located it. Charles Fenton Mercer, who had been associated with the Peters Colony, applied for an empresario grant for himself, and on January 25, 1844, President Sam Houston ordered the secretary of state to prepare a contract allowing Mercer five years to introduce at least 100 families to settle in Texas. A boundary dispute arose when it was learned that the Peters contract had used the word *westerly* meaning *easterly,* so each empresario believed he owned certain strips of land. Mercer had ordered maps printed of his colony and had distributed them throughout Indiana and Illinois to attract such families as the McKinneys.[8]

In the spring of 1845, Mercer engaged B. J. Chambers to survey and prepare townships for immediate settlement. Opposition came from Thomas I. Smith, captain of the Texas Rangers, and William R. Howe, who lived on Chambers Creek. Eight men, Smith among them, prepared a warning to Chambers that if he attempted to survey the section, they would cause him "to desist even though rough means be necessary."[9] Chambers, however, was determined to go about his work. When he tried to establish an office near Melton, he was "threatened and incommodated," and his team was "dispensed and driven away so rapidly as to result in the death of one ox." Chambers was left "some thirty miles above Franklin." C. C. Taylor,[10] surveyor of Robertson County, refused to submit his plat.[11]

Not long after moving into the area, Hamp McKinney and his three sons located two cedar cabins some distance apart. The four moved one cabin and linked it by dog trot to the second,[12] and while one cabin served as the family quarters, the McKinneys opened a tavern in the other, "where both man and beast could find comfortable quarters, a well prepared table and courteous attention." "Mother" McKinney would tolerate no rough characters; she insisted her guests be gentlemen. Among the prominent men who had quarters at the McKinney Inn were John L. Miller,[13] Roger Q. Mills,[14] Alexander Beaton,[15] John M. Crockett,[16] John H. Reagan,[17] and Clinton M. Winkler.

It was in 1847 that Clinton Winkler, a young lawyer, engaged board in the McKinney tavern.[18] For the first two years of the county's history, records and documents were maintained, and courts convened in the home of William Howe, but finally officials agreed to relocate the county seat in Hampton McKinney's tavern.[19] Citizens' complaints about the "great public inconvenience" were responsible for the county seat being moved to the Richardson community, nearer the geographic center of the new county.[20]

Winkler composed a bill for the legislature that provided for the permanent location of the county seat. Representatives passed the act in February of 1848, and named Thomas I. Smith, William F. Henderson, Ethan Melton, James A. Johnson, and James Riggs commissioners "to select the most suitable portion of a survey marked on the map of the Richardson Land District. . . ."[21]

Commissioners considered two sites—Richland, later known as Dresden, and Richardson Settlement. They voted for the Richardson plot, located on the Jesus Ortiz Survey. G. A. Campbell had become owner of the certificate calling for the land, and he eventually sold to Thomas I. Smith, James C. Neill, and David R. Mitchell, land speculators and surveyors. Mitchell had been land surveyor for the Robertson land district. Representative Winkler, who introduced the bill to the House and was a friend of all three owners, stipulated the county seat be on the Campbell location, and it was "no mere coincidence."[22]

The title, however, was not clear. It is likely that all three owners were aware of the cloud surrounding the deed. The location overlapped title surveys held by Rachel Leach and Jehu Peoples, and these surveys had been located long before there were settlements in the region. Too, the Robertson County School Land had been located in the same area, in conflict with the Ortiz survey. On January 26, 1839, a legislative act had set aside three leagues of land for each county for the purpose of supporting schools. In February 1840 the Texas Congress added one additional league of land. When the county commissioners met on February 25, 1848, Thomas I. Smith signed a $10,000 bond that he would clear the title.[23]

Unaware that his friend of long standing, Thomas Smith, had died on March 20, James Clinton Neill on March 28, 1848, prepared his will, naming Smith and David R. Mitchell as executors. Neill died in Grimes County on March 30.

Mitchell, as executor of both Neill's and Smith's wills, and as the surviving member of the trio of owners of the land on which the county seat of Navarro would be located, set about clearing the title. He received the patent on January 9, 1850.

On January 30, 1848, Mitchell deeded the 100-acre townsite to the county, and on May 1, the first sale of Corsicana town lots took place.[24] James M. Riggs was auctioneer for the sale, which some sources say lasted seven days. Hamptom McKinney was the first buyer, purchasing Lot 2 of Block 12 for $50.[25] McKinney went into the hotel business, erecting a two-story building with an ell used as a kitchen and dining room. The building had a long gallery in front and a big hall between the rooms, each with a large fireplace.[26]

21

LAST WILL

". . . this my last will . . ."
J. C. Neill's will

Three months after Neill's death, when the probate court of Navarro County met on July 31, 1848, it named David R. Mitchell[1] administrator of Neill's estate with a bond of $5,000. That session marked the beginning of a long, involved process.[2] Mitchell pointed out that "J. C. Neill late a citizen of Grimes County died possessed of property real and personal lying in Navarro and parts of the state and that decedant before his death with all the formalities required by law made and executed his last will and testament disposing of his effects." The court ordered Mitchell to set about his task as executor of the will.[3]

When the court assembled the following month, it was mentioned that the proper deposition of John Gillespie,[4] a resident of Grimes County, had been received. Gillespie, appearing before Joseph Morison, a notary public,[5] vowed that he witnessed James C. Neill "sign, seal and deliver the document and that he was of sound mind and memory."[6]

Claims against the estate began to cross Mitchell's desk, and by October 30, he was able to list some of them: a note on William Bloodgood payable in horses or cattle, $100; a note on Thomas I. Smith,[7] $30; a note on William Dunbar (balance), $35; a note on Jackson Griffin,[8] $63.23; a note on James M.

Osburn, $125; a note on N. A. Carrol,[9] $6.75; a note on Ira Millican, Texas money, $110; a note on James D. Elliott, $200; and a note on John Clifton, $500.

The following day, the court ordered James A. Johnson[10] and William J. Ladd[11] to appraise 640 acres of land. They did so, setting a value of 75 cents per acre.[12] On July 13, 1849, William M. Love, John Boyd, and John Carner were named to a commission to appraise ⅔ league of one labor of land in Limestone County.[13] In August, appraisers were appointed to look over holdings in Fannin County.[14] John L. Lovejoy and Alfred Johnson reported in September 1849 that ⅔ of a league of land lying on Pilot Grove, part of the headright tract, patented in Neill's name on February 24, 1842, was worth 75 cents per acre. One-third of a league, surveyed and patented on February 23, 1842, and lying on Six Mile Creek, also was valued at 75 cents per acre.[15]

In the September 1849 session, Willis A. Price petitioned the court that he held title bond, signed by Neill, June 20, 1847, for property he had assigned to James M. Love, a citizen of Limestone County.[16] Mitchell acknowledged being aware of the fact, and the court ordered him to make and execute a deed of conveyance to Love.[17]

Seemingly, as soon as one appraisal was read to the court, another assignment was made. E. S. Wyman, Thomas Bell, and John Treadwell were appointed to appraise the land in Navarro County. At the same time, the court called for an evaluation of 493 acres on Ash Creek, part of the Campbell headright, and also on 1,280 acres of Neill bounty land.[18]

A different type of property came before the court on September 26, 1849, when David Laughlin[19] and F. S. Williams were asked to appraise a Negro woman belonging to the estate. The fifty-year-old slave was examined and valued at $50.[20]

On September 28, 1849, the court appointed J. C. Ragan,[21] Allen M. Moore, and Philip T. Bufford to appraise the headright of Francis F. Williams' one-third of a league.[22] Horatio Nelson of Houston County, administrator of the estate of F. F. Williams, deceased, had offered at public sale in the town of Crockett on April 4, 1843, one-third of a league containing 1,476 acres. The land was on the waters of Catfish Bayou. J. C. Neill successfully bid $1,000,[23] and Nelson signed, sealed, and delivered the deed July 28, 1844.[24]

The Williams headright tract and the 1,256 acres in Neill's headright were valued at $1 per acre.[25]

Mitchell notified the court that there was no personal property to satisfy the debts, and he asked for permission to sell the 1,256 acres on Walnut Creek in Henderson County. Members of the probate court agreed it was time to dispose of some of the land in order to satisfy the estate's debts, which now totaled $763.44.[26]

During the same session, Mitchell listed the assets of the estate: 640 acres of land at 75 cents per acre, $480; 4,605 acres of Collin County land at 75 cents per acre, $3,454; 3,129 acres of Limestone County land at 75 cents per acre, $782.24; 1,280 acres in Navarro at 75 cents per acre, $1,280; 492 acres of Navarro land at $1 per acre, $492; one Negro woman, $50; and 2,732 acres of land in Henderson County at $1 per acre, $2,732.[27]

Notes on the estate also were exhibited: R. M. Tyrus[28] acct., $12.50; C. C. Taylor,[29] $34.40; James Morgan, $43.28; Thomas Johnson, $30; Doct. F. A. Graves, $29; E. L. Arndt, note, $20; James Highten, $86.56; H. J. Jones, $10; and Willis A. Price, $210. Notes came to $495.74.[30]

Mitchell also listed his expenses during the year, including cash for Patten, $2; expenses, not explained, $3; expenses to Palestine, $6; tax on 640 acres, $1.92; advertising, $3.50; expenses to Collin County, $10, cash for certificate, $50; tax on 1 league and labor in Collin County, $23.75; expenses to Austin, $25; judge's fee, $2; clerk's fee, $7.33; and "dye myself," $125; for a total of $284.50.[31] Added after expenses had been enumerated and totaled was a deed made to J. M. Love for 375 acres at Tehuacana Hills and "paid to" J. D. Lynch.

Amount of notes in favor of the estate included one on William Bloodgood, payable in horses or cattle, $100; note on Thomas I. Smith, $30; note on William Dunbar, $35; note on Jackson Griffin, $42.23; note on James M. Osburn, $125; note on N. H. Carrol, $11.75; note on Ira Williams, Texas money, $110; note on James D. Elliott, $200; and note on John Clifton, $500.[32]

Apparently, Mitchell received no offers for the land in Henderson County, and the order to sell was revived in the September term, 1849.[33]

The court must have sat in silence in December 1849. Petitions were read from Dr. William Nicks Anderson and William White that sounded like thunderbolts. Each claimed one-third interest in the Neill estate, in both real and personal holdings, and they charged that Mitchell had been supervising the estate long enough to have things in order to begin the partitioning.

Mitchell was ordered to appear in person in the Corsicana sessions the last Monday of the year to explain why "said estate should not be partitioned."[34] He said he was "not bound in law to answer said petition because the same is informal and insufficient." He argued that he had used "every exertion to settle the business of said estate," but he had been unable to do so because suits were pending in Limestone County in which the estate was involved. There were debts he had been unable to settle, and some demands were unmet.[35]

The court ruled the citation had been served as required by law, and that William White, William Nicks Anderson, and William B. Pillow,[36] who had filed a separate petition, were "entitled separately and individually to one third." Two different boards of commissioners were named to partition the land; one consisted of a man unidentified other than Evans, one identified only as McClure, and John F. Taylor; on the other were John Boyd, William M. Love, and John Carner.[37]

How did William Nicks Anderson, William White, and William B. Pillow come into possession of one-third each of the estate? On October 3, 1849, George Jefferson Neill, then a resident of Travis County, sold Anderson for $1,000 "all of my interest in the estate of James C. Neill deceased, including real estate, bonds, notes, chases in action, and everything also that I may have."[38]

Neill's daughter, Mary H. Price, and her husband Willis A. Price on that same date sold their interest in the estate to William White. They retained 200 acres that had been sold to A. J. Dixon,[39] who assigned it to Anderson.[40]

Samuel Clinton Neill, on May 5, 1849, sold and conveyed by deed and transfer "all my right title interest claims I demand in and to the property and estate, both real and personal of James C. Neill, late of the county of Grimes." A resident of

Caldwell County at the time, Samuel Neill sold his share of the estate to Asa Pullen, who sold it to William B. Pillow of Navarro for $600.[41]

Mark F. Roberts was appointed commissioner to partition and distribute the 1476 acres in the J. C. Neill headright and 3,129 acres in another tract.[42]

James Monroe Riggs,[43] attorney, Corsicana commissioner, and land agent, was appointed guardian of Miranda Neill "to divide her share of land as willed to her by her Grandfather James C. Neill decd."[44] An order of the court in February 1850 set 640 acres "a part to Miranda Neill, a daughter of Samuel Neill as granted to her by the last will and testimony of her grandfather."[45]

Meanwhile, Anderson and William White filed suit in county court against Mitchell, ordering him to deliver all papers belonging to the estate. In open court, Anderson declared he could not safely come to trial in January for want of testimony, although he had used diligence to pressure it in time for the case. He vowed the suit was held "not for the purpose of delay but that justice may be done."[46]

Anderson and White also complained that Mitchell had not returned a true and perfect inventory of "goods chattles lands tenements and effects."[47] They charged he had not "complied with the law" by failing to render a complete inventory, and they demanded his removal as administrator,[48] but their petition was dismissed and they were ordered to pay court costs.[49]

Again in open court, White explained the plaintiffs could "not safely come to trial for want of material witnesses."[50] In March 1850 he said that George Neill and W. A. Price, both residing in Travis County, held evidence material to the case. Depositions sent them had not been returned. The hearing was delayed until the next regular term of court.[51] The next term of court came, but the depositions did not.[52]

Joseph Lynch appeared as a petitioner, saying that on February 2, 1842, Neill bargained and sold him 1,280 acres of land on Briar Creek, a northern branch of Richland Creek in Navarro County. To make title, Neill executed to him his bond, as agreement in writing and signed in his own hand. He paid "down in hand" to Neill. At the time the bargain was made, the land had been located but not surveyed or patented. Since that time, however, proper offices had surveyed. Neill had received the land twenty-six miles west of the Trinity River and six and one-half miles north of Richland, by Warrant No. 496, issued by Bernard E. Bee, secretary of war, on November 24, 1836. In the bond, the land was described as lying in Burnet County, but it was in territory now embraced by Navarro.[53]

Mitchell vowed he was "well acquainted with the hand writing of said James C. Neill and knows that the bond sued on by plaintiff and exhibited in his petition was signed by him and James C. Neill." He knew of no reason the title to the land should not be made.[54] The court directed him to prepare a deed conveying the land to Lynch.[55]

Another term of court appeared on the calendars, and again Anderson, lacking material evidence, requested a delay. He had been diligent in attempting to get depositions from Willis A. Price and George J. Neill, he explained, and had forwarded them mail. "Fearing from the uncertainty of the mails that evidence would not arrive in time," White had left fifteen days earlier to see that the depositions were in Corsicana "without fail." For some unexplained reason, White had not returned, and Anderson mentioned that the "mail has failed beyond Springfield."

Anderson again called for a complete inventory, pointing out that Neill died possessing one horse and rigging, twenty-six head of cattle, one half interest in the William Kincannon survey of one league and labor,[56] one half interest in the Matthews survey, and other claims.[57] The case was continued until the next term of court.

Christopher C. Taylor of Navarro petitioned the court in May 1850, claiming the estate owed him $34.40. He charged that Mitchell "neglects and fails to apply to the court for an order to sell sufficient land or other property to pay this with other debts of the estate." Mitchell termed Taylor's prayers superfluous, since plans were already underway to make available in a private sale 1,215 acres.[58] The court ordered sale of 1,250 acres in Henderson County "at the earliest practicable time after the expiration of six months." Credit of twelve months would be permitted.[59]

Finally, Anderson and White had their hearing in court, explaining to Justice Sterling C. Cross that each had purchased undivided third interests "at great cost and paying large and valuable considerations." They charged that Mitchell had failed to provide "a full and complete inventory," there being, to their knowledge, "one horse, bridle and saddle and other rigging, 26 head of cattle," and pieces of real estate not yet named. They mentioned "the tract of land on which Elias Carroll lives," one half of a league and labor in Kincannon's headright, and John Huffman's headright of 640 acres,[60] C. J. Neill's headright certificate for 320 acres,[61] and a certificate located Tehuacana for 640 acres, and Zack Brook's certificate for 320 acres.[62]

Mitchell's attorney answered the charge, saying the administrator had no legal record of Anderson's or White's being "the heirs or as owners of the claims." Mitchell vowed he had inventoried all the property belonging to James C. Neill, and that the horse, saddle, bridle, and other items as charged in the plaintiffs' petition did not come into his hands as administrator. Mitchell explained:

> When I . . . visited the residence of the late J. C. Neill . . . to take into my possession the papers of J. C. Neill, I understood that there was five cows belonging to said estate which said cattle I made arrangements to have taken care of, . . . and before they came into my possession I learned that George Neill and Willis Price, two of the heirs of J. C. Neill decd, drove said cattle to Colorado and they have not as yet come into my possession.

Saying he did not know the number or value, he would, should they come into his possession, "return them on the inventory as property belonging to said estate."

Mitchell then turned his attention to the matter of real estate, saying he had patent for part of the Kincannon league and labor, but the tract was in litigation with one of the plaintiffs, Anderson. Only part of the tract belongs to the Neill estate, Mitchell explained. No part of the 640 acres belonging to John Huffman was included in the estate. George Neill's certificate was impatented. The Zack Brooks property had not come into his possession, and no claim for ⅓ of a league of land in the Toler name had come to his attention, nor had the Matthews' claim of 1,280 acres.[63]

The suit was dismissed.⁶⁴

No sooner had Mitchell solved one of his headaches than another suit reached county court in Tennessee. In 1850 Sarah Ann and John Jarrett, minor heirs of John G. Jarrett, through a friend, Alfred E. Pace, filed charges that Neill had on February 19, 1841 promised to provide Jarrett a "good and legal title to one tract of a league of land—⅓ of a league and a labor granted to Neill by joint resolution of both houses of Congress," January 27, 1841. Jarrett had indicated he would locate the land himself and pay all government dues on it. He had died in December 1841, and his children filed suit on January 2, 1851.⁶⁵

In November 1850, the court ordered Mitchell to make and execute a deed conveying the land to the minor heirs of Jarrett.⁶⁶

Mitchell continued to accept and disperse for the estate. He had continued to pay on the notes and attorney's fees.⁶⁷ He had received $350 from the sale of 350 acres and $93.25 from W. Bobo as rent for one mule.⁶⁸ He added to the inventory of real estate 640 acres granted Thomas Church⁶⁹ and transferred to Matthews and then to the estate. The property, described as "near where William Bright⁷⁰ now lives," was appraised at $1 per acre.⁷¹ The court named James M. Riggs and James B. Barry⁷² to evaluate the tract.

Later in the March term, Mitchell explained he had paid cash taxes for 1848 amounting to $19.70, clerks' fee of $12.13, judges' fee of $2.50, and had been out $6 in making a trip to Anderson County, and had paid on a number of notes totaling $793.80.⁷³

In March 1853, R. N. White, county clerk,⁷⁴ filed three deeds as ordered by the court and dated February 1851. They transferred land to William Nicks Anderson, William P. Pillow, and Abner Carroll. Pillow and White were ordered to pay the clerk $2 each for making the deeds and 50 cents each for the certification.⁷⁵

The estate was partitioned in February 1851, as ordered by S. C. Cross, chief justice of Navarro County. Named as distributees were William N. Anderson, William B. Pillow, and William White, who assigned his interest to Abner Carroll. The one-third of a league—or 1,476 acres in Anderson County—and a similar partition of 2,713 acres in Limestone were set aside, but space for a name has been left blank in official documents. Set aside for Anderson were 492 acres from the headright of Francis F. Williams lying in Anderson County. From the same headright, the court set aside 492 acres for Abner Carroll. For Carroll the court also partitioned Lot no. 1 of 904 1/3 acres near Tehuacana Hills in Limestone County. Lot B of 904 1/3 acres was deeded to Pillow, and to William Anderson went Lot No. 3 and one labore of John Boyd's survey.[76]

Before the estate could be cleared, fifty-six-year-old David R. Mitchell died on October 7, 1853, and J. C. Miller and Will H. Mitchell, a son,[77] filed letters of the account of Mitchell and the Neill estate.[78]

22

GEORGE J. NEILL

"To George J. Neill..."
J. C. Neill's will

The 1830 Greene County, Alabama, census taker recorded the James Clinton and Harriet Neill household as including a male 5 to 10 years of age, three females between 0 to 5 years, two females between 5 to 10, a female 10 to 15, and two sons between between 15 to 20. What happened to this large family is not explained, but when J. C. and Harriet left for Texas, only three children accompanied the parents.

George Jefferson Neill, born in Bedford County, Tennessee, July 8, 1808, was twenty-three years of age when his parents turned their backs on Alabama and followed the Lone Star of Texas to their destiny.

John Holland Jenkins, a Texas neighbor, described George Neill as "a man every whit suited to the scenes of his early manhood, possessing by nature the faculty not only to endure, but even to enjoy the struggles of frontier life."[1] His companions often called him Nail.[2]

George Jefferson Neill was not immune to the Texas Independence fever which infected his father, brother, neighbors, and friends. Although he is not listed in Sam Houston Dixon's and Louis Wiltz Kemp's *The Heroes of San Jacinto*, signed statements in the state archives and Neill's own affidavit show that he participated. When he appeared before state comptroller A.

Bledsoe in 1871 he certified he was in the war for independence, having "belonged to his fathers command of artilery."³ Jennings O'Bannion submitted a statement that he "knew him while he was a member of Capt. J. C. Neill's company of artilery."⁴

Capt. John C. Hunt, the Alabaman who supplied "Opiate Sedatives" to Gen. Sam Houston, "suffering, greatly, from the Effects of his Glorious Battle-Wound" at San Jacinto, signed a statement that Neill joined his company May 25 and served "faithfully and honorably." From Camp Colett on July 31, 1836, he recorded that Neill went on a fourteen-day leave of absence, at the end of which he was discharged.⁵

Neill received his discharge from the Texian Army in August 1835 and immediately joined Deaf Smith's spy company. It is possible he was in the command that left the Republic capital at Columbia December 8 for Bexar to investigate rumors that a large Mexican force was pressing toward the Texas frontier.⁶

When rumors of the advance of the Mexican forces spread, the *Telegraph and Texas Register* editorialized, "Let every man . . . perform his duty." The editorial continued:

> Are there not freemen enough in Texas, to rise and at once crush the abject race, whom like the musquetoe, it is easier to kill, than endure its annoying buzz?⁷

On February 1, 1838, George Jefferson Neill enlisted for three months, serving in the ranging company of John L. Lynch of Bastrop. At the end of the enlistment period, Neill was discharged.⁸

From the land commissioners of Bastrop County, he received one-third league of land⁹ on a site around which grew the town of Waterloo. In the spring, 1839, J. S. Jones wrote Mirabeau B. Lamar that Waterloo was "a small village at the foot of the mountains."¹⁰ On the following day, W. Jefferson Jones was calling the area "the most beautiful and at the same time the most sublime scene I ever saw." To Lamar, he continued:

> . . . and I frequently wished that you were present to enjoy the scenery as I saw it in all the majesty of nature and the verdue of Spring. The atmosphere was charged with the most delightful perfume and every hill and every flower seemed to extend a welcome to the weary traveller. I never expected to realize your eloquent description of Texas till I saw the lands of the upper Colorado— There are a hundred of the most beautiful sites for building round the town level and Rome itself with all its famous hills could not have surpassed the natural scenery of Waterloo. . . .[11]

In 1839 the capitol of Texas was approved for location in the town of Waterloo, situated in Bastrop County. On April 3, the special term of court was called to order, attended by L. C. Cunningham, chief justice of Bastrop County; S. R. Miller, clerk; and A. Mays, coroner and ex-officio sheriff.

Bastrop officials read a petition from Albert C. Horton,[12] William Menefee,[13] Louis P. Cooke,[14] Isaac Burton,[15] and Isaac Campbell,[16] commissioned under an act for the permanent location for the seat of government. On March 23, they selected land "situated, lying and being in the County of Bastrop, and Republic of Texas, on the East bank of the Colorado River, on a point of which stands the Town of Waterloo, and the remainder of which are near or adjoining to said Town."[17] Included was one-third league belonging to George Neill, then residing in Washington County. Other property in the selected tract belonged to Logan Vandeveer, Aaron Burleson,[18] George D. Hancock,[19] Joseph Porter Brown, James Rogers,[20] and Jacob Harrell.[21]

Neill and other land owners were summoned to appear in the Bastrop courthouse before jurors Bartlett Sims,[22] B. M. Clopton, John Brown, James Standoford,[23] Jeptha Boyce,[24] and James Lynn.[25] William Pinckney Hill[26] was chosen to speak for the defendants.

Jurors fixed the value of the land on the East Bank of the Colorado River, allowing Neill $3.50 per acre.[27] The sheriff was ordered to "proceed forthwith, and make to the Republic of Texas a deed of said land."[28] For his property on which now stands the capitol of Texas, Neill received $5,600. The purchase was approved on February 1, 1840.

The matter was not concluded, however. On February 3, 1871, Neill petitioned the Texas House and Senate saying "the commissioners after said ajudication, neglected and failed to furnish" him "a draft on the Treasury of the Republic as it was their duty to have done." He had been paid by promissory notes, at the time worth no more than 25 to 30 cents on the dollar. Neill claimed he was paid "no more than fair value;" he appealed to be compensated.[29]

On April 14, 1840, he married Marcella Jones, but she did not live long after the wedding date.

Perhaps to allay his grief over the loss of his wife, perhaps from a sense of patriotism, or perhaps because of an inherent adventuresome spirit, George Jefferson Neill participated in the Plum Creek Fight in the summer of 1840.

Smarting under defeats that Gen. Edward Burleson and Col. John H. Moore had inflicted on them, the Comanche Indians began large-scale raids through the Texas settlements—plundering, sacking, and burning Linnville, attacking Victoria, and killing and capturing settlers in their wake.

General Burleson began recruiting men along the Colorado to go in pursuit of the Indians, and soon the troops moved across country toward the Guadalupe Valley, where they were to join a force of Guadalupe and San Marcos recruits. Among the Guadalupe fighters were Mathew Caldwell, Jack Hays, Ben McCulloch, Henry McCulloch, Andrew Sowell, and others.[30]

Nine miles from the rendezvous point, the men under Caldwell caught sight of the Comanches. The place was Plum Creek, approximately three miles from present day Lockhart. Two Indians had been stationed on a high ridge to serve as scouts; they sat on their ponies awaiting the approach of the white men. The two were wearing plug hats[31] they had looted in Linnville.

Riding in the front echelon of eighty-two settlers was George Neill. As he dismounted, he vowed he would move the Indian scouts. Aiming high, he fired his long-range gun. The Indians wheeled their horses, and in haste to escape, lost their hats.[32]

Earlier that morning, scouts reported they had sighted approximately a thousand Indians with vast herds of horses and mules.[33] Galbreath described some of the Indians facing the settlers:

> Many of the Indians had on fine coats and boots, and some of them carried umbrellas over them. They had many horses and mules packed with goods, and these were rushed on ahead by the squaws, while the warriors fought the battle. At a mott of timber the Comanches rallied in large force and a sharp fight ensued, but they again fled and scattered.[34]

One of the chiefs rode a fine horse with an American bridle; to the animal's tail was tied a red ribbon eight or ten feet long. The chief wore elegant clothes plundered at Victoria and Linnville. He wore a fine pair of boots, a large top silk hat, and leather gloves. When he first appeared at the battle site, he had a large umbrella stretched over himself.

The Indians would charge the Texians, then retreat. After several such feints, the settlers determined that the Indians wore shields. One old Texian waited patiently, and as an Indian spun his horse, his shield flew from the body. The Texian fired. The warrior hit the ground. After several other Indians met a similar fate, the Indians began a retreat.

Before long, many of the pack animals wearied and had to be abandoned. Some of the Indian ponies became mired in a boggy area, but the pursuit continued to the foot of the mountains between San Marcos and Kyle.[35]

George Jefferson Neill married Mary A. Highsmith on April 18, 1841, in Washington County, the occasion uniting two illustrious frontier families. Mary was born in Missouri on May 7, 1825, the daughter of Abujah M. Highsmith[36] and Deborah Turner Highsmith. The girl was only three years of age when her parents crowded the family of two daughters and a son[37] into a covered wagon for the move to Texas. The family crossed the Sabine River by raft the day before Christmas. In the party were four other families, thirty-three persons in all, and all but one related.[38]

After settling on the bank of the Colorado River two miles above the present location of La Grange, the six families of colonists were threatened by Indians. The Highsmiths then moved to Aylett C. Buckner's[39] in 1829.

In July 1842, George Neill, James Curtis,[40] and two Mexicans were driving mustangs toward a pen they had prepared on Plum Creek Prairie. Unarmed but astride fine mounts, they were approximately fifteen miles from their home base when they were surprised by a band of Comanches. Of the incident John Holland Jenkins wrote:

> Nothing but the superior fleetness and endurance of their horses saved them from falling into the hands of the Indians, whose horses failed when about one and a half miles from the pen. All of the men except James Curtis were wounded, and arrows were sticking in all the horses when the race was done.[41]

In 1843, Capt. John C. Hays made plans to go to the head of the Guadalupe River to reconnoiter some of the canyons below the mountains and return to his camp on the Leon Creek west of San Antonio. With him were approximately thirty-five men, including George Jefferson Neill.[42]

From base camp, the Rangers rode northwest until they struck the Medina River near where Castroville stands. They kept along that stream and set up camp where Bandera is situated. Guards were posted at night. Around the campfire were all types of people. Ben Highsmith recalled "it was not uncommon to hear men quoting from the most popular poets and authors, and talking learnedly on ancient and modern history." Outwardly, the men wore "rough garb and wide hats to protect them from the sun" through the long days on the prairie. Buckskin or cowskin leggins protected their legs from mesquite and retame brush, and "the large clinking spurs put new life into a tardy pony if occasion demanded."[43]

The following morning, they turned north toward Bandera Pass, approximately 500 yards long and 125 yards wide, but with boulder and brush-covered canyon walls reaching fifty feet high. Scouts were farther ahead than usual when the Rangers rode into the pass two or three abreast.

Sudden fire threw the first men into confusion; their wounded, frightened horses attempted to wheel and escape the danger.

Captain Hays was riding with the front line when the Indians opened their attack and began to jump from behind brush and boulder concealment. Calmly, he yelled, "Dismount! Tie your horses."

As quickly as the Rangers could hit the ground and tether their mounts, they prepared their guns and began firing. Their first shots drove the Indians behind cover again. Then the chief urged his warriors to sweep forward, and a large force closed in on the Rangers. About 11:00 A.M. the Rangers began to push the Indians back toward the north end of the pass, frequently resorting to hand-to-hand combat.

Near the north end of the pass, Kit Ackland felled the chief with a pistol ball, and the two engaged in a wrestling match. Both were large, powerful men, and they rolled over and over on the ground, each trying to deliver a fatal thrust of a knife. Finally, the Ranger won, and when he stood up, he was covered with blood and dirt, a bloody knife clutched in his hand. The chief had been hacked to pieces.[44]

Thomas Galbreath, wounded, was lying on the ground facing north. An arrow had struck him above the pistol belt and near the hip bone. Galbreath removed the arrows and resumed loading his gun. No one was aware he had been wounded until the Indian retreat got underway.

Sam Luckey[45] was shot through the body. Luckily, Ben Highsmith was on the ground only feet away and caught him, easing the fall to the ground. Luckey called for water, and Highsmith held his canteen for the wounded man.

Highsmith, wounded after firing many times, pulled the arrow from his leg but continued to take careful aim. Sam

Walker[46] was wounded by a lance. Ranger Sam Fohr[47] was shot through the body with an arrow, a spike on one side and a feather on the other. Andrew Erskine[48] received an arrow in the thigh. As Creek Taylor,[49] a participant in the battle, recalled:

> He charged the Indian with a five-shooter, but the barrel dropped off with his knowledge, and he almost touched the Indian trying to shoot, but failed. The Comanche had his bow-stick shot in two and was also unable to shoot, but noticing the condition of the Ranger's pistol, grasped an arrow in his hand and tried to stab him with it.[50]

By noon the Indians had begun their retreat, and the Rangers took tally of their losses—several horses had been killed or disabled. Six Rangers lay seriously wounded, and five men were dead. The Indians removed their fallen warriors through the north end of the pass and buried their dead chief. The Rangers rode through the south end.

In 1842, when San Antonio was captured by the Mexicans under Gen. Adrian Woll, George Jefferson Neill again saw action.

Under command of Mathew Caldwell, a company rode to Salado, seven miles northwest of San Antonio, and joined Capt. Jack Hays' Rangers, commissioned by Gen. Sam Houston to raise a force for protection of the frontier following the Plum Creek incident.[51]

The Rangers drew Woll with approximately 1,500 men from San Antonio to Caldwell's position. Woll moved his army to the east side of the creek to face the Texians, set up cannon, and prepared for battle.

With only 200 men, the Texians planned their defensive.

Hoping to rout the Texians with artillery fire, Woll also prepared to charge. He dispatched his cavalry across the creek to cut off an escape route, posted Cherokee Indians in his troops on the creek, and ordered his cavalry above the creek to cut off any men in that area.

The bugle sounded, and soon the Mexican soldiers appeared, seemingly in the midst of the Texians. Protected by creek banks and pecan trees, the Texians poured volley upon volley into the Mexican ranks. Finally, the formation was broken and the Mexican soldiers fell into confusion and disorder. A cavalry company charged, but the horses recoiled at the fire, and the riderless mounts, in confusion, knocked down some of the infantry.[52]

The Texians began to yell, the Mexican cannon roared, and the Texians cheered louder.

When some of their mounts fell from fire, the Mexicans attempted to run but had trouble. Rowels on their spurs, several inches in diameter, dragged on the ground. The men had to run on their toes. A participant, Thomas Galbreath, said the ground where the battle took place looked "as if a garden rake had been used over the ground."

General Woll and his army retreated to Mexico.[53]

At one point in 1848, the Tarbox and Brown stage line began covering the route between Austin and San Antonio. D. P. Hopkins, writing "The Postroad" for the San Marcos *Free Press*—July 7, 1874—recalled riding over the line. After crossing Bolding's Creek on a bridge that his father had built, Hopkins observed the stage climb an embankment and pass on the west side of the John G. Swisher farm.

> Four miles farther on we crossed Williamson and found ourselves opposite the old home of Colonel George Neill, one of the grandest men of the earliest times in Texas. He was a veteran of the battle of San Jacinto.

"From Colonel Neill's residence," the road went south of the home of Q. J. Nichols. Nichols and McGee were contractors for the state capitol that later was destroyed by fire.[54]

In March 1866, the first cattle drives began, moving the herd from southern Texas northward. Ever the pioneer, George

Neill was the first to send a herd up the trail from Hays County, Texas. The herd left in May 1867 and was driven to Abilene, Kansas, where it was sold.[55]

The trail bosses figured that with the combined force of 100 hands, there would be less chance of an attack by a band of roving Comanches or Kiowas.

Boss Ed Chambers, in charge of one of the herds at Pond Creek, ordered his herd to stop while he and two hands rode ahead to determine which fork had been the heavier traveled. He was a participant in a cattle drive. The drovers had crossed the Texas line into Indian Territory, and ten herds making up the drive camped for the night along Pond Creek.

From one of the draws appeared ten Indians. Chambers, thinking the Indians were friendly Creeks or Caddoes on a buffalo hunt, galloped slowly. He called to the other riders that the Indians would not harm them. The Indians began firing, and at the first shot Chambers fell from his horse. Some of the Indians stopped to scalp him. The two drovers, seeing that they were too late to aid their companion, dug the spurs into their horses.

In pursuit the Indians had almost overtaken the two when one hit his target.

The two cowhands rode into camp. Soon word spread to the other herd bosses, and the George Perkins herd dispatched George Neill to the fight. When he reached the scene, the Indians were gone. The lone Indian who had been shot was not dead. His companions "had rolled him around on the ground and had probed his wound with coarse straws of prairie grass, the blood on the straws showing they had probed six inches." His companions had taken no money or his watch.[56]

With Neill on this drive was his brother-in-law, Houston Taylor Kennedy, a native of Jackson Parish, Louisiana, who had come to Texas in the late sixties to work for his uncle, George Perkins, in Hays County. Kennedy made five trail drives to Kansas—three with cattle and two with horses.

To George Jefferson Neill and Mary Highsmith Neill were

born nine children: Mary E., James C., Abjah Morris, Harriet, Harvey, Kate, Samuel, George, and Sarah (Sally).

Mary Highsmith Neill died on May 11, 1879, and was buried in York Creek Cemetery in Hays County. George Jefferson Neill died on January 28, 1891, and his body was laid to rest in Line Oak Cemetery, one and a half miles east of Manchaca in Travis County.

George Jefferson Neill had begun filing for a pension in January 1871.

Wayman F. Wells appeared before the pension officials in Comal County to say that he was acquainted with Neill and had "served with him in the battle of Concepcion and Grass fight."

John Ingram and Wayman F. Wells also testified in 1874 to being personally acquainted with George J. Neill and his family. He also stated to have known Neill since 1831 in Texas, and that he was a soldier of the War of Texas Independence. "He is now about sixty six years of age, that we believe him entitled to a pension."

Neill, a resident of near Stringtown in Comal County, appeared before Ed J. S. Green, clerk of Hays County, in January 1875, and was identified by J. M. Taylor and C. A. Groos. John M. Swisher signed an affidavit that he had known Neill since 1836, that he was "a man of truth and integrity," and that he was "satisfied that Neill was in the grass fight in 1835 and in the Texas Army during the war with Mexico."

On January 18, 1875, Neill named James P. McKinney of Austin his attorney to receive moneys, vouchers, or certificates due him from the state.

A son of George Jefferson Neill and Mary Highsmith Neill, James C. Neill was born in 1850, and was married to Itasca Perkins on December 25, 1876, in Hays County.

Kate Deborah Neill, the daughter of George Jefferson Neill and Mary Highsmith Neill, was born in Comal County on April 18, 1856. She and Houston Taylor Kennedy exchanged wedding vows at Seguin on January 4, 1875, with the Reverend Buck Harris performing the ceremony.

The young couple moved to Bandera County in June, 1875, and settled on the Anglin Prong of Sabinal River. Their first child, May, was born there. In 1878, the Kennedys bought a place near the Taylor School.⁵⁷

Kate Kennedy was described as weighing approximately 300 pounds. Frances Hicks recalled an incident involving Kate. Houston Taylor Kennedy had asthma and was unable to clean his well, so he lowered his wife into it. He was unable to retrieve her and had to run for help.⁵⁸

When Kate Kennedy died in 1908, she was survived by nine children: May, Edna, Sam, Lula, Dosa, Maud, Katie, Charlie, and Morris.⁵⁹

The will and inventory of goods belonging to Samuel Neill, the son of George Jefferson Neill, is in the Uvalde courthouse, filed on March 13, 1928. He provided that his debts and funeral expenses be paid; his niece Sallie Gooding, receive $500; his brother George receive $500; a niece, Mrs. Hattie Lou Buttler receive $300; and his brother Abysh Morris inherit $100. He directed his body be buried in Sabinal Cemetery and a suitable marker be erected over the grave. Sallie Gooding was named administrator.

In the May 1938 term of court, an inventory showed that Sam Neill had a $3,300 certificate of deposit at the Commercial Bank of Uvalde and notes of $400 in credits.

Claims against the estate were $1,391 from Sallie Gooding; $210 from G. J. Neill; $221 from Dr. S. B. Hudson; $21.90 from S. A. Hubbard; an attorney's fee of $51; $20.35 from Central Pharmacy; $28.75 from the Sabinal Mercantile Co.; $278 due L. F. Heard; $35 due Dr. B. M. Hines; and $150 to cover the cost of the monument.

23

SAMUEL C. NEILL

"To Samuel C. Neill . . ."
J. C. Neill's will

When George Jefferson Neill was seven years old, a brother, Samuel Clinton, joined the family in Bedford County, Tennessee.

Samuel Clinton Neill served with the Ranger force that had been organized to protect the frontier around Bastrop. The decree which had established the force called for a unit of 150 men to be commanded by a major, divided into three companies serving under a captain, a first lieutenant, and a second lieutenant. Each Ranger was to furnish his own food, clothing, horses, ammunition, and other supplies. "At all times they were to be armed and supplied with one hundred rounds of power and ball," and for their services would receive $1.25 per day.

The decree establishing the Ranger force was passed the day the regular army was created, and provisions for the Rangers were subject to the orders of the commander in chief of the army, so " the rangers were an anjunct to the army, created separately to afford the colonists protection against the Indians while the army was dealing with the Mexicans."

Unfortunately, the force did not reach full strength. There were few recruits available, and the men in service were dissatisfied that they were not allowed to elect their own officers.[1]

Early in March 1836, Capt. John J. Tumlinson[2] rode into

Bastrop and released his command to Capt. Robert McAlpin Williamson, and on March 20, Samuel Neill enlisted.[3]

The Rangers faced problems. General Houston continued to lead the Texians in a retreat. The Mexican Army was reported approaching Bastrop. Citizens, upset over the rumors of Texian retreat and of Mexican advances, attempted to escape to the Louisiana border, creating their own "runaway scrape." Noah Smithwick described the situation:

> People were poorly prepared for moving, and in order to give them all the time possible, it was decided to put a picket guard out on the San Antonio road, beyond Plum creek, to give notice of hostile approach. A squad of eight men were detailed for this duty, of which I was given command. Taking supplies for a two-days' sojourn, we started on our mission; but before we reached out station, a courier overtook us with an order to send all the men back but two.[4]

The captain read the dispatch to his men. "Well, boys, you hear the order. I've got to stay. Now who is going to stay with me?"

Overall, the men were reluctant to do so. Some complained that to remain would be to face certain murder. Sixteen-year-old Jim Edmondson[5] volunteered. "By gumie, Captain, I ain't afraid to stay with you anywhere."

"Very well, Jim," the leader said, "You can all go back, boys. Jim and I will keep watch."

After scouting the area several days and finding no sign of a foe, Smithwick and Edmondson returned to Cedar Creek. "The residents were all gone. There were chickens and eggs to make a preacher's mouth water, and we helped ourselves," Smithwick recalled. The following day the two rode into Bastrop, empty except for the twenty-two-man Ranger force. The men sank all the boats and started down the east side of the river when they encountered a courier with orders for the Rangers to remain in Bastrop and to move as many of the cattle to the east bank as possible.

Four of the men were detailed to Webber's place to retrieve a dugout. "It proved to be a new one, unfinished, and very heavy and clumsy, but we hitched onto it with our lariats and snaked it down to the river, where we launched it." Ganey "Choctaw" Crosby[6] and Smithwick manned it; the other two men handled the horses. The craft presented problems, and Crosby and Smithwick were dumped into the water, getting their guns wet. They managed to right the boat and with their hats bailed it out and maneuvered it to Marty Wells' place.[7] What happened next was described by Smithwick:

> The place was, of course, deserted. So we took possession and made ourselves comfortable. There was plenty of provender, and we made a roaring fire in the kitchen, cooked a sumptuous supper, dried our clothes and laid down to sleep.

Sleep was not in the cards, for a stick and mud chimney caught fire.[8]

Using a better canoe they had found, Crosby and Smithwick managed to reach Bastrop without additional mishap. A sense of security lulled the Rangers to post only one sentry at night. One morning they awoke to see 600 Mexicans on the opposite bank of the river. Smithwick recalled that the Rangers left in such haste they almost neglected to notify the sentry, Jimmy Curtis, of their departure.[9]

When Smithwick remembered the sentry, he reminded Major Williamson, "You ain't going to leave Uncle Jimmie on guard, are you, Major?"

"Good God! No. Ride back and tell the old man to come on."

Smithwick found Curtis leaning against a tree, a bottle of whiskey beside him. He was "as happy and unconscious of danger as a turtle on a log."

"Uncle Jimmie," Smithwick called. "Mount and ride for your life. The Mexicans are on the other side and our men all gone."

"The hell they are. Light and take a drink."

Smithwick protested. "There's no time for drinking. Come. Mount and let's be off. The Mexicans may swim the river and be after us any moment."

"Let's drink to their confusion," Curtis proposed.

Smithwick decided the quickest way to get Curtis moving was to humor him, so he accepted a drink.

As he mounted, Curtis remarked casually, "Well, we can say one thing. We were the last men to leave."

Two men in the Rangers, Andy Dunn[10] and Jimmy Leach,[11] lost their horses, and some of the younger men walked alternately, allowing them to ride. The ground was so boggy that the Rangers left the road. They grew hungry and tired.

They overtook two men, who dropped their bundles and ran. The Rangers looked through the bags and determined the men were runaway black men who would be so eager to keep out of the Mexican's sight they would give no information.

At this point, Captain Williamson, tired of waiting on the slow, decided to ride ahead. He called on "Choctaw Tom" Crosby and James Curtis to ride with him, placing Lt. George Petty in charge.

When the Ranger force reached Cole's settlement,[12] the men found a notice Major Williamson had attached to a tree. It reported the massacre of Fannin's men. Then the Rangers realized why the inhabitants were fleeing.

Smithwick describes the country through which the Rangers passed:

> Houses were standing open, the beds unmade, the breakfast things still on the tables, pans of milk moulding in the dairies. There were cribs full of corn, smoke houses full of bacon, yards full of chickens that ran after us for food, nests of eggs in every fence corner, young corn and garden truck rejoicing in the rain, cattle cropping the luxuriant grass, hogs, fat and lazy, wallowing in the mud, all abandoned. Forlorn dogs roamed around the deserted homes, their doleful howls adding to the general sense of desolation. Hungry cats ran mewing to meet us, rubbing their sides against our legs in token of welcome.

Wagons had been so scarce that the settlers abandoned their household goods to escape the approach of Mexican forces. Many women and children had to walk.[13]

John H. Jenkins, who was with Houston's army, ran into some of his neighbors when he reached Washington County. These friends had left their families at Washington and were on their way to Bastrop County to collect stock and prevent it from falling into the hands of the invading army. In the group were Samuel Neill, Andrew Neal,[14] Bob Pacer, and High Childress.[15]

They had word from Jenkins' mother that he should turn back and help them.[16]

The second wife of Samuel Neill could boast of a rich pioneer heritage, for her parents, Sarah and Francis Berry, and family had been the first Anglo-American settlers to locate on the site a mile east of the present town of Gonzales.[17] Here in August 1825, James Kerr had erected cabins and surveyed a community named for the first governor of Coahuila and Texas, Don Rafael Gonzales. In the Berry party from Missouri were John and Elizabeth Oliver, grown children of Mrs. Berry by a previous marriage.[18]

The colonists existed on bread made of Indian corn, honey, and game. From the prairies they loaded their tables with buffalo and deer. They considered coffee not a luxury but a necessity.

These early residents of Gonzales were the only American residents west of the Colorado. Guadalupe Victoria was sixty miles to the south; San Antonio de Bexar was seventy-eight miles away. So on the first day of July 1826, settlers were excited over the prospects of traveling to a Fourth of July celebration at Beason's on the Atascosita crossing of the Colorado. James Kerr was out of the colony on official business; Erastus Smith and Geron Hinds were hunting buffalo. Bazil Durbin, John and Betsey Oliver, and Jack, "a very sprightly Negro boy" belonging to Major Kerr, decided to ride horseback to the Colorado observance.

Looking forward to visiting with other settlers, the celebrants rode out Sunday, July 2, and camped that night at Thorn's Branch, fourteen miles east. At midnight, they were aroused from sleep by the firing of guns and the yelling of Indians. Durbin received a wound in the shoulder but crawled into a thicket for shelter. His companions also hid in the brush.

When the Indians left with the blankets, horses, and goods, the settlers began the walk back to the Kerr cabins. Here they found John Wightman in the passage between the pens of his log cabin. He had been scalped.

The settlers hurried to Berry's cabin, only to find the place deserted and a message scrawled in charcoal on the door, "Gone to Burnham's, on the Colorado." When the Durbin party had set out for the Colorado the previous day, Strickland, Musick, and Major Kerr's black slaves, Shade, Anise and several of their children, had gone to Berry's.

After reading the message on the door, the entire group set out for the Colorado, and a few days later met Deaf Smith and Hinds. Weak from his wounds, Durbin leaned on Betsey Oliver's arm. Because of the warm weather, there was danger of gangrene, so his wound was poulticed with mud and oak sap.

On the afternoon of July 6, the party trudged into Burnham's.[19]

Jenkins welcomed the change, having found that moving the families was hard, monotonous work. The small group rode to Bastrop, fearing the Mexicans would be stationed in the town. Instead, they found Captain Williamson and his small company of men, and they took on the duty of rounding up cattle.

On September 13, after fifty days in Captain Williamson's company of mounted riflemen, Samuel Clinton Neill received a discharge.

On June 13, 1841, Samuel Neill and Nancy B. Fitzgerald exchanged wedding vows in Washington County. In 1842 a daughter Maranda was born.

Nancy Fitzgerald Neill died circa 1845, possibly in childbirth.

In 1847 Samuel Neill took as his bride Lourahama Berry Neal, the widow of Anson G. Neal,[20] and to the couple were born four children, Jane, Jemima, James W., and Mary.

In 1846, before her marriage in 1847 to Samuel Clinton Neill and after the death of her first husband, Anson G. Neal, Lourahama received a deed from Sarah and Francis Berry[21] to 640 acres of land, part of the headright on Clear Fork of Plum

Creek, two miles southwest of Lockhart. In 1854 Lourahama and Samuel G. Neill sold 317 acres to Samuel L. McNeal from Hardeman County, Tennessee. The price was $1,000.

Later, Lourahama transferred to Amanda Bouldin 138 acres, listed on the deed as part two of Lourahama's homestead.

Samuel Clinton Neill died circa 1856.

24

MARY NEILL PRICE

"To my daughter Mary H. Neill, otherwise Mary H. Price . . ."
J. C. Neill's will

Mary Harriet Neill was born in Greene County, Alabama, circa 1820. She was married to Wilkes (Willis) A. Price, the son of Drury Price and Sarah Price. He was born in Tennessee between 1818 and 1820. The wedding took place sometime between 1841 and 1843, and to the union were born five children: Sarah J., Mary R., Andrew (Drew), Rebecca Harriet, and James K.

The Price family was living in Travis County in 1850 but moved to Limestone County, probably to land inherited from her father.

Mary's memories of her father were revived in the 1870s, when she was involved in a county court suit over land in Travis County. She initiated the suit in May 1874, appointing William E. Rogers[1] of Hill County "attorney in fact to procure my one half undivided interest in 1,800 acres in Travis County granted to William Cannon March 28, 1835, being the upper one-half of said part of league deeded by Cannon to my Father in 1845." She offered Rogers one half of her share of the land or money. T. M. Pentill and Joseph Wood witnessed the document, signed in Mexia two days after Mary named Rogers her attorney.[2]

In 1875 Mary declared that she was an equitable owner of the 1,800 acres, that she was the child of J. C. Neill, and that defendants, John C. Wilson[3] and Thomas E. Stanley,[4] did with force and arms enter upon her land, and oust and eject her from the same. She avowed that until the time of the case, the defendants had with force and arms kept her from her possession, had taken for themselves rent, profits, and use of the land, had cut timber, but had refused to pay her. She sought $300.

Stanley and Wilson said Mary's charges of trespassing were untrue. In March she filed a supplemental petition against Thomas E. Stanley and David M. and Don Wilson[5] of Travis County, saying they also claimed an interest in the land.

In June 1875, summons were sent for Booker F., Thomas E. Sr., Mary E., George F., and Elias S. Stanley, Thomas W. Wilson, John C. Wilson, and Rhoda Wilson to appear in court.

George Jefferson Neill, a citizen of Comal County but temporarily in Travis County, appeared before Z. T. Fulmore,[6] a notary public, as a material witness for the defendants.

Shelley[7] and Moore,[8] attorneys for the defendants, asked the following questions of him:

"Do you know the principals in this case? And for how long?"

Neill answered, "I know Mary H. Price. I know Stanley but not his wife's name. Know their children but not given names. I know Nolan. Have a limited acquaintance with Wilson but don't recollect his first name. I do not know Rhoda Wilson."

"Did you know William Cannon?"[9]

"Yes, he lived in Bastrop and died there about 22 or 23 years ago."

"Tell what you know about this transaction."

"Cannon owed my father a debt—about $1,100 and probably more which Cannon agreed to pay in land at four bits an acre. Cannon deeded land to me. Father owed Robert Redding[10] and Preston Conley[11] and I in consideration of the fact, that the deed was made to me, agreed to pay Conley and Redding what my father owed them, which I did. This was all out of the Cannon League (headright) located in Travis County, the number of acres being 2,200 acres. Transaction took place at Bastrop with myself, my father, Redding and Conley all present. The consideration of the deed to me by Cannon was his indebtedness to my father.

"My father owed me $600 and I was to assume the payment

of his debt to Redding and Conley. Father lived in Montgomery County[12] at this time. There was an understanding at the time Cannon conveyed the land to me between my father and me that I should pay the two debts and that the balance should go to myself in consideration for what he owed me. This was understood and appreciated by all present, and was carried out in full."

"Did you live on the land?"

"I did live on the land. I moved on the place on Dec. 28, 1846, and stayed there four years. My father was living at the time I moved on it and he died about March 28, 1849, as well as I can recollect.[13] At the time of his death I was in Mexico and for some time thereafter."

"What happened to the land?"

"I sold to Conley and Redding a portion of this land during my father's lifetime—sometime in 1847. I can't remember exact consideration I received from them as I transferred the land in consideration of them deliverying to me my Father's notes to them. I know it took 925 acres at 50 cents an acre to pay these debts." [14]

"Where was Mrs. Price living at this time?"

Neill answered, "I do not know certainly where Mrs. Price lived at the time of my father's death. I think it was Tehuacana Hills, county unknown.[15] She did not continue to live at this place, but in the Fall of 1850 they moved neighbors to me. I sold her husband, Mr. Willis A. Price, 100 acres of the land conveyed to me by Cannon. She came onto this land in 1850 and lived there about a year. She does not live on this land now. Her husband sold it to a man named Arrington in 1851."

"Have you lived on the land?"

"I lived on it, claiming it as my own property."

"Can you identify Mrs. Price? Are there other descendants?"

"She is my sister. There are descendants of my deceased brother now living. There are four—named Miranda, Sarah, Harriet, and Mary. I don't know their ages. There were none other living at the time of the transaction."

"When did Mary Price marry?"

"I don't know exactly when Mary married but think 1842. Her husband has been dead about five years."

"Who was living at the time of the transaction?"

"My father was living at the time of the transaction, and I think Cannon was alive. Redding's claim was by note and account. Conley's was a note."

"Who else has lived on the land?"

"No one else lived on the land except Redding and Conley who claimed deed from me. There were two others to whom I sold tracts out of the part I owned, Gregg and Shuttles, who were in possession when I sold to them. I think in 1848."

"Did your father continue to claim the land?"

"My father never claimed any portion of the land after it was conveyed to me."

Attorneys for Mary then questioned George Neill.

"Who drew up the deed from Cannon to you?"

"I don't remember."

"Did your father know which portions were conveyed to you?"

"Land was surveyed during father's lifetime. I knew what portions were conveyed to me, and I suppose my father did but couldn't swear particularly that he did."

George then said that his father owed D. T. Portis of Houston $500 and Portis was pushing him for payment. "I held note on Portis for $600. I loaned father this note to offset Portis' note and he took it and did so—that being the grounds of his debt to me. He became indebted to me about 1843."

"Are you interested in any way in favor of the defendants?"

"I am not. Only I gave a warranty deed to Redding and Conley."

"Did Mrs. Price ever authorize you to sell any of the land for her?"

Neill shook his head. "She did not."

"Are you and Mrs. Price the only survivors of your father?"

"There are only two of my father's children living—myself and Mrs. Price, whom I last saw in 1851, who is now living. She and I are the only children of my father who have been living within the past seven years, within the past fifteen years. My brother, Samuel C. Neill, was killed about 16 years ago—and left four children—and I think they are all living."

Interrogation revealed how distant were the members of James C. Neill's family. George was uncertain about the date of his father's death. Perhaps understandable. He likewise was vague about the demise of his brother Samuel. But the family characteristic of aloofness—of separation from kin—is evident in his relationship with his sister. No wonder the maiden name and death date and place for Margaret Harriet Neill are veiled in time. No wonder the details of Colonel Neill's early years are obscure.

On April 8, 1875, James E. Rector[16] and A.M. Jackson[17] posted $100 bond for Mary, and when the case was dismissed in 1876, adjudged against the plaintiff, $66.55 in court costs were withheld.

25

MIRANDA NEILL

"To my grandaughter Miranda Neill . . ."
J. C. Neill's will

Amanda Neill, daughter of Samuel Clinton Neill and Nancy B. Fitzgerald Neill, was born in 1842. Her mother died when the child was three years of age.

A cousin, Mary E. Neill, daughter of George, was born on March 1, 1848, in Travis County. Another cousin, Sarah J., Mary's daughter, was born in 1843, but Amanda was the only grandchild James Clinton Neill had a chance to know. She, naturally, was the only one included by name in his will, written March 28, 1848, and providing her with 640 acres of land "together with sixty dollars in money to be disposed of for her education."

Amanda, called Miranda, was living in the home of Benjamin Teel in Caldwell County in 1850, and it was here she probably became acquainted with Bennet Tomerlin.

She was married to Tomerlin, who often is listed as Burnett Tomerlin. He was in Co. K. 36th Texas Cavalry, during the days of the Confederacy.[1] His service record shows that the resident of Caldwell County enlisted on February 3, 1862. Between February 1864 and March 1865, Private Tomerlin was on detached duty in pursuit of deserters but was due to report April 1.[2]

Miranda and Bennett Tomerlin are buried in the Tomerlin

Cemetery between More and Devine. A great-great-grandson, Monte Tomerlin, says, "The tombstone which I am told belongs to Miranda Neill Tomerlin has the simple inscription Grandma Tomerlin, and a date difficult to read."[3]

Notes

Chapter 1

1. "The Name and Family of Neal(e) or Neil(l)," a pamphlet issued in typewritten form by Media Research Bureau, Washington, D.C., undated.
2. Mary McKernan, "The Big Deal for Everyone O'Neill," *The Los Angeles Times,* March 14, 1982.
3. "O'Neill, The Origins of a Dynasty," *Family Links,* Vol. 1, No. 2, May, 1982, p. 22.
4. William Jolliffee, *Historical Genealogical and Biographical Account of the Jolliffe Family of Virginia* (Philadelphia: J. B. Lippincot Co., 1893), p. 175. See also *The Lookout,* Oct. 31, 1925, otherwise unidentified, a clipping in the possession of the author.
5. Harold Rose, *Your Guide to Ireland* (New York: Funk & Wagnalls, 1965), pp. 200-201.
6. "O'Neill, The Origins of a Dynasty," *Family Links,* Vol. 1, No. 3, September, 1981, p. 19.
7. Seumas McManus, *The Story of the Irish Race* (New York: The Devin-Adair Company, 1944), p. 77.
8. Ibid., pp. 77-78.
9. Ibid., p. 79.
10. Sir Iain of that Ilk Moncrieffe, "The High Kings in Ireland," *Family Links,* Vol. 1, No. 2, May 1981, p. 20.
11. Seumas McManus, *The Story of the Irish Race,* p. 81.
12. Seumas Moncrief, Sir Iain of that Ilk "The High Kings in Ireland," p. 14.
13. "O'Neill, The Origins of a Dynasty," p. 26.
14. Seumas McManus, *The Story of the Irish Race,* pp. 363-364.
15. Ibid., p. 369.
16. Ibid., p. 370.
17. "The O'Neills of Ulster," *Ireland,* Vol. 16, No. 1, May-June, 1967, p. 18.
18. William Jolliffee, *Historical Account of the Jolliffee Family,* p. 175.
19. Seumas MacManus, *The Story of the Irish Race,* p. 389.
20. Ibid.
21. James Plunkett, *The Gems She Wore* (New York: Holt, Rhinehart and Winston, 1973), p. 144.
22. Aodh de Blacam, *The Black North* (Dublin: M. H. Gill & Son, 1939), pp. 22-23.

23. James Plunkett, *The Gems She Wore*, pp. 145-148.
24. *The Pilgrim's Guide to Rome* (New York: Harper & Row, Publishers, 1975), p. 122.
25. Seumas MacManus, *The Story of the Irish Race*, p. 419.
26. Kathleen Neill, "An Informal Account of the Gathering," *Family Links*, Vol. 1, No. 6, September, 1982, p. 20.
27. "O'Neill, The Origins of a Dynasty," *Family Links*, Vol. 1, No. 5, May, 1982, p. 9.
28. Reference Public Record Office, Microfilm 16/2-5, based on information supplied Peggy Neill by Miss Ivy Embleton, Ireland, January 3, 1973.
29. William Jolliffe, *Historical Account of the Jolliffe Family of Virginia* (Philadelphia: J. B. Lippincott Co., 1893), p. 176.
30. Ibid., p. 178.
31. Ibid., pp. 178-179.
32. Ibid., p. 178.
33. Lyman C. Draper, *King's Mountain and Its Heroes*, (Cincinnati: P. G. Thompson), 1811, p. 22.
34. Ibid., p. 557.
35. Catherine C. Letter, Constable to Peggy Neill, March 9, 1971. Deed Book BB, County of Bedford, Tenn, p. 143.
36. Pension application for Andrew Neill, March 2, 1840.
37. Ibid.
38. Peggy Neill, letter to C. R. K., 27 Feb. 1984.
39. *DAR American Monthly Magazine*, January-June, 1912, Vol. 40.
40. Will probated in Nottingham, New Jersey, July 1, 1696. The appraisal was filed July 13, 1896.
41. Book C, p. 95, Wills of Rowan County, 1786.
42. Ibid.
43. Steel yard or scale.
44. Iredell County Wills, Book A, p. 80, October 30, 1800.

Chapter 2
1. Manuscript by Doris Ketchum Bryant, *Ancestors & Descendants of James Rowland Neill and Eliza Matilda McLain*, Unpublished, 1984, pp. 207. Additional information on the Neill family is included in Howard C. Clinton, *The Clinton Lineage and Related Families*, (Orlando, Fla.: Howard C. Clinton, 1974), and in Laura Dingle Ewing, *Our Ewing Family*, (Wimberley, Texas: Spindletop Museum, Lamar University, 1978). These works offer conflicting lists of siblings of William Neill and Mary (Polly) Clinton Neill. Also see a manuscript, *The Neills* by C. Richard King, unpublished, 1977.
2. *The Goodspeed Histories of Maury, Williamson, Rutherford, Wilson, Bedford & Marshall Counties of Tennessee*, (Columbia: Woodward & Stinson Printing Co., 1971), p. 862.
3. Ibid., p. 886.
4. Ibid., p. 887.
5. Andrew, who married Mary Moffet McDowell, the widow of Joseph

McDowell, moved here from Marengo County, Alabama. Alexander who married Ann Cathey, died in 1848. Jane, a sister, married John Orr. She died in 1828. James died sometime between November 13, 1835 and 1839. Hannah Clayton was still alive in 1855, when a letter by Mrs. Miton Hall Dysart addressed to Mrs. Bryan Nowlin III inquired of the condition of her grandmother Hannah. All were buried in a plot near a big spring behind the house on Dr. Bryan Nowlin property. The place later became known as the Musgrove place. Manuscript of Doris Ketchum Bryant, p. 5.

6. In 1832 James Neill wrote that he had known John Dysart "before the Revolutionary War and was with him in the Indian War" and also "in a skirmish on Maine Creek" prior to the Battle of King's Mountain.

7. *The Goodspeed Histories of Maury, Williamson, Rutherford, Wilson, Bedford & Marshall Counties of Tennessee*, p. 887.

8. In a book from the library of James Rowland Neill, a nephew of James Clinton Neill's, David Jasper Neill wrote, "Taken from my uncle's library in Neill's Gap, Tenn., 1909." The volume is in the author's possession.

9. *The Goodspeed Histories of Maury, Williamson, Rutherford, Wilson, Bedford & Marshall Counties of Tennessee*, p. 898.

Chapter 3
1. H. S. Halbert and T. H. Ball, *The Creek War of 1813 and 1814* (University: University of Alabama Press, 1969), pp. 148, 151.

2. Ibid., pp. 148-149.

3. Ibid., p. 151.

4. William Garrott Brown, *A History of Alabama* (New Orleans: University Publishing Company), 1900, p. 108.

5. Ibid., p. 108.

6. Halbert and Ball, *The Creek War of 1813 and 1814*, p. 152.

7. Ibid., p. 168.

8. William Garrott Brown, *A History of Alabama*, pp. 108-109.

9. Ibid., p. 109.

10. Stanley J. Folmsbee, Robert E. Corlew and Enoch Mitchell, *Tennessee, A Short History* (Knoxville: The University of Tennessee Press, 1969), p. 136.

11. Ibid., p. 138.

12. War of 1812 Service Records for James Clinton Neill.

13. Ibid.

14. Ibid.

15. Ibid. In a list titled "Muster Roll of a Company of Artillerists under Command of Capt. Joel Parrish in the Service of the United States Commanded by Major Gen. Andrew Jackson from the 1st of March, 1814, when Mustered Into Service to 16 May 1814, When Discharged," is No. 26, James Neil, private. He was appointed on April 6, 1814, and discharged May 16, 1814. There were no remarks by his name, such as sick or wounded, as there were by some names.

16. William Garrott Brown, *A History of Alabama*, p. 109.

17. Various stories continue on the origin of the name Red Sticks. One

version is that the chiefs assembled their warriors by sending them red sticks. Albert Burton Moore, *History of Alabama and Her People* (Chicago: The American Historical Society, Inc., 1927) p. 48. Albert James Pickett, *History of Alabama* (Tuscaloosa: Wells Publishing Co., 1962), p. 580, says that the war clubs the Creeks carried into combat were painted red.

18. Albert James Pickett, *History of Alabama*, p. 588.
19. William Garrott Brown, *A History of Alabama*, p. 118.
20. Lucille Griffith, *History of Alabama, 1540-1900*. (Northport, Alabama: Colonial Press, 1962), p. 76.
21. Albert James Pickett, *History of Alabama*, pp. 580-590.
22. Lucille Griffith, *History of Alabama*, 1540-1900, p. 70.
23. Albert James Pickett, *History of Alabama*, p. 588.
24. William Garrott Brown, *History of Alabama*, p. 120.
25. Marquis James, *The Life of Andrew Jackson* (Indianapolis: The Bobbs-Merrill Company, 1938), pp. 170-171.
26. M. K. Wisehart, *Sam Houston, American Giant*. (Washington: Robert B. Luce, Inc., 1963), pp. 17-18.
27. John Holmes Jenkins, editor, *Recollections of Early Texas* (Austin: University of Texas Press, 1958), p. 155.
28. War of 1812 Service Records for James Clinton Neill.
29. Ibid.
30. Ibid.
31. Emma Inman Willias, *Historical Madison* (Jackson: Madison County Historical Society, 1946), p. 333.
32. Samuel Cole Williams, *Beginnings of West Tennessee*. (Johnson City: The Watauga Press, 1930), p. 136.

Chapter 4
1. Thomas McAdory Owen, *History of Alabama and Dictionary of Alabama Biography* (Chicago: The S. J. Clarke Publishing Company, 1921.) Vol. 1, p. 667.
2. Nathaniel Greene (1742-1786), called "the man who saved the South," was ranked by many as a great military leader, second only to George Washington. Born of a Quaker family in Rhode Island, he served in his state's legislature and was commander of the Rhode Island militia. He became a brigadier general in 1775, and Washington promoted him to major general the following year. In 1780 he was sent to replace Gen. Horatio Gates, whose army had been defeated so frequently that is was known as "only the shadow of an army." Greene first defeated the British general Sir Banastre Tarleton at Cowpens. He drove the British deeper into the South and in nine months had freed Virginia and Carolina from British control, except three bases on the coast. *The World Book Encyclopedia* (Chicago: Field Enterprises, Inc., 1952. Vol. 7), p. 3173.
3. Tombickbee, now spelled Tombigbee, comes from a Choctaw word meaning box-maker or coffin-maker. Mary Morgan Glass, editor, *A Goodly Heritage, Memories of Greene County*. Greene County Historical Society, 1977, p. 112.

4. Thomas McAdory Owen, *History of Alabama and Dictionary of Alabama Biography*, Vol. 1, p. 667.

5. Israel Pickens, the son of Captain Samuel and Jane Carrigan Pickens, was born Jan. 30, 1780, in Mecklenburg County, N. C. He was educated in private schools and was graduated from the law department of Washington College, Pensylvania. He was in the North Carolina senate 1808-1810 and in Congress 1811-1817. He moved to Alabama in 1817, just before the state was admitted into the union, and represented Washington County in the constitutional convention that formed the state of Alabama in 1819. Three years later he was elected the state's third governor, and to him fell the job of completing the organization of the state. (Thomas McAdory Owen, *History of Alabama and Dictionary of Alabama Biography*, Vol. IV, p. 1360) F. S. Lyon of Marengo, an observer of events at the time, called Pickens "the most useful executive the State has ever had." (Willis Brewer, *Alabama, Her History, Resources, War Record and Public Men*, p. 272.)

Pickens in 1826 accepted an appointment by President John Quincy Adams to the U.S. Senate to fill an unexpired term.

In 1827 he went to Cuba in search of health but died April 24, 1827. He was buried in Matanzas; the Alabama legislature later provided for having the body removed for interment in the burying ground near the Pickens homestead, Greensboro. (Thomas McAdory Owen, *History of Alabama and Dictionary of Alabama Biography*, Vol. IV, p. 1360.)

Willis Brewer said of him, ". . . he possessed the solid, ingenious, and practical talents of which all new states stand in need; the experience to shape her domestic policy; and the wisdom and virtue which the founders of all governments should leave as a legacy to posterity." Willis Brewer, *Alabama, Her History, Resources, War Record, and Public Men*, p. 272.

6. Willis Brewer, *Alabama, Her History, Resources* (Spartanburg, S.C.: The Reprint Company, Publishers, 1975), p. 47. In 1821 Pickens received 9114 votes to 7129 for Dr. Chambers; in 1823 he polled 6942 to 4604 for Chambers. Ibid., p. 272.

7. Ibid., pp. 47-48.

8. When the returns were final, Jackson had 99 electoral votes, John Quincy Adams had 84, and William H. Crawford of Georgia was a poor third. No candidate pulled a majority, so the election went to the House of Representatives, where voting was by states. Adams won 13 states, Jackson, 7, and Crawford, 4. *The World Book Encyclopedia* (Chicago: Field Enterprises, Inc., 1951), Vol. 9, pp. 3953-3954.

9. Marquis de Lafayette (1757-1834) fought in the French and American Revolutions. He was born at Chavaniac, in Haute Loire, Sept. 6, and upon the death of his father thirteen years later inherited a great fortune. He came to America in 1777 on a ship that he had provided with a party of soldier-adventurers. He offered his services in the struggle for American independence; Congress made him a major general without pay or command, and Washington asked him to become a member of his staff. Upon Washington's recommendation, Lafayette received command of a division. In 1778 he was placed in charge of a planned invasion of Canada.

10. Greene County Wedding Book A, p. 69.
11. Ibid., p. 47.
12. Ibid., p. 48.
13. Ibid.
14. Ibid., p. 50.
15. Ibid., p. 83.
16. Ibid., p. 83. She was the daughter of James and Elizabeth Knox. Pauline Jones Gandrud, compiler, *Marriage Records of Greene County, Alabama, 1823-1860* (Memphis: The Milestone Press, 1969), p. 119.
17. Could have been Richard Warren, who came from Burke County, Georgia, about 1817, and built a fort near Burnt Corn. After living here one year, he moved across Murder Creek. Thomas McAdory Owen, *History of Alabama and Dictionary of Alabama Biography*, Vol. IV, p. 1727.
18. William Garret, *Reminiscences of Public Men in Alabama*. (Spartanburg, S.C.: The Reprint Company, Publishers, 1975), p. 751, contains a different list of representatives; it names J.H. Sims, J.C. Neill, and R.H. Nancy. *The Journal of the House of Representatives of the State of Alabama*, Seventh Annual Session, Cahawba: William D. Allen, State Priner, 1826, includes the name Warren in accounting for votes, but does not include a Nance.
19. *Journal of the House of Representatives of the State of Alabama*, Seventh Annual Session, p. 66.
20. Ibid., p. 67.
21. Neill was appointed to a standing committee on the military Nov. 23, 1825, serving with Edridge Greening of Conecuh, John M. Dupuy of Jefferson, Joseph Coe of Lawrence, Nicholas Davis of Limestone, King, and Lambert. *Journals of the House of Representatives of the State of Alabama*, Seventh Annual Session, p. 69.
22. James Dellett, the son of Irish parents, was born in Philadelphia, Pa., in 1788, and died at Claiborne Dec. 21, 1848. He grew up in South Carolina and was graduated with first honors from South Carolina College in 1810. He was admitted to the bar in 1813. In 1819 he moved to Alabama, settling at Claiborne. Soon after his arrival, he became judge of the circuit court and was elected to represent the county in the first general assembly of the state. After the assembly gathered at Huntsville in 1819, he was elected speaker of the House of Representatives. During the following 12 years he was four times elected to the assembly and in 1821 again was named speaker.

In 1833 Dellett was a candidate for Congress but lost to John Murphy. Four years later, Dellett defeated Murphy for election to the twenty-sixth Congress. He defeated Judge Henry Goldthwaite to win re-election in 1843.

Recognized as a debater, Dellett once, in April, 1843, delivered to the House of Representatives a speech which filled 30 pages when printed in pamphlet form.

When Dellett retired from Congress, he began managing his large holdings near Clairborne. Thomas McAdory Owen, *History of Alabama and Dictionary of Alabama Biography*, Vol. III, p. 478.

23. *Journal of the House of Representatives of the State of Alabama*, Seventh Annual Session, p. 69.

24. William B. Martin was the son of Warner and Martha Bailey Martin. His uncle was Henry Bailey, attorney general of South Carolina 1836-1845. Martin was descended of Louis Montaiagne, who fled France in 1824, and after settling in South Carolina changed his name to Martin. Thomas McAdory Owen, *History of Alabama and Dictionary of Alabama Biography*, Vol. IV, p. 1166.

25. *Journal of the House of Representatives of the State of Alabama*, Seventh Annual Session, p. 70.

26. Nicholas Davis, son of John Dabney and Ann Tinsley Davis, was born Sept. 19, 1781, in Virginia. He was descended from John of Gaunt, fourth son of Edward, King of England; of John Shelton, mayor of Dublin, Ireland; and of Sir John Davis of Glamorganshire, Wales. Davis was a U.S. Marshal in Virginia, lived in Kentucky briefly, and prior to 1817 moved to Alabama. He was a member of the first constitutional convention in 1819 and served in the state's first legislature. He served in the state senate 1820-1828, and five times headed that body. He ran for Congress in 1829 but C.C. Clay defeated him by a narrow margin of 80 votes. Thomas McAdory Owen, *History of Alabama and Dictionary of Alabama Biography*, Vol. III, pp. 464-465.

27. Willis Brewer, *Alabama, Her History, Resources*, p. 321.

28. Thomas McAdory Owen, *History of Alabama and Dictionary of Alabama Biography*, Vol. III, p. 467.

29. *Journal of the House of Representatives of the State of Alabama*, Seventh Annual Session, p. 70.

30. Ibid., p. 22.

31. Ibid., p. 100.

32. Ibid., p. 122.

33. *Journal of the House of Representatives of the State of Alabama*, Eighth Annual Session (Tuskaloosa: Granting & Robinson, state printers, 1827), p. 5.

34. Albert Burton Moore, *A History of Alabama and Her People* (Chicago: The American Historical Society, Inc., 1927), Vol. I, p. 142. Neill was elected colonel of the 19th regiment, Alabama militia, on Nov. 20, 1820, and on Dec. 8, 1821 was re-elected colonel. He continued to serve until June 28, 1824, when he resigned.

Col. Neill's sword is on display in the Witte Museum, San Antonio. Dr. Bill Green, assistant curator, phoned Mrs. Charles O. Miller, San Antonio, that "a lady and some children were playing in a vacant lot or field about the year 1900-1910 in Austin, when they saw something sticking up in the ground. They unearthed it, and it was this old rusty sword that had been buried for a long, long time. The handle had rotted away. She kept it for a long time but gave it to a Howard L. Pawelke who presented it to the Witte Museum in 1957." The weapon is believed to be of the type used at least 20 years before the days of the Alamo.

A card in the museum identifies the sword as "saber and scabbard of Col. J.C. Neill. Gift of Howard L. Pawelka." Letter, Mrs. Charles O. Miller, San Antonio, to author, May 10, 1982.

35. Muscle Shoals was a series of rapids on the Tennessee River where the river dropped 132 feet over a 36-mile stretch. The Shoals became the site of a federal water-power project controlled by the Tennessee Valley Authority and created in 1933. Two dams, Wheeler and Wilson, were created to raise the water level at the rapids, forming lakes. Under the National Defense Act of 1916, the federal government completed two nitrate plants at Muscle Shoals. *The World Book Encyclopedia.* (Chicago: Field Enterprises, Inc., 1952), Vol. II, p. 5342.

The TVA followed 15 years of Congressional debate on what to do with the nitrate plant and Wilson Dam. An act transferred Wilson Dam and the plant to the TVA from the War Department.

The governor of Alabama proved correct in his message to the Assembly. The amount of freight carried on the Tennessee River increased rapidly with the improvement of the river channel, "which provides a 630-mile navigation route." Vol. 16, pp. 7967-7968.

36. *Journal of the House of Representatives of the State of Alabama,* Eighth Annual Session, p. 8.

37. *Greene County Deed Book D,* pp. 291-292.

38. *Greene County Wills, Book B,* p. 54.

39. Green County *Gazette,* May 3, 1830.

40. Ibid., May 24, 1830.

41. Lafayette Lodge No. 26, A.F.&A.M., was located in Greensboro, once in Greene but now Hale County. Correspondence from the Grand Lodge of Alabama, A.F.&A.M., to author, undated.

42. The chief festival of the Operative or Stonemasons during the Middle Ages was the Feast of St. John the Baptist on June 24. The occasion continues to be observed by Speculative Masons and by the A F.&A.M. fraternity. Albert Gallatin MacKey, *An Encyclopedia of Freemasonry and Its Kindred Sciences* (Chicago: The Masonic History Company, 1926), p. 264.

43. Greene County *Gazette,* June 21, 1830.

44. Ibid., July 12, 1830.

45. Ibid., July 26, 1830.

46. Ibid., August 9, 1830.

47. Ibid., August 23, 1830.

48. Neill could have read the brief story in the Greene County *Gazette,* Oct. 25, 1830.

49. Moses Lewis was "a smart New England Yankee who loved a dollar." He was among the "moving forces" in building Springfield; he opened a store in 1830 and developed a large volume of business with the Choctaw Indians. From his association with the Indians, he was able to purchase the bluffs and lands where Gainesville later was built. He settled his family there in 1836. Mary Morgan Glass, editor, *A Goodly Heritage, Memories of Greene County,* p. 21.

50. *Greene County Deed Book D,* pages 291-292, No. 6887.

51. Greene County *Gazette,* July 5, 1830.

52. Ibid., June 21, 1830.

Chapter 5

1. Eugene C. Barker, *The Life of Stephen F. Austin* (Austin: The Texas State Historical Association, 1949), p. 220.

2. Juan Davis Bradburn, who had entered Mexican service with Francisco Xavier Mina in 1817, secured a contract from the state of Coahuila to navigate the Rio Grande for 15 years. Early in 1840 he had joined Manuel de Mier y Teran at Matamoros and was sent to New Orleans to investigate conditions of the Texas colonists. In November, 1830, he was ordered to take charge of the garrison at Anahuac. *The Handbook of Texas,* Vol. I, p. 203.

3. Margaret Swett Henson, *Samuel May Williams* (College Station: Texas A&M University Press, 1976), p. 33.

4. Juan Francisco Madero was appointed general land commissioner of Texas on September 27, 1830. He reached Texas in January 1831, and announced plans to issue titles in the Trinity River area. *The Handbook of Texas,* Vol. II, p. 127.

5. Margaret Swett Henson, *Samuel May Williams,* p. 10.

6. Ibid., p. 13.

7. John G. Holtham was the central figure in one of the Republic's legal matters. Plans for a fiesta to celebrate the 20th anniversary of the beginning of Mexican independence were being formed in San Felipe but were interrupted by three murders and a jail break. One of the crimes was the murder of Holtham and involved alderman Hosea H. League and Seth Ingram, surveyor. Margaret Swett Henson, *Samuel May Williams,* p. 28.

Following a quarrel over Holtham's "drunken intrusion on his property," Ingram ordered Holtham "to remove objectionable notices." Holtham refused to do so, and Ingram killed him. *The Handbook of Texas,* Vol. I, p. 885.

Hosea H. League was implicated Sept. 2, 1830, as an accessory. League and Ingram were arrested and held for trial, but after 16 months in chains, were released on bond. Again arrested, they were not released until the summer of 1833. During his long legal affairs, League decided to sell enough property to settle claims against him. His business ruined, his health broken, and his savings destroyed, he turned over the work of the Nashville Company to Sterling C. Robertson. *The Handbook of Texas,* Vol. II, p. 41.

8. Sue Watkins, editor, *One League to Each Wine* (Austin: Texas Surveyors Association, 1965), pp. 8-9.

9. James C. Neill files, General Land Office, petition to House and Senate Feb. 6, 1885.

10. Born in Hungary in 1795, George Fisher had studied for the priesthood but ran away from school to enlist in the Serbian Revolution in 1813. When his legion was disbanded, Fisher sailed for America. Unable to redeem his contract, Fisher escaped by passing himself as a fisher. He settled in Mississippi before moving to Texas. He took out Mexican naturalization papers in 1829 and contracted to sign 500 families on lands formerly held by Haden Edwards. He was appointed collector of customs at Galveston in 1829 but did not receive his credentials. *The Handbook of Texas,* Vol. I, pp. 600-601.

11. Margaret Swett Henson, *Samuel May Williams,* p. 35.

12. James C. Neill file, General Land Office, petition to House and Senate, Feb. 6, 1885.

13. Mrs. V. W. Hammer Jr., "Gone to Texas," *Valley Leaves*, March, 1980, p. 104.

Chapter 6

1. Walter Prescott Webb, editor, *The Handbook of Texas* (Austin: The Texas State Historical Association, 1952), Vol. II, p. 491.

2. See C. Richard King, *The Lady Cannoneer* (Burnet, Texas: Eakin Press, 1981).

3. William Harris Wharton was born in Virginia in 1802. His parents died when the child was young, and he was reared by an uncle in Nashville, Tennessee. He was a graduate of the first class of the University of Nashville and was admitted to the bar. As a young lawyer, he moved to Texas and was married to Sarah Ann Groce, daughter of a wealthy plantation owner. Wharton was killed in 1839 when he accidentally discharged a pistol as he was dismounting at the home of a brother-in-law, Leonard W. Groce. During this convention of 1832, Wharton was author of the resolution seeking separate statehood. *The Hankbook of Texas*, Vol. II, p. 890.

4. Rafael Manchola, who made his home in Goliad, was an agent for Martin de Leon. He had been representative to the Second Constitutional Congress of Coahuila and Texas in 1829 and the following year was the Texas deputy to the Congress of Coahuila and Texas. *The Handbook of Texas*, Vol. II, p. 135.

5. Viesca was one of the Mexican governmental subdivisions created in November, 1830, with boundaries beginning at the crossing of the Coushatta Trace on the east bank of the Brazos. The line then went in a direct route to the Atascosito Road at a point four leagues from the Brazos, thence along the road "to divide between the San Jacinto and Trintiy rivers, northward to the Old San Antonio Road along the San Antonio Road to the Brazos." Following the meanders of the river, the line returned to the place of origin. *The Handbook of Texas*, Vol. II, p. 842.

In *History of Milam County, Texas*, Lelia M. Batte explains that during the First Congress the area was called the Municipality of Milam. Prior to that time it was the Municipality of Viesca. "The exact size of the original Municipality of Viersca and Milam . . . has been long a difficult problem, because the early acts by which they were created did not define the boundaries in detail." In 1941, the Historical Records Survey published a map that shows "that the original boundary of the Municipality extended as far north as the northern part of Callihan County, the northwest corner of Eastland County, the southern part of Palo Pinto County, and the southwestern corner of Parker County. As the county boundaries were defined in time, the northern boundary was extended somewhat further north. Out of Milam County, in addition to the present limits of Milam, were entirely created fifteen counties—Bell, Bosque, Burleson, Coryell, Erath, Falls, Hamilton, Hood, Jones, McLennan, Robertson, Shackelford, Somervell, Stephens, and Williamson, and there were partially created eighteen counties—Brazos, Brown, Burnet, Callahan, Comanche, Eastland, Haskell, Hill, Johnson, Lampasas, Lee, Limestone, Mills, Palo Pinto, Parker, Stonewall, Throckmorton, and Young." (San Antonio: The Naylor Company, 1956) pp. 33-34.

6. Leonard Waller Groce, the eldest son of Jared E. Groce, was born in Lincoln County, Georgia, on Sept. 27, 1806. In 1838 he was paying taxes on 67,000 acres of land. *The Handbook of Texas*, Vol. I, p. 739.

7. James D. Carter, *Masonry in Texas* (Waco: Grand Lodge of Texas, A.F. and A.M., 1955), p. 253.

8. A *Sitio de ganado minor*, a ranch for small stock, was an area of 11,111,111 square *varas*. A *Sitio de ganado major*, a ranch for cattle, was a square league. The *vara* is now defined as 33-1/3 inches. *Legua*, or league, was the equivalent of 5,000 *varas* or 2 ⁵/₈ statute miles. Edwin P. Arneson, "The Early Art of Terrestrial Measurement and Its Practice in Texas," from Sue Watkins, editor, *One League to Each Wind*, (Austin: Von-Boeckmann-Jones Printers, 1965), pp. 8-9.

9. *The Handbook of Texas*, Vol. I, p. 739.

10. James M. Day, compiler, *The Texas Almanac, 1857-1873* (Waco: Texian Press, 1967), p. 23, contains this statement: "Burnet drew up and submitted the memorial on the subject of state, which was unanimously adopted. He also prepared and submitted a series of resolutions denunciatory of the African slave trade, which was then actively prosecuted by some wealthy citizens." These resolutions "produced some excitement without the halls of the Convention."

11. Eugene C. Barker, "The African Slave Trade in Texas," *The Southwestern Historical Quarterly*, Vol. VI, No. 2 (October 1902), p. 151.

12. Jonathan Peyton, James Whitesides, Joseph White, and others subscribed to a fund to dig a public well in 1830. Perhaps the earliest editorial appearing in a Texas newspaper was the one in the *Texas Gazette*, August 14, 1830, chastizing the youths who had defiled the well. C. Richard King, *The Lady Cannoneer*, (Burnet, Texas: Eakin Press, 1981), p. 58.

13. John Henry Brown, *History of Texas* (St. Louis: L. E. Daniell, publisher, 1893), Vol. I, p. 228.

14. The proceedings of this convention were never published, and there is some confusion over who served on Houston's committee. John Henry Brown attempted to assemble a list of delegates, using some notes from James Kerr, "an alleged delegate." Kerr, however, is not named at the end of the proposed Constitution of 1833. Malcolm D. McLean, *Papers Concerning Robertson's Colony of Texas* (Arlington: The UTA Press, 1980, Vol. VII), p. 435-436.

15. John Henry Brown, *The History of Texas*, Vol. I, p. 228.

16. James Carter, *Masonry in Texas*, p. 253.

17. *The Handbook of Texas*, Vol. I, p. 399, says the constitution divided the state "into ten electoral districts." Malcolm D. McLean, in *Papers Concerning Robertson's Colony in Texas*, Vol. VII, p. 435, cites Article 104, which provides for eleven districts.

18. Duncan W. Robinson, *Texas' Three-Legged Willie*, (Austin: Texas State Historical Association, 1948), p. 82.

19. H. Yoakum, *History of Texas*, (New York: Redfield, 1855, facsimile by The Steck Company, Austin, no date), Vol. I, p. 311.

20. Eugene C. Barker, *The Life of Stephen F. Austin* (Austin: University of Texas Press, 1926), p. 361.

21. *The Handbook of Texas*, Vol. I, p. 404.

22. Ethel Zivley Rather, "Explanations to the Public Concerning the Affairs of Texas by Citizen Stephen F. Austin," *Southwestern Historical Quarterly*, Vol. VIII, No. 3 (January, 1905), pp. 241-243. See also John Henry Brown, *History of Texas*, Vol. I, p. 229.

23. Branch T. Archer, a native of Fauquier County, Virginia, had studied medicine in Philadelphia. He later served as a member of the first Texas Congress and was speaker of the House of Representatives during the second session. *The Handbook of Texas*, Vol. I, p. 63.

24. Robert McAlpin Williamson was born in Georgia in 1804 or 1806. He moved to Texas in 1826, locating in San Felipe. Here he established the *Texas Gazette* and *Mexican Citizen*. *The Handbook of Texas*, Vol. II, p. 918. See Duncan Robinson, *Texas' Three Legged Willie*.

25. David G. Burnet was born in Newark, New Jersey, the youngest of eight children. He was reared by an older brother. He established a trading post at Natchitoches in 1813. Between 1819 and 1825 he divided his time between studying and practicing law and in living in Louisiana and Texas. *The Handbook of Texas*, Vol. I, p. 252.

26. Nestor Clay was born in Daviess County, Kentucky, in 1799. His father was a Virginia soldier of the Revolution and one of the framers of the first constitution of Kentucky. John Henry Brown, *History of Texas*, Vol. I, p. 203. Clay had been called the "Master Spirit" of the convention of 1832. He died in Washington Conty in 1835, *The Handbook of Texas*, Vol. I, p. 358.

27. Herbert Gambrell, *Anson Jones: The Last President of Texas*, (Garden City: Doubleday & Company, Inc., 1948), p. 35.

28. Noah Smithwick, *The Evolution of a State* (Austin: Gammel Book Company, 1900), pp. 67-68.

29. James D. Carter, *Masonry in Texas*, p. 254.

Chapter 7

1. Robert W. Amsler, "Life and Times of Arthur Goodall Wavell," Unpublished dissertation, The University of Texas, Austin, June 1950, pp. 102-104.

2. Ibid., p. 107.

3. Ibid., p. 109.

4. Lois Garver, "The Life of Benjamin Rush Milam," Unpublished thesis, The University of Texas, Austin, June 1930, p. 62.

5. Ibid., pp. 64-65.

6. Ibid., pp. 70-71.

7. The property has been identified as those 500 acres owned by Hugh

King McDonald at Hills Prairie. McDonald came to Texas in 1851 and ran a ferry and sawmill. During the War Between the States he supplied the Confederate army with cattle and supplies, but during Reconstruction was forced to sell his ferry and saw mill. John Holmes Jenkins III, editor, *Recollections of Early Texas* (Austin: University of Texas Press, 1958), p. 257. See Bill Moore, *Bastrop County, 1791-1900* (Wichita Falls: Nortex Press, 1977), p. 171.

8. Albert C. Horton, William Menefee, Lewis B. Cooke, Isaac W. Burton and Isaac Campbell, commissioners to select the permanent location of the capital of the Republic of Texas, selected five thirds of leagues and two labors on the east bank of the Colorado.

Among the owners of the land named by commissioners on March 23, 1839, was George J. Neill, then residing in Washington County.

Bartlett Sims, B. M. Clopton, John Brown, Jeptha Boyce, James Standiford, and James Lyon, appointed to establish the value of the property, set $3.50 per acre for Neill's holdings. The property was conveyed to the Republic of Texas April 3, 1839. Bastrop County Deed Book B, pp. 419-420.

9. Rogers had received one league of land a month before Neill applied for his title. Bill Moore, *Bastrop County*, p. 29. he served as a first lieutenant in Tumlinson's Rangers. Worth S. Ray, *Austin Colony Pioneers*, (Austin: The Pemberton Press, 1970) p. 305. He was "run down and killed" by Indians between Coleman's Fort and Hornsby's Station. Ibid., p. 304. James Rogers was appointed administrator of the estate of Joseph Rogers on March 26, 1838. Ibid., p. 339.

10. Jessie C. Tannahill had applied for a league of land at the same time Rogers submitted his application, Oct. 30, 1832. Bill Moore, *Bastrop County*, p. 29.

11. Smith applied for land two weeks before Neill. Bill Moore, *Bastrop County*, p. 30. He was named chief justice of Bastrop on August 8, 1846. Ibid., p. 59.

12. Andrew Rabb was the first chief justice, appointed April 14, 1837. Bill Moore, *Bastrop County*, p. 48, p. 59

13. The ayuntamiento in 1836 granted Samuel Wolfenbarger deed to property in Mina (Bill Moore, *Bastrop County*, p. 38), and on July 1, 1843, he was appointed coroner. Ibid., p. 58. *Proceedings of the Corporation of Bastrop, Texas, 1839-1856*, a copy of which is in the Bastrop County Museum, shows Wolfenbarger a man of many talents. He was appointed with B. M. Clopton to repair the courthouse (p. 137) and superintend the building of a schoolhouse, p. 141.

14. John Holmes Jenkins, III, editor, *Recollections of Early Texas*.

15. Ayuntamiento Minutes for August 19, 1834, as quoted in Bill Moore, *Bastrop County*, pp. 33-34.

16. Bill Moore, *Bastrop County*, p. 35.

17. Ibid., p. 36.

18. Ibid.

19. Duncan W. Robinson, Judge Robert McAlpin Williamson, *Texas' Three-Legged Willie* (Austin: Texas State Historical Association, 1948), preface.

20. On Feb. 6, 1885, W. C. Walsh, commissioner of the General Land Office, certified that "it appears from the archives of this office that James C. Neill received, as colonist in Milam's Colony, a title to one league of land, issued by Talbot Chambers, Commissioner of said Colony, on the 1st of June 1835." The land on the Colorado River is now in Travis County.

21. Bartlett Sims was one of Austin's Old Three Hundred settlers. Large, rotund, and with a good nature, he had a laugh that could be heard a great distance. He was a member of the General Council of the Provisional Government in 1835 and participated in several expeditions against the Indians. He was in the Brushy Creek fight. Worth S. Ray, *Austin Colony Pioneers*, p. 211.

22. Bastrop County Deed Book B, p. 180, in Bastrop County courthouse.

23. John Henry Brown, *History of Texas* (St. Louis: L. E. Daniell, Publisher, 1892), p. 286. See also James T. DeShields, *Border Wars of Texas* (Waco: Texian Press, 1976), pp. 130-131.

24. James Goacher, a native of Alabama who settled on Rabbs Creek in southern Lee County, opened a trail from his home to San Felipe and into Bastrop County. This trail became known as Goache's Trace. Walter Prescott Webb, editor, *The Handbook of Texas* (Austin: Texas State Historical Association, 1952), Vol. I, p. 697.

25. The Berry family moved from Indiana in 1826 and became members of Sterling C. Robertson's colony. In 1834 they located in Bastrop. Walter Prescott Webb, editor, *The Handbook of Texas*, Vol. I, p. 151.

26. John Henry Brown, *History of Texas*, p. 286. See also John Holmes Jenkins III, editor, *Recollections of Early Texas*, 22fn.

27. James DeShields, *Border Wars of Texas*, p. 132, and John Henry Brown, *History of Texas*, p. 286.

28. James DeShields, *Border Wars of Texas*, p. 132. John Holmes Jenkins III, editor, *Recollections of Early Texas*, offers another version, indicating that Canoma was returned to Mina, held under guard a time, but finally released. p. 22.

29. A native of Kentucky, Coleman moved to Texas in May, 1831. He was a member of the consultation in San Felipe in 1835 and when the first Ranger company was authorized, he was named captain. He was elected a delegate to the convention that signed the Declaration of Independence in March, 1836. He served as aide-de-camp to Sam Houston at the Battle of San Jacinto. Later he raised a company of Texas Rangers and was the group's colonel. Coleman drowned while bathing in the Brazos River in May, 1838. His widow, Elizabeth Coleman, and son, Albert, were killed when Indians raided their cabin in 1839. Sam Houston Dixon and Louis Wiltz Kemp, *The Heroes of San Jacinto*, (Houston: The Anson Jones Press, 1932), pp. 49-50.

30. John Holmes Jenkins III, editor, *Recollections of Early Texas*, p. 23. A slightly different version appears in John Henry Brown, *History of Texas*. Brown indicates that Coleman's force consisted of 25 men, three of whom were well known Brazos settlers. He sets the campaign at Tehuacana. Though killing "a considerable number of Indians," Coleman "was compelled to retreat." p. 287.

31. J. W. Wilbarger, *Indian Depredations in Texas,* (Austin: The Steck Company, 1935), pp. 218-219.

32. Bill Moore, *Bastrop County,* p. 41.

33. George Washington Barnett was born in South Carolina Dec. 12, 1793. A physician, he settled for a time in Williamson County, Tenn., and in 1823 moved to Mississippi. He came to Texas in January, 1834, and settled in Washington County. Later he bought a farm near Brenham. He joined Capt. James G. Swisher's company and was discharged in December, 1835, following the capture of San Antonio. He was a signer of the Texas Declaration of Independence. Ray Worth, *Austin Colony Pioneers* (Austin: The Pemberton Press, 1970) p. 56. He was killed by maurading Indians in October, 1838. Walter Prescott Webb, editor, *The Handbook of Texas,* Vol. I, p. 112.

34. John Henry Brown, *History of Texas* (St. Louis: L.E. Daniell, Publisher, 1892, Vol. I), p. 288.

35. Ibid.

36. John Holmes Jenkins III, editor, *Recollections of Early Texas,* p. 24.

37. William Harrison Magill was born in Madison County, Ky., on Jan. 3, 1813, and came to Texas in 1834. On Sept. 16, 1834, with his partner, William Redmond, he received a half league of land located in Wharton and Goliad counties. He joined Jesse Billingsley's Mina volunteers and was second sergeant in the battle of San Jacinto. John Holmes Jenkins III, editor, *Recollections of Early Texas,* p. 257.

38. Ibid., p. 25.

39. Ibid., p. 26.

40. James H. C. Miller settled in Gonzales between 1831 and 1835. Eugene C. Barker, "James H. C. Miller and Edward Gritten," *The Southwestern Historical Quarterly,* Vol. 8, No. 2 (October, 1909), p. 145. Julia Sinks' scrapbook B-36/209 in the archives of The University of Texas, Austin, contains a document showing he was secretary of a group submitting a petition from the ayuntamiento to the governor of Coahuila and Texas. When Texians splintered into war and peace factions, he joined the peace group, believing the disturbances of the time were prompted by speculators. Walter Prescott Webb, editor, *The Handbook of Texas,* Vol. II, p. 196.

41. Andrew Jackson Houston, *Texas Independence* (Houston: Anson Jones Press, 1938), p. 62.

42. Archie P. McDonald, *Travis* (Austin: Jenkins Publishing Company, 1976), p. 107.

Chapter 8

1. W.S. Cleaver, "The Political Career of Lorenzo de Zavala," MA thesis, The University of Texas, August, 1931. p. 126. Zavala was born near Merida, Yucatan, Oct. 3, 1788, (Ibid., p. 5) and was an advocate of democratic reforms. Because of his liberal viewpoints, he was arrested in 1814 and imprisoned in the Castle of San Juan de Ulloa. In the summer of 1835 he had begun his support the cause of Mexican Federalism while living in Texas. Walter Prescott

Webb, editor, *The Handbook of Texas* (Austin: The Texas State Historical Association, 1952), Vol. I, p. 498.

2. W.S. Cleaver, "The Political Career of Lorenzo de Zavala," p. 132.

3. John Henry Brown, *History of Texas* (St. Louis: L.E. Daniell Publisher, 1892), Vol. I, pp. 305-307.

4. In November, 1831, George Fisher, customs collector, announced new regulations on customs clearing the port at Anahuac, at the head of Galveston Bay. These rules antagonized colonists. Juan Davis Bradburn impressed slaves belonging to some settlers and harbored some runaway slaves. When he arrested Patrick C. Jack and William B. Travis, Bradburn invited trouble. Local citizens demanded the release of the two Texians and persuaded authorities to relieve Bradburn of his command. In 1835, after the opening of the customs house, Andrew Birscoe was arrested for violating a tariff law. Walter Prescott Webb, editor, *The Hankbook of Texas*, Vol. I, p. 43.

5. Ibid.

6. Office memo signed by Governor William P. Clements, in possession of John Wheat, archives translator, Barker Texas History Center, The University of Texas, Austin.

7. Ibid.

8. James Tumlinson, born in Tennessee, moved to Texas with his wife and three sons in 1821. He received a Donation Warrant for 1280 acres of land for his part in the storming of Bexar. He served as captain of a group of Rangers in 1836 and commanded a company of volunteers who fought the Indians in 1840. Sam Houston Dixon and Louis Wiltz Kemp, *The Heroes of San Jacinto* (Houston: The Anson Jones Press, 1932), p. 222. His home, across the street from the jail plaza and 130 feet north, was appraised at $16. Edward A. Lukes, *DeWitt Colony of Texas*, pp. 142, 144. See also "The Tumlinsons—Texas Rangers" in *Old West* (Winter, 1984), pp. 14-17.

9. John Wheat to Dr. Patrick Wagner, April 11, 1980, citing Bexar Archives, March 4, 1831, frame 206, Green DeWitt to Ramon Musquic. Wheat's personal file.

10. From personal files of John Wheat, citing the Bexar Archives, dated March 10, 1831, frame 13.

The field piece was a "six-pounder, unmounted cannon," according to Edward A. Lukes, *DeWitt Colony of Texas*, p. 136. He cites a letter from DeWitt to Ramon Musquic, March 4, 1831, in the Bexar Archives. On p. 177 he refers to it as "the six-pound cannon," citing Noah Smithwick's *The Evolution of a State*, p. 101. Mamie Wynne Cox in *The Romantic Flags of Texas* (Dallas: Banks, Upshaw and Company, 1936), says that the piece probably was "one of those cannon spiked by Lieutenant (Augustus) Magee's army in 1813. p. 156. A footnote from *The Evolution of a State*, p. 101, contains the same information. T. R. Fehrenbach calls it "a small brass cannon, a six-pounder" in *Lone Star, a History of Texas* (New York: The Macmillan Company, 1958), p. 192.

11. Noah Smithwick, who landed at Matagorda in the fall of 1835, recalls in *The Evolution of a State*, that the artillery piece "was practically useless, having been spiked and the spike driven out, leaving a touch-hole the size of a

man's thumb." (p 101) A gunsmith, Smithwick went to the Sowell blacksmith shop in Gonzales and "set to work to help put the arms in order." He recalled:
> There was no coal, so some of the boys were set to burning charcoal. We brushed the old cannon (an iron six-pounder), scoured it out, and mounted it on wooden trucks." (p 102)

Noah Smithwick, *The Evolution of a State* (Austin: The Steck Company, 1935). Nicholas Perkins Hardeman in *Wilderness Calling* (Knoxville: The University of Tennessee Press, 1977) describes the cannon as a six-pounder made of brass. (p 124).

12. Ethel Zivley Rather, *DeWitt's Colony*, Bulletin of The University of Texas No. 51, January 15, 1905, p. 56.

13. Edward A. Lukes, *DeWitt Colony of Texas* (Austin: Jenkins Publishing Company, 1976), p. 179.

14. Ethel Zivley Rather, *DeWitt's Colony*, p. 57.

15. The property was identified as in Block 12 of the city and upon the site later containing a cotton gin and the Gardian Livery Stable. Ethel Zivley Rather, *DeWitt's Colony*, p. 56. A folder, "Gonzales, Where the Fight for Texas Liberty Began," undated but issued by the Joseph Boothe Society, children of the American Revolution, a copy of which is in the Barker History Center, The University of Texas, indicates that George P. Davis's peach orchard was between St. Micheal Street and U.S. Highway 183. An orchard belonging to Jacob Darst also has been mentioned as the place where the cannon was hidden.

16. Andrew Jackson Houston, *Texas Independence* (Houston: The Anson Jones Press, 1938), pp. 71-72.

17. John Henry Brown, *History of Texas* Vol. I, pp. 348-349.

18. Edward A. Lukes, *DeWitt Colony of Texas*, pp. 189-191.

19. H. Yoakum, *History of Texas* (New York: Redfield, 1855), Vol. I, p. 363.

20. Edward A. Lukes, *DeWitt's Colony of Texas*, p. 183.

21. Joseph Washington Elliot Wallace was approximately 50 years of age when he was named lieutenant colonel. The Pennsylvania native had come to Texas in 1830. He was a member of the militia when he participated in the Plum Creek Fight in 1840. He died in Columbia in 1877. Walter Prescott Webb, editor, *The Handbook of Texas*, Vol. II, p. 856.

22. James T. DeShields, *Tall Men with Long Rifles* (San Antonio: The Naylor Company, 1971), p. 17.

23. Another source says that the cannon was mounted on a wagon donated by Jo Martin. Ethel Zivley Rather says that Sowell and Chisholm, blacksmiths, mounted the piece on a broad-tired ox-wagon. p. 60.

24. James T. DeShields, *Tall Men with Long Rifles*, pp. 26-27.

25. Miles S. Bennet, "The Battle of Gonzales, The Lexington of the Texas Revolution," *The Quarterly of the Texas State Historical Association*, Vol. II, No. 4 (April 1898), p. 313.

26. Walter Prescott Webb, editor, *The Handbook of Texas*, Vol. I, pp. 606-607.

27. Sulpher Springs *Telegram*, Sept. 4, 1934. Cynthia Burns was the daugh-

ter of Arthur Burns, one of DeWitt's colonists. Mamie Wynne Cox, *The Romantic Flags of Texas*, p. 155. Evaline DeWitt's father was founder of the colony. Edward A. Lukes, *DeWitt Colony of Texas*, p. 189, says the flag was made by Sarah Seely DeWitt, wife of Green DeWitt, and her daughter Naomi. The flag was made of Naomi's wedding dress.

28. James T. DeShields, *Tall Men with Long Rifles*, p. 17.

29. James M. Day, compiler, *The Texas Almanac, 1857-1873* (Waco: Texian Press, 1967), pp. 442-443.

30. "It is not recorded, but is nevertheless a fact that Colonel Neill fired the first gun for Texas at the beginning of the revolution—the famous little brass cannon at Gonzales." So wrote John Holland Jenkins. John Holmes Jenkins III, editor, *Recollections of Early Texas* (Austin: University of Texas Press, 1958), p. 155.

D.C. Barret of Mina wrote Sam Houston Nov. 29, 1835, about his "neighbor and friend, Col. James C. Neill." He said, "He was the first in camp whose experience was sufficient to mount & point a cannon at the enemies of Texas, and of liberty in our land—and has a command in the Artillery during the time...."

John H. Jenkins, general editor, *The Papers of the Texas Revolution* (Austin: Presidial Press, 1973), No. 1006.

31. Andrew Jackson Houston, *Texas Independence*, p. 72, and Edward A. Lukes, *DeWitt Colony of Texas*, p. 187.

Chapter 9

1. Noah Smithwick, *The Evolution of a State* (Austin: The Steck Company, 1935), p. 104.

2. Edward A. Lukes, *DeWitt Colony of Texas* (Austin: Jenkins Publishing Company, 1976), p. 188.

3. Noah Smithwick, *The Evolution of a State*, p. 110.

4. Ibid.

5. Ibid.

6. Ibid.

7. Ibid., p. 107.

8. Edward A. Lukes, *DeWitt Colony of Texas*, p. 188.

9. Noah Smithwick, *The Evolution of a State*, p. 108.

10. William Houston Jacks, born April 12, 1806, in Wilkes County, Georgia, was a graduate of the University of Georgia. He had been elected to the Georgia Legislature in 1829, but the following year he moved to Texas. Brazoria County citizens elected him to the Committee of Safety and Correspondence in 1834. He later served in the Fourth Congress of the Republic of Texas and was a senator in the Sixth, Seventh, and Eighth Congresses. He died in Brazoria County on Aug. 20, 1844. Walter Prescott Webb, editor, *The Handbook of Texas* (Austin: The Texas State Historical Association, 1952), Vol. I, pp. 899-900.

11. Noah Smithwick, *The Evolution of a State*, p. 108.

12. Ibid.

13. Ibid., p. 102. Creed Taylor said the wheels were 4-inch discs cut from a large cottonwood tree and "strengthened by strips of timber nailed on transversely." James T. DeShields, editor, *Tall Men with Long Rifles*, (San Antonio: The Naylor Company, 1935), p. 25.

14. Noah Smithwick wrote, "Sometimes when the forward column opened a rather wide gap, we prodded up the oxen with our lances (the only use that was ever made of them) until they broke into a trot and the old trucks bumped and screeched along at a lively gait till the gap was closed. But rapid locomotion was not congenial to them; they protested by groans and shrieks and at length began to smoke . . . . ." *The Evolution of a State*, pp. 110-111.

In telling James T. DeShields his life story for *Tall Men with' Long Rifles*, Creed Taylor had another version. He said, "My recollection is that this truck was drawn by horses and not by oxen as some have contended. And this stands to reason, since there was comparatively no scarcity of horses, and owing to the slow gait of the oxen, no troop would have thought of using them as draft animals on the cavalry march when every volunteer was eager to cover the distance in the shortest space of time." p. 32.

15. A leaflet, "Texas Arms" of the Texas Gun Collectors Association, meeting in San Antonio, May 18-22, 1979, lists on display an iron cannon dug up at Gonzales and included in the collection of Henry Guerra of Reynosa, Tampalipas, Mexico. "Calendar of Discoveries on the Research of the Gonzales Cannon of 1835" indicates that Dr. Patrick Wagner of Shiner bought the cannon Dec. 18, 1979, and began extensive research to authenticate it as the artillery piece identified as "The Flying Artillery." Gene Key, a resident of Dewville, recalled finding the cannon on Sandies Creek after a severe flood in July, 1936. It was stored in the Gonzales post office until sold to the Mexican collector. The cannon was cast iron construction with surface pitting. X-rays in April, 1980, show that the cannon had been brushed as Smithwich mentions in *The Evolution of a State*, p. 102.

Dr. Wagner wrote John Wheat, archives translator in the Barker History Center of The University of Texas, Austin, that the cannon measures 21.5 inches and weighs 68 pounds. At the time he had employed a craftsman to use wood from the Guadalupe River banks to chisel a hand-hewn carriage. Personal files of John R. Wheat.

In November, 1981, members of the Texas National Guard moved the cannon from Austin to the Alamo for a display. *The Dallas Morning News*, Nov. 15, 1981. See also James T. DeShields, Tall Men with Long Rifles, pp. 30, 42.

16. Noah Smithwick, *The Evolution of a State*, p. 112.

17. Walter Lord, *A Time to Stand* (New York: Harper & Brothers, 1961), pp. 26-27.

18. Mission San Francisco de la Espada was "moved" from east Texas and re-established near San Antonio in 1731, changing its name in the moving process. Origin of the name, Saint Francis of the Sword, is unknown, but one explanation concerns the vision St. Francis had of a sword in the sky. Espada, a church for Indians, had been built of stone with a carved wood roof. Under construction in 1745, it was in use in 1756. In 1778, however, Father Morfi

noted that the chapel was in ruins. A new church was under construction in 1785. Charles Ramsdell, *San Antonio, A Historical and Pictorial Guide* (Austin: University of Texas Press, 1959), pp. 140-141.

19. The journalist George Wilkins Kendall was in San Antonio in 1841 and described the Mission of Concepcion. He wrote, "The Mission of Concepcion is a very large building with a fine cupola, and though plain, magnificent in its dimensions and in the durability of its construction." *Narrative of the Texan Santa Fe Expedition* (New York: Harper & Brothers, 1847), Vol. I, p. 50.

John Bartlett, visiting the mission nine years later, wrote, "The two towers and dome of the church make quite an imposing appearance when seen from a distance, but, on approaching it, we found it not only desolated but desecrated, the church portion being used as an inclosure for cattle, the filth from which covered the floor to a depth of a foot or more. Myraids of bats flitted about, which chattered and screamed at our invasion of their territory." John Russell Bartlett, *Personal Narrative of Explorations and Incidents* (London: George Routledge and Co., 1854), pp. 44-45.

20. Noah Smithwick, *The Evolution of a State*, p. 113, and Sallie Glasscock, *Dreams of an Empire* (San Antonio: The Naylor Company, 1951), p. 119.

21. Henry W. Karnes came from Tennessee to Texas by way of Arkansas. Born in 1812, he was a fighter. He was with Captain John York's company in the Battle of Concepcion, he was elected captain of a company of cavalry at Goliad in March, 1836, and prior to the Battle of San Jacinto, he and Erastus (Deaf) Smith went on a scouting mission. In 1837 he was dispatched to Matamoros to help with the exchange of prisoners but was incarcerated. Late in 1838 he was authorized to organize eight companies of men to oppose the Comanches. He died in 1840. Walter Prescott Webb, editor, *The Handbook of Texas*, Vol. I, p. 938.

22. The man was identified by Creed Taylor as Pen Jarvis, who became known as "Bowie-Knife Jarvis" following the incident. James DeShields, *Tall Men with Long Rifles*, pp. 41-42.

23. John Henry Brown, *History of Texas* (St. Louis: L. E. Daniell, Publisher, 1892), Vol. I, p. 371.

24. Richard Andrews' father was one of the Old Three Hundred who came to Texas prior to December, 1821. Richard was a member of that early household. A man of immense size and strength, Dick Andrews was wounded in the Battle of Gonzales and was killed Oct. 28, 1835. A county in the Texas Panhandle was named in his memory. Walter Prescott Webb, *The Handbook of Texas*, Vol. I, p. 48.

25. Noah Smithwick, *The Evolution of a State*, p. 114.

26. Ibid., p. 120.

27. Cleburne Huston, *Deaf Smith* (Waco: Texian Press, 1973), p. 30, gives the figure of captured horses as 200 scrawny animals. Texians sent the animals to pasture on the Colorado.

28. Sallie Glasscock, *Dreams of an Empire*, p. 121. See John Henry Brown, *History of Texas*, Vol. I, p. 373.

29. The Old Mill was a cane-crushing facility on the San Antonio River. Cleburne Huston, *Deaf Smith*, p. 34.

30. Sallie Glasscock, *Dreams of an Empire*, p. 125. Austin was not alone; the Consultation passed a resolution of thanks to Austin, James W. Fannin, and Benjamin Fort Smith for offering their landed property to aid the cause. John Henry Brown, *History of Texas*, Vol. I, p. 396.

31. Sallie Glasscock, *Dreams of an Empire*, p. 127.

32. John Henry Brown, *History of Texas*, Vol. I, p. 381.

33. Ibid., p. 396, and John Henry Brown, *Life and Times of Henry Smith* (Austin: The Steck Company, 1935), pp. 17, 24.

34. John Henry Brown, *Life and Times of Henry Smith*, pp. 107-108.

35. Ibid., p. 77.

36. John Henry Brown, *History of Texas*, Vol. I, p. 398.

37. Ibid., p. 399.

38. Burleson was born in Buncombe County, North Carolina, and lived in Tennessee and Alabama. While he resided in Missouri, he was commander of a company of Howard County militia and later was colonel of the first regiment in Saline County and colonel of a regiment in Hardeman County.

At Gonzales, Oct. 10, 1835, he was elected colonel of the only regiment organized under Stephen F. Austin. Later he succeeded Philip A. Sublett as colonel of infantry and in March, 1836, was named colonel of the 1st Regiment of Texas Volunteers, which participated in the Battle of San Jacinto. He became brigadier general of the militia in 1837 and in 1838 was appointed colonel of the infantry.

During the War with Mexico, Burleson was on the staff of James Pinckney Henderson.

Burleson also had a rich career in politics, having served in the House of Representatives in the Second Congress and in the Senate in the Third. In 1841 he was elected vice president of the Republic and was a candidate for president, opposing Anson Jones. After Texas became a state, Burleson served in the First, Second, Third, and Fourth Legislatures. He was president pro tempore of the legislature at the time of his death, Dec. 26, 1851. Walter Prescott Webb, editor, *The Handbook of Texas*, Vol. I, p. 249.

39. John Henry Brown, *History of Texas*, Vol. I, pp. 408-409; H. Yoakum, *History of Texas*, Vol. II, pp. 17-18; Cleburne Huston, *Deaf Smith*, pp. 30-32.

40. Don Carlos Barrett, son of Jonathan and Elizabeth Murdock Barrett, was born in Vermont. An attorney, he settled in Velasco, Texas, and became a citizen of Coahuila and Texas April 13, 1835. He moved to Mina, where he later became a law partner of Elisha M. Pease. A representative of Mina in the Consultation, he was elected to the General Council. On Dec. 11, he was elected judge advocate general of the Texas Army with the rank of colonel. Walter Prescott Webb, editor, *The Handbook of Texas*, Vol. I, p. 114.

Henry Smith regarded it as his "disagreeable and painful though bounden duty to object" to the appointment. Smith said that the office, with the rank and pay of colonel in the line, was "new and unheard of in the country," and he listed six charges against Barrett. John Henry Brown, *Life and Times of Henry Smith*, p. 152.

41. John H. Jenkins III, editor, *The Papers of the Texas Revolution*, (Austin: Presidial Press, 1973), No. 1064.

42. The Navarro home is attached to a square store of two rooms, one upstairs and one down. The building has overhanging eaves and a gentle broken roof line. It was the homestead of Jose Antonio Navarro, one of the two native Texans who signed the Texas Declaration of Independence. Navarro was sentenced to life imprisonment by Santa Anna but escaped and made his way back to his home in 1845. He died in the house in 1877. Charles Ramsdell, *San Antonio* (Austin: University of Texas Press, 1959), pp. 165-166.

The San Antonio *Light* of Sept. 3, 1886, reported that workmen remodeling the Navarro home had uncovered a rafter, into which had been carved in Spanish "Commenced June 8, finished August 7, 1778 A.D. Gen. Agrieto." Alderman Schreiner bought the house in 1870 from Navarro.

Indian prisoners were used in constructing the house, which served as headquarters for the governor. Legend has it that two days before Navarro died, he sold a ranch for $1,200. After paying some minor bills, he buried the remainder of the money in his sleeping room. Donald E. Everett, *San Antonio: The Flavor of Its Past, 1845-1898* (San Antonio: Trinity University Press, 1976), p. 12.

43. The home of Antonio de la Garza was owned by the same family more than 150 years. The only mint in Texas during the Spanish era was located here when Garza coined money. He and his son were also in banking endeavors. The house was demolished in 1912 and workmen found a number of doubloons under the structure. Boyce House, in *City of Flaming Adventure* suggests these coins were hidden during Indian raids. (San Antonio: The Naylor Company, 1949), p. 28.

44. While Juan Martin Veramendi was governor of Coahuila and Texas, his home became known as the Veramendi Palace. The building later was the headquarters of David E. Twiggs, commandant of the United States forces in Texas during the War Between the States. A daughter, Ursula, was married to James Bowie in March, 1831. Walter Prescott Webb, editor, *The Handbook of Texas*, Vol. II, p. 837.

The San Antonio *Express* of April 23, 1897, reported that the Veramendi palace had been ordered torn down because of the dangerous condition of the roof and the walls. The original doors of the house on Soledad Street are now in the south transept of the Alamo. Donald E. Everett, *San Antonio: The Flavor of Its Past, 1845-1898*, p. 122.

The Veramendi mansion, however, was the scene of an interesting piece of surgery in 1854. Dr. Ferdinand Herff had arrived in the community only a short time before. He was called upon to operate on a Texas Ranger. Spectators filled the open doors and windows to see the "perineal lithotomy," the removal of a stone from the bladder. In this case, two stones which were bound together—one the size of a hen egg and the second as large as a turkey egg. Dr. Herff tried chloroform for the first time, and when the patient began to snore, the physician became frightened and continued the surgery without anesthesia. Henry G. Dielmann, "Dr. Ferdinand Herff, Pioneer Physician and Surgeon," *The Southwestern Historical Quarterly*, Vol. LVII, No. 3 (January, 1954), p. 277.

45. Hendrick Arnold, a free black, (Walter Prescott Webb, editor, *The Handbook of Texas*, Vol. I, p. 71) and Erastus (Deaf) Smith had returned from a buffalo hunt on Little River in October, 1835, when they learned that their home town, San Antonio, was occupied by Cos's army and was under siege by Texians. Arnold came to Texas from Mississippi in the winter of 1826 and settled on the Brazos. He was in Smith's spy company in the Battle of San Jacinto. He married Maria Ignazcia Duran, the daughter of Guadalupe Smith (Mrs. Erastus Smith) and her first husband. Arnold died in the cholera epidemic in Bexar in 1839. Cleburne Huston, *Deaf Smith*, p. 2, 16, fn. 46.

46. T. R. Fehrenbach, *Lone Star* (New York: The Macmillan Company, 1968), p. 197.

47. Henderson Yoakum, *History of Texas*, Vol. II, p. 24. Another version is that Bates Berry, scouting below the Old Mill, rode upon the Mexican lieutenant and took him before Gen. Burleson for questioning. James DeShields, editor, *Tall Men with Long Rifles*, p. 54.

48. James M. Day, "Benjamin R. Milam," *Heroes of Texas* (Waco: Texian Press, 1964), p. 115.

49. James T. DeShields, editor, *Tall Men with Long Rifles*, p. 57. See John Henry Brown, *History of Texas*, Vol. I, p. 417. An article on the storming of San Antonio de Bexar in 1835 was taken from the *State Gazette*, 1849, and appears in D.W.C. Baker's *A Texas Scrap Book*. The article says, "Colonel Neil (*sic*) was sent to make a feint on the Alamo, which he did in good style, and then joined Milam in town." (Austin: The Steck Company, 1935), p. 37. See also "Storming of San Antonio de Bexar in 1835," p. 37. See also "Storming of San Antonio de Bexar in 1835" in *Frontier Times*, Vol. 9, No. 11 (August, 1932) citing *Texas State Gazette*, 1849.

50. D.W.C. Baker, compiler, *A Texas Scrap Book*, p. 37.

51. Henderson Yoakum, *History of Texas*, Vol. II, p. 26.

52. Ibid., Vol. II, pp. 27-28.

53. Sallie Glasscock, *Dreams of an Empire*, p. 132.

54. The place was named for tall, blond, athletic Juan Manuel Zambarno, a minor church official. Born in San Antonio in 1772 or 1773, Zambrano had become a subdeacon and was selected by royal army officers to organize a counter-revolution in 1811. He had been exiled to Mexico by the governor of Texas. David M. Vigness, *The Revolutionary Decades* (Austin: Steck-Vaughn Company, 1965), p. 5.

55. Henderson Yoakum, *History of Texas*, Vol. II, p. 29.

56. Ibid.

57. Sallie Glasscock, *Dreams of an Empire*, p. 133.

58. Henderson Yoakum, *History of Texas*, Vol. II, p. 32.

Chapter 10
 1. Andrew Jackson Houston, *Texas Independence*, (Houston: Anson Jones Press, 1932) p. 88. See also Archie P. McDonald, *Travis* (Austin: Jenkins Publishing Company, 1976), p. 140.
 2. Archie P. McDonald, *Travis*, pp. 140-141.
 3. Ibid., p. 141.
 4. Ibid., p. 142.
 5. Ibid.
 6. Green Jameson was born in Kentucky circa 1807, and by October, 1830, he was practicing law in San Felipe. He joined James Bowie as an aide and chief engineer with the rank of ensign. Walter Prescott Webb, editor, *The Handbook of Texas* (Austin: The Texas State Historical Association, 1952), Vol. I, pp. 904-905.
 7. Walter Prescott Webb, editor, *The Handbook of Texas*, Vol. I, pp. 904-905, and John H. Jenkins, general editor, *The Papers of the Texas Revolution* (Austin: Presidial Press, 1973), No. 2110, G. B. Jameson to Gov. Henry Smith, Feb. 16, 1836.
 8. The debris was not cleared until 1848-1850, when the United States government removed the rubble and repaired the building for use as a quartermaster department. Amelia Williams, *Following Sam Houston* (Austin: The Steck Company, 1935), p. 99.
 9. Ameilia Williams, *Following Sam Houston*, p. 100.
 10. John H. Jenkins, general editor, *The Papers of the Texas Revolution*, No. 1576, Sam Houston to J. C. Neill, Dec. 21, 1835.
 11. Martha Anne Turner, *William Barret Travis, His Sword and His Pen*, (Waco: Texian Press, 1972), p. 155.
 12. John H. Jenkins, general editor, *Papers of the Texas Revolution*, No. 1516, J. C. Neill to D. C. Bazrett, Dec. 17, 1835.
 13. Donald Day and Harry Herbert Ullom, *The Autobiography of Sam Houston* (Norman: University of Oklahoma Press, 1947), p. 96.
 14. Walter Prescott Webb, editor, *The Handbook of Texas*, Vol. I, p. 718.
 15. Amelia Williams, *Following Sam Houston*, p. 94.
 16. John H. Jenkins, general editor, *The Papers of the Texas Revolution*, No. 1697, F. W. Johnson to the General Council.
 17. Ibid., No. 1708, J. C. Neill to Governor Henry Smith and members of the General Council, Jan. 6, 1836.
 18. Ibid.
 19. Ibid., No. 1709, Sam Houston to Gov. Henry Smith, Jan. 6, 1836.
 20. Amelia W. Williams and Eugene C. Barker, editors, *The Writings of Sam Houston, 1813-1863* (Austin: Pemberton Press, 1970), Vol. I, pp. 232-233.
 21. Francisco Ruis was named a delegate from Bexar to the convention at Washington-on-the-Brazos in March, 1836 (p 56). He was one of the signers of the Texas Declaration of Independence, (p. 357) at the time 54 years of age and listed as a native of Bexar (p 595). His son, Francis Antonio Ruis, was alcalde of San Antonio and decided to remain neutral in the struggle for Texas

independence (p 395). James M. Day, compiler, *The Texas Almanac, 1857-1873* (Waco: Texian Press, 1967).

22. John H. Jenkins, general editor, *Papers of the Texas Revolution*, No. 1729, J. C. Neill to the governor and general council, Jan. 8, 1836.

23. John William Smith, born in Virginia March 4, 1792, lived in Missouri before moving to Texas. After residing briefly in Gonzales, he settled in Bexar, where he opened a mercantile business. Three times between 1837 and 1844, he served as mayor of San Antonio, and in 1842 was elected to the Texas Senate. He died Jan. 13, 1845, at Washington-on-the-Brazos. Walter Prescott Webb, editor, *The Handbook of Texas*, Vol. II, p. 625.

When Erastus (Deaf) Smith wanted to have his family safely removed from San Antonio during the siege, he called upon John W. Smith. Guadalupe Smith and her four children, secretly removed at night, were delivered by the San Antonio merchant. Cleburne Huston, *Deaf Smith* (Waco: Texian Press, 1973) p. 5. At the time, Smith delivered valuable information on Cos and his forces; he remained with the Texians, serving as guide and spy. Ibid., p 28.

To distinguish John W. Smith from the other Smiths, early Texians called him "Colorado" or "Red." Ibid., p 32 fn.

24. John H. Jenkins, general editor, *The Papers of the Texas Revolution*, No. 1817, James W. Robinson to Edward Burleson, J. C. Neill, John W. Smith, and Francisco Ruis, Jan. 17, 1836.

25. John H. Jenkins, general editor, *The Papers of the Texas Revolution*, No. 1783, J. C. Neill to Sam Houston, Jan. 14, 1836.

26. Ibid., No. 1784, J. C. Neill to Gov. Henry Smith and members of the general council, Jan. 14, 1836.

27. Ibid.

28. Ibid., No. 4366, Resolutions passed Jan. 16, 1836.

29. John Marsh was discharged Dec. 14 after having served 72 days. His document was witnessed by Thomas Crawford, J. Anderson, and Samuel Coffey.

John Stanley, who had served the same period of time, signed over his right to bounty lands in a document witnessed by G. B. Jameson, Burke Trammel, and S. C. Cook. Jameson, 29, held the rank of ensign (engineer). A native of Kentucky, he was residing in Brazoria at the time of his enlistment. Amelia Williams, "A Critical Study of the Siege of the Alamo and of the Personnel fo its Defenders," *The Southwestern Historical Quarterly*, Vol. 37, No. 4 (April, 1934), p. 266. Burke Trammel, 26, was a private. A native of Ireland, he had come to Texas from Tennessee. Ibid., p. 281.

Alexander Franklin, after 74 days, signed over his right to property. His signature was witnessed Dec. 13 by Burke Trammel, J. North Crass, and Henry (*sic*) Warnell. Warnell, a 24-year-old private, was listed as single on some documents, but he had been married. His wife died in November, 1834, leaving an infant son John. Henry hired himself to Edward Burleson when he arrived in Texas in January, 1835. Weighing less than 118 pounds, with blue eyes, red hair, and freckles, he was described as a great hunter, a fine jockey, and "an incessant tobacco chewer." (Ibid., p. 282). One story persists that Warnell was carrying a message to Gen. Houston. Although severely wounded, he completed his mission but died in Port Lavaca several months later. Ibid., p. 311.

Samuel Fry, upon being released from service Feb. 12, signed over his property to Neill in a document witnessed by Green Jameson, Burke Trammel, and James L. Ewing.

Landey Jones was discharged Dec. 14 after 75 days with the Texas forces. His statement was witnessed by Thomas Crawford, J. Anderson, and Eliel Melton. A Thomas Crawford is listed in the 1837 grants as having received 1280 acres of land in Bastrop county. Bill Moore, *Bastrop County, 1691-1900* (Wichita Falls: Nortex Press, 1977), p. 262. Melton was lieutenant quartermaster. The 40-year-old was a native of South Carolina. At the time of his enlistment he made his home at Nashville-on-the-Brazos. Amelia Williams, "A Critical Study of the Siege of the Alamo," p. 271.

Also after completing 75 days of service, Joe Hegan was granted a discharge Dec. 14. His statement was witnessed by John Crunch, S. Steward, and S. S. Smith.

30. Ibid., No. 1783, J. C. Neill to Sam Houston, Jan. 14, 1836.

31. Ibid.

32. Martha Anne Turner, *William Barret Travis, His Sword and His Pen* (Waco: Texian Press, 1972), p. 168.

33. Ibid., p. 170.

34. John H. Jenkins, general editor, *The Papers of the Texas Revolution*, No. 1989, James Bowie to Gov. Henry Smith, Feb. 2, 1836.

35. Martha Anne Turner, *William Barret Travis, His Sword and His Pen*, p. 170.

36. Cleburne Huston, *Deaf Smith* (Waco: Texian Press, 1973), p. 41. James DeShields, however, says that Smith was performing his old job—scouting for Santa Anna, who had been reported in the vicinity.

37. John H. Jenkins, general editor, *The Papers of the Texas Revolution*, No. 1783, J. C. Neill to Sam Houston, Jan. 14, 1836.

38. Lt. Gov. James Robinson wrote Stephen F. Austin, William Wharton and Branch T. Archer on Jan. 23, 1836, ". . . it becomes incumbent on me, to communicate to you the painful and humiliating fact that Henry Smith Esq. has been and is now suspended from acting as Governor, and the council has preferred serious and weighty charges and specifications against him, and cited him to Trial, and with a view to give him an impartial Trial they gave him the Election to be tried either by the Council, or the next convention, and he chose the latter . . . ." John H. Jenkins, general editor, *Papers of the Texas Revolution*, No. 1898.

Walter Prescott Webb, editor, *The Handbook of Texas*, concisely states that the governor "did not believe in compromise and did not know the language of diplomacy." The strife between the executive and the council was due, in part, to Smith's belief that Texas already was a free and independent state. "Governor Smith attempted to dissolve the Council and the Council retaliated by impeaching the governor." Vol. II, p. 623.

See also John Henry Brown, *Life and Times of Henry Smith* (Austin: The Steck Company, 1935).

39. John H. Jenkins, general editor, *The Papers of the Texas Revolution*, No. 1843. Proclamation was issued from San Felipe de Austin, Jan. 19, 1836.

40. John H. Jenkins, general editor, *The Papers of the Texas Revolution*, No. 1896, J. C. Neill to the governor and general council, Jan. 9, 1836.

41. Ibid., No. 1743, Gov. Henry Smith to the general council, Jan. 9, 1836.

42. Ibid., No. 2073.

43. Ibid., No. 1898, James Robinson to the commissioners, Jan. 23, 1836. In 1841 Gov. Smith requested an investigation into the charges that he had misappropriated the funds contributed by H. R. W. Hill of Nashville, Tennessee. A joint committee, headed by Anson Jones in the Senate and Sterling C. Robertson in the House, unanimously adopted a report showing that the money had been used properly and that the government actually owed Gov. Smith $131 on account. John Henry Brown, *Life and Times of Henry Smith* (Austin: The Steck Company, 1935), p. 279.

44. Carlos Castañada, *Our Catholic Heritage in Texas* (Austin: Von Boeckman-Jones, 1950), Vol. VI, p. 285.

45. John H. Jenkins, general editor, *The Papers of the Texas Revolution*, No. 1897, J. C. Neill to Gov. Henry Smith, Jan. 23, 1836.

46. Ibid., No. 1898, James W. Robinson to the commissioners, Jan. 23, 1836.

47. Ibid., No. 1925, meeting of San Antonio citizens and soldiers.

48. Ibid., No. 1930, J. C. Neill to the Executive Council, Jan. 27, 1836.

49. Ibid., No. 1931, J. C. Neill to Henry Smith, Jan. 27, 1836.

50. Donald Day and Jarry Herbert Ullom, editors, *The Autobiography of Sam Houston* (Norman: University of Oklahoma Press, 1947), p. 92.

51. Ibid., p. 97, and John H. Jenkins, general editor, *The Papers of the Texas Revolution*, No. 1942, Henry Smith Sam Houston, Jan. 28, 1836.

52. Ibid., No. 2134, editor of the *Red River Herald*.

53. Dorman H. Winfrey, editor, *Texas Indian Papers, 1825-1843* (Austin: Texas State Library, 1959), p. 10.

54. John H. Jenkins, general editor, *The Papers of the Texas Revolution*, No. 1941, J. C. Neill to government, Jan. 28, 1836.

55. Ibid., No. 1953.

56. Ibid., No. 1944, William B. Travis to Gov. Henry Smith, Jan. 28, 1836.

Chapter 11

1. Martha Anne Turner, *William Barret Travis, His Sword and His Pen* (Waco: Texian Press, 1972), p. 186. Sources differ on the day that Davy Crockett and his Tennessee followers arrived in San Antonio. Some authors have Neill leaving the day after Crockett arrived, and some suggest for one reason or another, he was not invited or did not attend the fandango. John Sutherland said that Crockett and his men arrived "a few days after Colonel Neill's departure." *The Fall of the Alamo* (San Antonio: The Naylor Company,

1936), p. 11. James T. DeShields, "Fall of the Alamo," in the *Dallas Morning News* magazine supplement of Feb. 5, 1911, agrees with Sutherland.

2. James T. DeShields, *Tall Men with Long Rifles* (San Antonio: The Naylor Company, 1935), p. 74.

3. John H. Jenkins, general editor, *The Papers of the Texas Revolution* (Austin: The Presidential Press, 1973), No. 2066, G. B. Jameson to Gov. Henry Smith, Feb. 11, 1836.

4. Ibid., No. 2074, William B. Travis to Gov. Smith, Feb. 12, 1836.

5. John J. Baugh was born in 1803. He moved to Texas from Virginia. After the siege of the Alamo, he refused to continue in the regular army but became adjutant of the Bexar post, where he died March 6, 1836, only a few hours after assuming command upon the death of Col. William B. Travis. Walter Prescott Webb, editor, *The Handbook of Texas* (Austin: The Texas State Historical Association, 1952), Vol. I, p. 123.

6. John H. Jenkins, general editor, *The Papers of the Texas Revolution*, No. 2076, John J. Baugh to Gov. Smith, Feb. 13, 1836.

7. Ibid., No. 2084, William B. Travis to Go. Smith, Feb. 13, 1836.

8. James T. DeShields, "Fall of the Alamo," Feb. 5, 1911.

9. Dr. John Sutherland was born in Virginia, May 11, 1792, but moved with his family to Tennessee. He was engaged in mercantile and banking businesses in Knoxville and in Tuscumbia, Alabama. He studied medicine in Alabama before moving to Texas in December, 1835, settling in Bexar in January, 1836. He and John W. Smith scouted the approaching Mexican forces to keep William B. Travis alerted to the enemy's movements. Dr. Sutherland and Smith attempted to rally the people of Gonzales to support the Alamo and were able to recruit the last men to enter the Bexar fortress. In 1860 he wrote an account of the Alamo. He died in Sutherland Springs April 11, 1867. Walter Prescott Webb, editor, *The Handbook of Texas*, Vol. II, pp. 691-692. See also John Sutherland, *The Fall of the Alamo* (San Antonio: The Naylor Company, 1936), pp. 7-8.

10. James T. DeShields, "Fall of the Alamo."

11. Will T. Hale and Dixon Marritt, *A History of Tennessee and Tennesseans* (Chicago: The Lewis Publishing Co., 1913), Vol. II, p. 356.

12. Ibid., Vol. II, p. 394.

13. Harry Howard Evans," Robb, Banker and Pioneer Railroad Builder of Ante-Bellum Louisiana," *The Louisiana Historical Quarterly*, Vol. 23, (January-October, 1940), p. 200.

14. Will T. Hale and Dixon Merritt, *A History of Tennessee and Tennesseans*, Vol. III, p. 809.

15. George Campbell Childress was born in Nashville, Tennessee, Jan. 8, 1804, the son of John and Elizabeth Robertson Childress. In December, 1834, while he was editor of the *National Banner and Nashville Advertiser*, he made a trip to Texas. Upon the death of his wife in 1835, Childress decided to relocate in Texas. Only several weeks after his arrival, he was elected to represent Robertson's Colony in the Convention of 1836. He introduced the Declaration

of Independence, written in his own hand. Walter Prescott Webb, editor, *The Handbook of Texas*, Vol. I, pp. 338-339.

16. H. R. W. Hill to George C. Childress, Nashville, Tennessee, November 19, 1835, cited in John Henry Brown, *Life and Times of Henry Smith* (Austin: The Steck Company, 1935), p. 292. See also John H. Jenkins, general editor, *The Papers of the Texas Revolution*, No. 1245.

17. John Henry Brown, *Life and Times of Henry Smith*, p. 304.

18. John H. Jenkins, general editor, *The Papers of the Texas Revolution*, No. 2085, William H. Wharton to Gov. Smith, Feb. 13, 1836. See also John Henry Brown, *Life and Times of Henry Smith*, p. 288.

19. John Henry Brown, *Life and Times of Henry Smith*, p. 288.

20. Ibid., pp. 289-290.

21. John W. Smith, a native of Virginia, was in Missouri when he married Harriet Stone. His wife refused to join him in settling in Green DeWitt's Colony in Texas, so Smith left his family. He was sent by Travis as the final messenger from the Alamo to the convention of 1836. He continued as an army scout; he returned to San Antonio to become that community's first mayor. *The New Handbook of Texas*, Vol. 5, pp. 1104. See also Wallace O. Chariton, *Exploring the Alamo Myths* (Plano: Wordware Publishing, Inc., 1992), p. 100.

22. Cleburne Huston, *Deaf Smith* (Waco: Texian Press, 1973), p. 49, citing Eugene C. Barker, "The San Jacinto Campaign," *The Texas Historical Association Quarterly*, Vol. IV, p. 307. J. H. Kuykendall, writing in Leonie Rummel Weyand and Houston Wade's *An Early History of Fayette County* (LaGrange: LaGrange Journal Plant, 1936), p. 125.

23. Three men, Horace Eggleston, Thomas R. Miller, and Stephen Smith, were engaged in retail trade in Gonzales at this time. Eggleston's store was located upon land he rented from George W. Davis. Edward A. Lukes, *DeWitt Colony of Texas* (Austin: Jenkins Publishing Company, 1976), p. 229 and fn 74. Edna DeWitt, *Lest We Forget* (Gonzales: Gonzales Inquirer), contains no publication date, but a photograph, opposite p. 61, indicates that Eggleston's home, built in 1838, was standing at the date the book was published. The home was made of hewn logs of burr oak with rafters of split saplings. Eggleston reopened his business in March 1836.

24. William Newland signed a Declaration of Independence in the town of Goliad Dec. 20, 1835. The document appeared in the Jan. 13, 1836, issue of the *Texas Republican*. In the document, signers agreed that "nothing short of independence can place us on solid ground," so signers resolved that "the former province and department of Texas is, and of right ought to be, a free, sovereign and independent state, and as such has, and of right ought to have all the powers, facilities, attributes, and immunities of other independent nations." Those who signed pledged their lives, fortunes, and sacred honor, to sustain the declaration. James N. Day, compiler, *The Texas Almanac, 1857-1873* (Waco: Texian Press, 1967), pp. 353-354.

25. Stephen Smith received title to land in the DeWitt Colony April 15, 1831. He built a home across from the jail plaza and fifty yards east of the fort. Later he erected a store adjacent to his residence. He served as *sindico procu-*

rador and with John McCoy received $95.75 to build a ferry over the Guadalupe River in 1833. Edward A. Lukes, *DeWitt Colony of Texas*, pp. 98, 143, 144, 151, 153.

26. J. B. Crawford is not listed in Dixon and Kemp, *The Heroes of San Jacinto*, so he apparently did not complete the march from Gonzales to the battlefield on which the Texaians won their independence. A. J. B. Crawford is on the tax list in Washington County for 1840. Worth S. Ray, *Austin Colony Pioneers* (Austin: The Pemberton Press, 1970), p. 85.

27. The reference probably is to a roundabout coat, "cut circulary at the bottom, having no tails, train or the like." a short, close fitting jacket. *The Random House Dictionary of the English Language* (New York: Random House, 1966), p. 1248.

28. D. W. Smith has not been identified.

29. Jennings O'Banion, listed on the receipt as Jennings Obannon, was born in South Carolina August 28, 1816. He served in Captain James Gillespie's 6th Company, 2nd Regiment of Texas Volunteers. He settled in Hays County and became known for his "enormous stature." He died Feb. 10, 1891. Sam Houston Dixon and Louis Wiltz Kemp, *The Heroes of San Jacinto* (Houston: The Anson Jones Press, 1932), p. 409, and Walter Prescott Webb, editor, *The Handbook of Texas*, Vol. I, p. 689.

30. Receipts in the Texas State Archives, 2-12/370, Texas State Library, Austin.

31. Solomon Bardwell, who received a pair of shoes, was in Neill's Artillery Company at San Antonio. Oddly enough, his enlistment papers show that he was in service from April 7 to July 12, 1836. He died in Lawrence County, Mississippi. Sam Houston Dixon and Louis Wiltz Kemp, *The Heroes of San Jacinto*, p. 76.

James Rich Pinchback, who also received a pair of shoes, enlisted Feb. 15. He received a headright certificate for one-third league of land in 1838. Ibid., p. 140.

Cornelius DeVore may have been another Texian for whom a purchase was made. He came to Texas from New Orleans in 1834 and enlisted the day the purchase was made at Stephen Smith's store. He was mustered out of service June 6, 1836, and died in Liberty County in 1884. Ibid., p. 368.

Another pair of shoes was purchased for Thomas Freeman, who came to Texas in 1836. He received one third of a league. Bill Moore, *Bastrop County, 1691-1900* (Wichita Falls: Nortex Press, 1977), p. 257.

Except for the names, identifications for the other eight soldiers for whom items were purchased that day have not been made.

32. Edna N. DeWitt, *Lest We Forget* (Gonzales: Gonzales Inquirer, no date), pp. 25-27.

33. Travis' letter was read to the convention and a copy appeared in the *Telegraph and Texas Register*, March 12, 1836.

34. Charles Edward Lester, *The Life of Sam Houston* (Philadelphia: Davis, Porter & Coates, 1866), p. 91. See also Donald Day and Harry Herbert Ullon, *The Autobiography of Sam Houston* (Norman: University of Oklahoma Press, 1947), p. 101.

35. The figure 374 is based on a report Lt. H. S. Stouffer, acting adjutant, and J. C. Neill, lieutenant colonel of the Regular Army of Texas, submitted to Gen. Houston March 12, 1836. Broken down, there were eight captains, eight first lieutenants, and five second lieutenants for a total of 21 officers. One quartermaster's sergeant, 25 sergeants, 13 corporals, one musician, and 313 privates made up the enlisted personnel. The report indicated that 25 of the men were "as yet unorganized." John H. Jenkins, general editor, *The Papers of the Texas Revolution*, No. 2309.

36. William Physick Zuber, *My Eighty Years in Texas* (Austin: University of Texas Press, 1971), pp. 52-53. The Zuber anecdote is questioned.

37. John Sutherland, *The Fall of the Alamo* (San Antonio: The Naylor Company, 1936), p. 41.

38. See C. Richard King, *Susanna Dickinson: Messenger of the Alamo* (Austin: Shoal Creek Publishers, 1976).

39. John H. Jenkins, general editor, *The Papers of the Texas Revolution*, No. 2289, J. C. Neill to Sam Houston, March 10, 1936.

40. Ibid., No. 2280, George W. Hockely to J. C. Neill, March 9, 1836.

41. Ibid., No. 2287.

42. Leonie Rummel Weyand and Houston Wade, *An Early History of Fayette County*, p. 126.

43. C. Richard King, *Susanna Dickinson: Messenger of the Alamo*, pp. 45-46.

44. T. R. Fehrenbach, *Lone Star* (New York: The Macmillan Company, 1968), p. 214.

45. Leonie Rummel Weyand and Houston Wade, *An Early History of Fayette County*, pp, 126-127.

46. M. K. Wisehart, *Sam Houston, American Giant*, p. 186. In fn 1, p. 660, Wisehart quotes Houston's speech to the U.S. Senate, Feb. 28, 1859, in which the former commander in chief expressed his feelings of horror that someone would poison something enemy troops would be so determined to consume.

47. Ibid., p. 186.

48. James T. DeShields, "Fall of the Alamo," *Dallas Morning News Magazine Supplement*, Feb. 5, 1911.

49. When James W. Fannin Jr. and his men repaired and stengthened La Bahia presidio, they renamed it. Walter Prescott Webb, editor, *The Handbook of Texas*, Vol. I, p. 624.

50. Donald Day and Harry Herbert Ullom, editors, *The Autobiography of Sam Houston*, p. 105.

51. Ibid.

52. Llerena B. Friend, *Sam Houston, the Great Designer* (Austin: University of Texas Press, 1954), p. 68.

53. William Physick Zuber, *My Eighty Days in Texas*, pp. 52-53.

Chapter 12

1. Andrew Jackson Houston, *Texas Independence* (Houston: The Anson Jones Press, 1938), p. 189.

2. John M. Allen, a Kentuckian, came to Texas in 1830. He enlisted in the Texas Army and was sent on a recruiting assignment, bringing approximately 230 men into uniform. He was elected Galveston's first mayor. He was United States marshal at the time of his death, Feb. 12, 1847. Walter Prescott Webb, editor, *The Handbook of Texas* (Austin: Texas State Historical Association, 1952), Vol. I, p. 30.

3. Almanzon Huston was quartermaster general of the army. Born in New York in 1799, he and his wife Elizabeth settled in San Augustine in 1824 and opened an inn. He represented the municipality in the Consultation of 1835. He died in August, 1861. Webb, editor, *The Handbook of Texas*, Vol. I, p. 869.

4. John H. Jenkins, general editor, *The Papers of the Texas Revolution*, No. 2489, J. M. Allen to Sam Houston, March 31, 1836. A letter from Henry Vallette to David Burnet, mailed from Cincinnati, Ohio, May 31, 1836, mentions, "We sent you two four Pounders last March which we hope will reach you in time to do some service." The letter, with the mistaken weight of the cannon, is No. 3230, John H. Jenkins.

5. On Jan. 16, 1836, William Bryan had been appointed a general agent. In May, he and Toby and Brother Company bought the brig *Packet* for Texas, and in January, 1843, he and James Morgan were appointed to negotiate a secret sale of the Texas Navy. Walter Prescott Webb, editor, *The Handbook of Texas*, Vol. I, p. 234.

6. The letter is quoted in W. N. Bate, *General Sidney Sherman* (Waco: Texian Press, 1974), p. 46. In his report to the House of Representatives, Oct. 20, 1836, David G. Burnet said that the Twin Sisters cannon were "completely mounted and ready for service." John H. Jenkins, *The Papers of the Texas Revolution*, No. 4329.

7. Andrew Houston, *Texas Independence*, pp. 198-199.

8. Ibid., p. 199.

9. John A. Wharton had been accused of writing articles in the *Advocate of People's Rights* to abuse Stephen F. Austin's character and to oppose his policy of conciliation with Mexico. In 1834 Wharton had faced William T. Austin in a duel caused by dispute over property and by factional jealousy. Born in Tennessee, Wharton was a child when both his parents died and he was taken by an uncle, a former United States Congressman, to live in his home. Wharton studied law, set up an office in New Orleans, then in 1829 decided to relocate with his brother in Brazoria. Walter Prescott Webb, *The Handbook of Texas*, Vol. II, pp. 888-889. Also from *Ranting Lions and Bleating Lambs*, an unpublished manuscript on the history of newspapers during the Republic of Texas period by C. Richard King.

10. In his official letter of appreciation, written to Daniel Drake, William Corry, Pulaski Smith, Nathan Leamans, and W. Chase, from Velasco, July 22, 1836, President Burnet called them "the two beautiful pieces of 'Hollow-ware.'" In this letter, he makes the first reference to the artillery as the *twin sisters* of Cincinnati.

11. A number of sources explain the history of the Twin Sisters. *The Texian*

and Emigrants' Guide of Dec. 19, 1835, quotes the *Cincinnati Evening Post,* Nov. 17, 1835. See E. W. Winkler, "The 'Twin Sisters' Cannon, 1836-1865, *The Southwestern Historical Quarterly,* Vol. 21, No. 1 (July 1917), pp. 61-64. See also H. Yoakum, *History of Texas* (New York: Redfield, 1855), Vol. II, p. 123.

12. "Recollections of S. F. Sparks," *The Southwestern Historical Quarterly,* Vol. 12, No. 1 (July 1908), p. 66. Sam Houston Dixon and Louis Wiltz Kemp, in *The Heroes of San Jacinto* (Houston: The Anson Jones Press, 1932), pp. 350-351, say that Sparks, born in Mississippi in 1819, entered the service at Nacogdoches on March 8, 1836, and on April 6 he and Thomas D. Brooks, Howard Bailey, Henry Chapman, and Henry L. Brewer, were ordered to report to Gen. Houston. Sparks was the last president of the Texas Veterans Association. He died in 1908.

13. M. K. Wisehart, *Sam Houston, American Giant* (Washington: Robert B. Luce, Inc., 1962), p. 208.

14. "Recollections of S. F. Sparks," *The Southwestern Historical Quarterly,* p. 66.

15. Walter Prescott Webb, editor, *The Handbook of Texas,* Vol. II, p. 106, and Sam Houston Dixon and Louis Wiltz Kemp, *The Heroes of San Jacinto,* pp. 81-82.

16. Sam Houston Dixon and Louis Wiltz Kemp, *The Heroes of San Jacinto,* pp. 78-79.

17. Ibid., pp. 84-85.

18. Ibid., pp. 80-81.

19 Ibid., pp. 85-86. See also *Ranting Lions and Bleating Lambs,* a manuscript on the history of journalism during the Republic of Texas period, by C. Richard King.

20. Odie Faulk, *General Tom Green, a Fightin' Texan* (Waco: Texian Press, 1963), p. 6.

21. John Henry Brown, *History of Texas* (St. Louis: L. E. Daniell, publisher, 1893), p. 6.

22. Andrew Jackson Houston, *Texas Independence,* p. 211.

23. Ibid.

24. Ibid., pp. 212-214.

25. Frank X. Tolbert, *The Day at San Jacinto* (New York: McGraw-Hill Book Company, 1959), p. 108, 112.

26. Dr. Shields Bookers was assistant surgeon for Sidney Sherman's second regiment. On July 30, 1839, he was named surgeon general for the Texas Army. He was on trial in San Antonio Sept. 11, 1840, when Adrian Woll captured the city, taking as prisoners the officials and spectators of the court. He was in Perote Prison when he accidentally was shot by a Mexican soldier. He was buried in the castle ditch. Walter Prescott Webb, editor, *The Handbook of Texas,* Vol. II, p. 188.

27. Marquis James, *The Raven* (Garden City: Blue Ribbon Books, 1929), p. 245.

28. Marquis James, *The Raven* (Garden City: Blue Ribbon Books, 1929), p. 245.

29. Samuel Adams Hammett, *A Stray Yankee in Texas*, (New York: Redfield, 1859), p. 253.

30. *The Southwestern Historical Quarterly*, Vol. 15, No. 2 (October 1911), p. 158.

31. Frank X. Tolbert, *The Day of San Jacinto*, pp. 113-114.

32. William A. Park, a New Yorker, emigrated to Texas in 1830 and received land in Austin's Third Colony. He volunteered for service in Capt. Peyton R. Splane's company march 20, 1836, but transferred to Captain Moreland's artillery company. He was discharged May 3, 1836.

33. Marquis James, *The Raven*, p. 247.

34. Nathaniel Lynch was one of Austin's Old Three Hundred, receiving title to a league of land in 1824. On Feb. 1, 1830, Lynch applied to the *ayuntamiento* of San Felipe for permission to begin operation of a public ferry over the point where Buffalo Bayou flows into San Jacinto River. The site became known as Lynch's Ferry and later as Lynchburg. Walter Prescott Webb, editor, *The Handbook of Texas*, Vol. II, p. 97.

35. Walter Prescott Webb, editor, *The Handbook of Texas*, Vol. I, p. 498.

36. W. S. Cleaver, "The Political Career of Lorenzo de Zavala," Unpublished thesis, The University of Texas, August 1931, p. 132. The document was reprinted in the *Telegraph and Texas Register*, Oct. 26, 1835.

37. Singleton was one of the Old Three Hundred. He received title to a sitio of land in 1824. Census entries show him to be a farmer and a stockman. Walter Prescott Webb, editor, *The Handbook of Texas*, Vol. II, p. 615.

38. Not until Sept. 4, 1839, did the heirs receive the deeds to the property. Deed Record Book E, Harris County courthouse.

39. When Samuel Hammett described the property in 1859, it was controlled by Zavala's widow. Hammett saw "a pretty cottage, which is quite worthy of notice." Samuel Adams Hammett, *A Stray Yankee in Texas* (New York: Redfield, 1859), p. 189. The cottage probably was considered "worthy of notice" because it was one of the few in Texas covered with plank and shingles and with a sash. *John Burke's Texas Almanac and Immigrant's Hand Book, 1879*, with an introduction by Dorman Winfrey (Austin: Steck-Warlick Company, 1969), p. 79.

40. Zavala had three children by his first wife, Teresa Correa, and three by his second wife, Emily West. Walter Prescott Webb, editor, *The Handbook of Texas*, Vol. I, p. 498; W. S. Cleaver, "The Political Career of Lorenzo de Zavala," pp. 125-126; Raymond Estep, "The Life of Lorenzo de Zavala," unpublished dissertation, The University of Texas, June 1942, fn. 347.

41. M. K. Wisehart, *Sam Houston, American Giant*, p. 129.

42. John D. Morris, a native of Virginia, was a member of Jesse Billingsley's volunteers, but when Neill was hit, he was assigned to look after the colonel. Because of this assignment, Morris was not present at the Battle of San Jacinto. He did, however, receive a certificate for land in Bexar County. When Frio County was created from Bexar, it took in the 641.64 acres owned by Morris. General Land Office Files 2-720 and 2-380. See also Bill Moore, *Bastrop County, 1691-1900*, p. 215, and Walter Prescott Webb, editor, *The Handbook of Texas*, Vol. I, p. 237.

43. As late as May 19, 1836, Zavala was in Velasco to confer with Mirabeau B. Lamar, secretary of war, about the use of the residence as a hospital. Lamar reported that Zavala "complains that he is put to considerable inconvenience in consequence of his house being made use of as a hospital for the sick and wounded prisoners." Lamar urged Col. James Morgan to use the *Cayuga* "to bring the sick and wounded to Galveston." Morgan was instructed to move only prisoners; should any sick or wounded Texians request to be relocated, however, Morgan was urged to instruct Capt. Harris to "bring them, otherwise you will give orders to have arrangements made for their comfort in the neighborhood." Mirabeau B. Lamar to James Morgan, Valasco, May 19, 1836, in W. N. Bate, *General Sidney Sherman*, p. 117. Bate also cites a letter from Lt. S. B. Raymond to Col. Morgan, May 14, 1836, p. 118.

44. John Shea was a justice of the peace in Houston during the days of the Republic. His docket book is in the Texas State Library, Austin.

45. Document signed by J. C. Neill, Houston, March 18, 1839, in Harrisburg County, Republic of Texas. The document is in the Texas State Library, Austin.

46. Born in Augusta, Georgia, Charles Mason moved to Texas in 1834. He was a member of Albert Martin's Company in the Battle of Gonzales, an orderly sergeant in F. L. Parrott's company in November, 1835, and in Henry Teal's company from April to June, 1836. He married Eveline DeWitt in 1838. Mason died in Gonzales in 1883. Walter Prescott Webb, editor, *The Handbook of Texas*, Vol. II, p. 154, and Sam Houston Dixon and Louis Wiltz Kemp, *The Heroes of San Jacinto*, p. 101. During Lamar's administration, Mason served as first auditor; under the second administration of Sam Houston, he was auditor, a position he continued to fill when Anson Jones was president. James M. Day, compiler, *The Texas Almanac, 1857-1873* (Waco: Texian Press, 1967), p. 58.

47. The town of Columbia was founded by Josiah Hughes Bell in 1826. The capitol of the Republic of Texas was located here from October through November 30, when the Congress voted to move the seat of government to Houston. The first Congress convened Oct. 22, the House of Representatives meeting in a two-store frame house and the Senate holding its sessions in a smaller building. Walter Prescott Webb, editor, *The Handbook of Texas*, Vol, II, p. 882. See Also C. Richard King, *The Lady Cannoneer* (Burnett: Eakin Press, 1981), pp. 86-94.

48. One week after Neill signed the document, Asa Brigham accepted Houston's appointment as treasurer of the Republic of Texas. He, his wife, and two children arrived in Texas from Louisiana in April, 1830. The *ayuntamiento* of San felipe elected him *sindico procurador* of Victoria, and in October, 1832, he was named treasurer of the Brazoria district. He served as a representative to the Convention of 1836, at which he signed the Declaration of Independence. In civic affairs he was alderman in Houston and mayor of Austin. He died July 2, 1844. Walter Prescott Webb, editor, *The Handbook of Texas*, Vol. I, p. 216.

49. Papers are in the Archives of the Texas State Library, Austin.

Chapter 13

1. James Gaines was a brother of General Edward Pendleton Gaines of the United States Army. He had gone with his brother to Nashville, Tennessee, in 1803, and in 1805 was with him in visiting Natchitoches, Louisiana. He established his ferry and mercantile store where the old San Antonio Road crossed the Sabine River. After serving with the Magee expedition, he returned to his business and ferry on the Sabine. George Louis Crocket, *Two Centuries in East Texas* (Dallas: The Southwest Press, 1932), p. 70.

The Handbook of Texas, Vol. I, p. 659, identifies him as the son of Richard and Jemina Pendleton Gaines. He was born in Culpepper County, Virginia, circa 1776. He was married to Suzanna Norris, and they were the parents of at least five children. Gaines joined the gold rush to California, where he died in November 1856.

2. John A. Williams in September, 1824, wrote Stephen F. Austin that he, his wife, and several slaves intended joining the Austin colony if he could get good land on the Brazos or San Bernard rivers. By 1829 he relocated at Pine Bluff on the Trinity, and in 1832 he had become alcalde at Anahuac. William H. Wharton offered $500 for Williams' arrest on grounds that he had prevented volunteers from joining the Texas Army at Gonzales. He escaped into New Orleans. *The Handbook of Texas*, Vol. II, p. 913.

3. Almanzon Huston served on the Permanent Council organized Oct. 11, 1835. After arriving at San Felipe several days later, Huston was chosen secretary. (p. 171) He later was on the committee drawing up plans for the military department of a provisional government. His report was read to the Consultation. (p. 173) George Louis Crocket, *Two Centires in East Texas*.

4. Alexander Horton, son of Julius and Susan Purnell Horton, was born April 18, 1810, in Halifax County, North Carolina. In 1823, he, his widowed mother and other members of the family came to Texas, and in 1824 Alexander, his brother Sam W., and his brother-in-law, James Whitis Bullock built a cabin. When the other two returned to Louisiana, 13-year-old Alexander took charge of the property. He participated in putting down the Fredonian Rebellion and fought in the Battle of Nacogdoches in 1832. He served as sheriff of the Ayish Bayou and represented his community in the Consultation of 1835. He was aide-de-camp when Sam Houston was appointed commander in chief of the Texas Army. He died on his farm near San Augustine Jan. 11, 1894. *The Handbook of Texas*, Vol. I, p. 841.

5. George Louis Crockett, *Two Centuries in East Texas*, pp. 85-87, 104-109.

6. Ibid., pp. 315-316.

7. There is some disagreement over the number of McFarland Lodge. *The Texas Lodge System of Candidate Information*, Book 1, prepared by the Grand Lodge of Texas, AF.&AM., mentions that Anson Jones received the Charter for Holland Lodge No. 36 on the prairie between Groce's and San Jacinto. Dr. Jones retained the Charter in his saddlebags through the battle, and in October, 1837, the Lodge was re-opened in Houston. "There were then in existence two other Lodges in Texas chartered by the Grand Lodge of Louisiana—Milam No. 40 at Nacogdoches and McFarland No. 41 at San

Augustine." (p. 15). Through the transcript of the minutes of McFarland Lodge, a copy of which is in the Eugene C. Barker Texas History Center at The University of Texas, Austin, the lodge is given variously as No. 40 and as No. 41. The transcript was prepared in 1953 under the direction of James D. Carter, outstanding historian of Masonry in this area.

8. A J. B. Denton is in the 1840 census from Red River County. That census shows him to be the owner of 640 acres under a completed title (patented), one town lot, and one silver watch. Gifford White, editor, *The 1840 Census of the Republic of Texas*, (Austin: The Pemberton Press, 1966), p. 141. There is no explanation of the emergency.

9. Transcript of Minutes of McFarland Lodge No. 41, (San Augustine, Texas, August 13, 1837, to December 27, 1848), p. 22.

10. George Louis Crocket, *Two Centuries in East Texas*, p. 319.

11. Transcript of Minutes of McFarland Lodge No. 41, p. 23.

12. Wyatt Hanks and Donald McDonald were partners in a saw mill on Ayish Bayou, south of San Augustine. (p. 88) Hanks had moved from the Kentucky-Indiana area with his mother and brothers, James and Horatio. The family was related to Nancy Hanks, the mother of Abraham Lincoln. Wyatt served as a delegate from Bevil in Jasper County to the Constultation of 1835. (pp. 125, 172) George Louis Crocket, *Two Centuries in East Texas*.

13. Transcript of Minutes of McFarland Lodge No. 41, p. 23.

14. Robert Bruce Irvine was a citizen of San Augustine as early as 1835. He was a lieutenant in the volunteer army, voting against the siege of Bexar. On Dec. 6, 1835, Sam Houston ordered him to recruit men for the regular army and to report with a command by March, 1836. Irvine was commended by Almanzon Huston for his vigilance in July, 1835, and in August, 1836, was appointed assistant quartermaster general with orders to report to Velasco. In October, 1837, he was in a group of San Augustine citizens who invited Mirabeau B. Lamar to a ball in the Mansion Hall to commemorate the Battle of Concepcion. *The Handbook of Texas*, Vol. I, p. 896.

15. Donald McDonald was a partner with Wyatt Hanks in a sawmill on Ayish Bayou, (p. 88), and the two were neighbors. McDonald was a Scotchman who had fought with the British Army in the war of 1812, and he always contended that the British had won the Battle at Lundy's Lane. For a year or two, he operated a ferry on the Sabine River. (p. 70). He became sheriff in 1856 and served two terms. (p. 214). George Louis Crocket, *Two Centuries in East Texas*.

16. Transcript of Minutes of McFarland Lodge No. 41, p. 33.

Ed Knipstein, who served as tiler of lodges in Hamilton and Stephenville, explained in an interview with the author May 19, 1984, that frequently tilers were paid to serve as custodians of the hall. He received a small payment each month for his "keeping of the lodge hall" in Hamilton.

Chapter 14

1. In the fall of 1822 the first settlers located on a site that grew into the town of Washington, located on the banks of the Brazos. In March, 1836, when delegates arrived for a convention, they found Washington containing only

one house large enough for the sessions, but they adopted the Declaration of Independence as written by George C. Childress. The 58 delegates affixed their signatures, witnessing the birth of the Republic of Texas. On March 17, this group adopted the constitution for Texas.

For 19 days, Washington was the capital of the provisional government, which was removed to Harrisburg, to Galveston, to Velasco, to Houston, and in 1839 to Austin. Three years later, however, it was removed to Washington then to Houston, but on Sept. 16, by order of Sam Houston the government was returned to Washington and remained there until Texas became a state.

The town of Washington at the time of the Indian conclaves were in progress was "at the zenith of her glory and attained her greatest commercial importance. With a population of 1,500 souls (some say 4,000 to 5,000), she was one of the largest towns in Texas. Her water facilities made her a distributing point for Middle Texas. The old town was prospering and building on safe and sure lines until she in 1858 made the fatal error of refusing to give a bonus of $11,000 to the Houston & Texas Central Railroad. "Washington-on-the-Brazos," *Frontier Times*, Vol. 6, No. 7 (April 1929) pp. 302-303.

2. Osnaburg is "a heavy, coarse cotton in a plain weave" used for grain sacks and sportswear. *The Random House Dictionary of the English Language* (New York: Random House, 1970), p. 1018. The name comes from Osnabruck, an industrial city in Lower Saxony, Germany, which once specialized in linen textiles. *Collier's Encyclopedia* (New York: The Crowell-Collier Publishing Co., 1963), Vol. 18, p. 242. Probably with reason, the cloth is known in the south as slave's material. An advertisement for a runaway slave in *The South Carolina Gazette*, Dec. 19, 1732, described the fugitive as wearing an "oznhburg jacket." The early settlers made "coats, breeches, and gowns" of osnaburg. Lucy Barton, *Historic Costumes for the Stage* (Boston: Walter H. Baker Company, 1935), p. 589.

3. Jonnie Lockhart Wallis, *Sixty Years on the Brazos* (Ann Arbor: University Microfilm, Inc., 1966), p. 156.

4. Ibid.

5. T. R. Havins, "Noah T. Byers at Torrey's Trading Post," *Texana*, Vol. VIII, No. 4, 1950, p. 329.

6. Eldridge, "a man of education, experience, courage, and the highest order of integrity," received Houston's appointment as General Superintendent of Indian Affairs. Hamilton Bee said of him, "He was an admirable character, brave, cool, determined in danger, faithful to public trusts and loving in his friendshps." His work as superintendent is treated interestingly by John Henry Brown, *History of Texas* (St. Louis: L. E. Danioell, Publisher, 1893), Vol. I, pp. 262-279.

Eldridge was born in New York City on May 8, 1818. He moved to Texas from Connecticut in 1837. In 1847 he was appointed assistant paymaster of the U.S. Navy. He participated in the laying of the Atlantic telegraph cable. He died in New York on August 14, 1881. Walter Prescott Webb, editor, *The Handbook of Texas* (Austin: The Texas State Historical Association, 1952), Vol. I, p. 551.

7. T. R. Havins, "Noah T. Byars at Torrey's Traiding Post," p. 329. Walter Prescott Webb, editor, *The Handbook of Texas*, Vol. I, p. 880.

8. Jonnie Lockhart Wallis, *Sixty Years on the Brazos* (Ann Arbor: University Microfilm, Inc., 1966).

9. George Whitifield Terrell, a native of Kentucky, was 40 years of age when he served as Indian commissioner. As a youth, he had moved to Tennessee and in 1828 Sam Houston, governor of Tennessee, appointed him district attorney. *The Handbook of Texas*, Vol. II, p. 726.

10. Herbert Gambrell, *Anson Jones: The Last President of Texas* (Garden City: Doubleday and Co., Inc., 1948), p. 279.

11. John Henry Brown, *History of Texas* (St. Louis: L. E. Daniell, Publisher, 1893), Vol. II, p. 264.

12. Dorman H. Winfrey, editor, *Texas Indian Papers, 1825-1843* (Austin: Texas State Library, 1960), p. 152.

13. Ibid., p. 157.

14. Ibid.

15. Ibid., p. 160.

16. Jonnie Lockhart Wallis, *Sixty Years on the Brazos*, p. 101.

17. Ibid.

18. Dorman H. Winfred, editor, *Texas Indian Papers, 1825-1843*, p. 161.

19. Ibid., p. 163.

20. Jonnie Lockhart Wallis, *Sixty Years on the Brazos*, p. 102.

21. Ibid.

22. *The Quarterly of the Texas State Historical Association*, Vol. IV, No. 4, April 1903, p. 300. See also Herbert Gambrell, *Anson Jones: The Last President of Texas*, p. 280. By May, 1836, the remains of the Alamo were crumbling, stones from the walls scattered over the plaza. Later these stones were gathered, and Nangle, the artist, and Joseph Cox, a stonecutter, fashioned them into souvenir items offered for sale. An article in the New Orleans *Crescent*, May 28, 1851, quoted in the *Quarterly*, mentions that Nangle and Cox had made the items in San Antonio. *The Northern Standard*, Dec. 23, 1843, reports that Nangle, "an Englishman by birth" and a self-taught artist, was dead by the time the Alamo monument he created was displayed in New Orleans. The monument Nangle hoped to sell to the Texas government became the property of Lezch and Cavanaugh of New Orleans. (*Texas State Gazette*, Jan 29, 1853). Eventually the monument was placed in the Texas capitol, and only a fragment was rescued from the fire which destroyed the building on Nov. 9, 1881. (*The Quarterly of the Texas State Historical Association*, Vol. VI, No. 4, April, 1903) p. 300.

23. Herbert Gambrell, *Anson Jones: The Last President of Texas*, p. 280.

24. Luis Sanchez was listed in the Nacogdoches census of 1831 as a 27-year-old worker with a wife and two children. Walter Prescott Webb, editor, *The Handbook of Texas*, Vol. II, p. 563. *Old Northwest Texas* by Nancy T. Samuels and Barbara R. Knox, Vol. I-B, pp. 597-598, says he was born of Mexican-Indian parentage. The book was published by the Fort Worth Genealogical Society in 1981. Roy D. Holt, *Heap Many Texas Chiefs* (San Antonio: The Naylor

Company, 1966), says Sanchez as a boy was stolen by the Indians and later was made chief of the Keechi tribe. (p. 279).

25. Jesse Chisholm was born in Tennessee of Scotch and Indian ancestry. His mother was a sister of Houston's Indian wife and a relative of the forebearers of Will Rogers. Roy D. Holt, *Heap Many Texas Chiefs*, pp. 218-219. He settled near Fort Gibson, Arkansas, and became a trader. He spoke 14 Indian languages. He died of food poisoning on March 4, 1868, and was buried at the trading post in present Blaine County, Oklahoma. Walter Prescott Webb, editor, *The Handbook of Texas*, Vol. I, p. 341.

26. Herbert Gambrell, *Anson Jones: The Last President of Texas*, p. 280.

27. Ibid., pp. 280-281. The embrace consisted of one man putting his arm in front of his chest, his friend putting an arm on top, etc. Then friends pressed their arms together.

28. Jonnie Lockhart Wallis, *Sixty Years on the Brazos*, p. 104.

29. Ibid.

30. Dorman H. Winfred, *Texas Indian Papers, 1825-1843*, p. 229.

31. Ibid., pp. 214-216.

32. Ibid., p. 217.

33. John Henry Brown, *History of Texas*, (St. Louis: L. E. Daniell Publishers, 1893), Vol. I, pp. 275-276.

Chapter 15

1. Born circa 1792, Thomas G. Western came to Texas in 1831 and settled near Goliad, which elected him to the Consultation of 1835. He was unable to attend, however. He raised a company of 48 calvary troops to serve for the duration of the Texas Revolution and officiated at the burial of the remains of the victims of the Alamo. After work as a ranger, 1838-1839, he settled in Harris county and was an interpreter and translator in the General Land Office. He was a charter member of the Masonic Grand Lodge of Texas. He died in Houston Dec. 19, 1847. Walter Prescott Webb, *The Handbook of Texas*, Vol. II, p. 884-885.

2. A trading post was organized by John F., David K., and Thomas S. Torrey with George Barnard and Sam Houston as two of the stockholders. The firm established posts at New Braunfels and at the Falls of the Brazos. The post at Tehaucana Creek, actually at the mouth of the Trading House Creek tributary of Tehaucana Creek, was authorized by the Republic of Texas and was designated Post No. 2. Thomas S. Torrey died in 1843, after returning from a trip with Barnard to locate a site for a new post. In 1843 President Houston sent David K. Torrey to New York to purchase articles for Indian trade. He was killed by Indians in 1849. John F. Torrey died in San Antonio in 1893. Walter Prescott Webb, *The Handbook of Texas*, Vol. II, p. 790.

John Torrey Jewelry and Fancy Goods Store was located on Main Street, Houston, and between 1840 and 1844, offered jewelry, books, stationery, hardware, and similar items. This store marked the beginning of the firm. Henry C. Armbuster, "Torreys Trading Post," *Texana*, Vol. VII, No. 2, Summer, 1964, p. 113. See also Henry C. Armbuster, "John F. Torrey's New Braunfels Years," *Texana*, Vol. IV, No. 3, Fall, 1966, pp. 201-212.

John Henry Brown, *History of Texas,* Vol. I, p. 278, says there were several Torrey brothers: David K., born in 1815, and killed by the Mescaleros near Presidio del Norte on Christmas Day, 1849; John F., born in 1817, and famed as a Houston merchant and as a woolen manufacturer in New Braunfels; Thomas B., born in 1819 and died at the treaty grounds; James N., born in 1821, and recipient of a black bean on the Mier expedition in March, 1843. James N. and Thomas S. were buried on Monument Hill near La Grange. Three other brothers, Judson, George B., and Abraham, came to Texas. The father of the family died in New Braunfels in 1873.

3. Dorman H. Winfrey, editor, *Texas Indian Papers, 1844-1845* (Austin: Texas State Library, 1960), pp. 9-10.

4. Washington-on-the-Brazos had been proposed as capital of the Republic of Texas, but an election approved the town of Houston instead. In 1842, when Republic officials left Austin for fear of Mexican invasion, Washington again became the temporary seat of government. As president of the Republic, Houston ordered the archives removed to Washington from Austin, the incident resulting in the archives war. See C. Richard King, *The Lady Cannoneer,* (Burnet: Ed Eakin Press, 1981).

5. James Whitesides was one of Stephen F. Austin's Old Three Hundred Colonists, original settlers. He received title to land in Grimes, Brazos, and Waller counties. Walter Prescott Webb, editor, *The Handbook of Texas,* Vol. II, p. 899.

Worth S. Ray in *Austin Colony Pioneers* (Austin: The Pemberton Press, 1970) calls "Uncle Jimmie" Whitesides "one of the great characters of the colony." Daniel Shipman tells in his memoirs in the Houston *Telegraph* in 1870 that he called on the Whitesides. Uncle Jimmie and Aunt Betty "met us at the door, asking us what she could do for us—she knew we were wet and chilly—said she had no coffee, but she ran off and got us a good drink of butter milk...."

The Whitesides were from Tennessee. His brother Jenkins was a prominent lawyer.

James and Betty Whitesides ran the Whitesides Hotel in San Felipe, and he was jailer. p. 244-247.

6. Dorman H. Winfrey, *Texas Indian Papers,* p. 10.

7. M. K. Wisehart, *Sam Houston, American Giant* (Washington: Robert B. Luce, Inc., 1952), pp. 3-5.

8. Dorman H. Winfrey, *Texas Indian Papers,* pp. 12, 16-17, 19.

9. Ferdinand Roemer, *Roemer's Texas* (San Antonio: Standard Printing Company, 1935), p. 191.

10. Dorman Winfrey, *Texas Indian Papers,* p. 13.

11. Ibid.

12. Jonnie Lockhart Wallis, *Sixty Years on the Brazos,* p. 108.

13. Amelia W. Williams and Eugene C. Barker, editors, *The Writings of Sam Houston* (Austin: Jenkins Publishing Co., 1970), Vol. IV, p. 313.

14. Dorman H. Winfrey, *Texas Indian Papers,* pp. 11, 12.

15. Lillian Schiller St. Romain, *A History of Western Falls County, Texas* (Austin: The Texas State Historical Association, 1951), p. 2.

16. Ferdinand Roemer, *Roemer's Texas,* p. 191.

17. Jonnie Lockhart Wallis, *Sixty Years on the Brazos*, p. 111.
18. Ibid.
19. Dorman H. Winfrey, *Texas Indian Papers*, p. 13.
20. Jonnie Lockhart Wallis, *Sixty Years on the Brazos*, p. 110.
21. Born in Connecticut in 1818, George Barnard had come to Texas in 1838 and in 1841 had participated in the Santa Fe Expedition. He was in poor health following his release from Perote Prison, but he became associated with David K. and John F. Torrey. Walter Prescott Webb, editor, *The Handbook of Texas*, Vol. I, p. 111.
22. Henry C. Armbruster in "Torreys Trading Post," published in *Texana*, Vol. II, No. 2, Summer, 1964, describes Barnard as "something of a dandy." He "wore silken underwear, and, while he sold 'fine dress coats' to frontier farmers and substantial plantation owners for eight and ten dollars each, he was paying Lockwood and Dubois on Broadway, New York, thirty-five dollars each for his dress coats and twenty dollars for his business coats . . . and from ten to fifteen dollars a pair for cashmere trousers." P. 119.
23. Ibid., p. 305.
24. Ibid., p. 307.
25. Ibid.
26. Dorman H. Winfrey, editor, *Texas Indian Papers*, pp. 13-17.
27. Ibid, p. 17.
28. Ibid.
29. Ibid., pp. 16, 19.
30. Ibid., p. 18.
31. Roy D. Holt, *Heap Many Texas Chiefs*, (San Antonio: The Naylor Company, 1966), pp. 298-300. Webb, *The Handbook of Texas*, Vol. II, p. 563.
32. Dorman H. Winfrey, *Texas Indian Papers*, p. 20.
33. Ibid.
34. Williams and Barker, *The Writings of Sam Houston*, Vol. II, p. 563.
35. Ibid.
36. Ibid., p. 294.
37. Dorman H. Winfrey, *Texas Indian Papers*, p. 20.
38. Ibid., pp. 20-21.
39. Ibid., p. 21.
40. Ibid., p. 26.
41. Ibid., pp. 30-31.
42. Ibid., pp. 35-40.
43. Ibid., pp. 39-40.
44. Ibid., pp. 40-42.
45. Ibid., pp. 42-49.
46. Ibid., pp. 49-56.
47. Ibid., pp. 56-59.
48. Ibid., pp. 59-61.
49. Ibid., p. 63.
50. Ibid.
51. Ibid., pp. 69-70.

52. Ibid., pp. 70-71.

Chapter 16
1. Dorman H. Winfrey, editor, *Texas Indian Papers. 1844-1845* (Austin: Texas State Library, 1960), p. 74.
2. Ibid., p. 76.
3. Ibid., p. 79.
4. Ibid., p. 88.
5. Ibid., p. 89.
6. Ibid., pp. 93-94.
7. Ibid., p. 95.
8. Ibid., p. 98.
9. Ibid., pp. 95-96.
10. Ibid., p. 99.
11. Ibid., p. 100.
12. Ibid., p. 104.
13. San Marcos.
14. Dorman H. Winfrey, editor, *Texas Indian Papers*, pp. 109-114.
15. Ibid., p. 119.
16. Ibid., p. 123.
17. Ibid., pp. 125-126.
18. Daniel G. Watson served as witness to a letter Mopechucope, Comanche chief, wrote Sam Houston March 21, 1844. With John Conner, Watson attempted to round up the Comanches in the spring of 1844 (p. 44) and was interpreter at the Falls conclave in the autumn (p. 104). T. G. Western said he was an "excellent and competent" man in his field. Dorman H. Winfred, *Texas Indian Papers, 1844-1845*, p. 231.
19. John Conner is identified as a "fearless and intelligent Delaware Indian" who served the whites faithfully. Col. Richard I. Dodge said he had "a more minute and extensive personal knowledge of the North American continent than any other man." When Conner was 18 he struck out across the west, making his way to the mouth of the Columbia River, hiking southward along the Pacific coast, returning to his home by way of Texas. Later he visited Mexico City. In 1848 he was in Washington with a delegation of Indians from Texas. He and Jesse Chisholm were interpreters in a peace council between the United States and the Indians of Texas in 1850. To "Chief John Conner for services rendered," the Legislature on June 17, 1853, granted him a league of land. Roy D. Holt, *Heap Many Texas Chiefs*, pp. 191-1941.
20. Dorman H. Winfrey, editor, *Texas Indian Papers*, p. 129.
21. Ibid., p. 130.

Chapter 17
1. Dorman H. Winfrey, editor, *Texas Indian Papers, 1844-1845* (Austin: Texas State Library, 1960), p. 321.
2. Ibid., p. 354.
3. Born in the Spartanburg district of South Carolina, May 17, 1808,

Byars had lived in Georgia and had learned the trade of blacksmithing and gunsmithing. He settled in Washington, Texas, in 1835, going into partnership with Philip M. Mercer. It was in their business house that the convention met to adopt the Declaration of Independence in 1836. He served as sergeant-at-arms of the Republic of Texas Senate. His appointment as gunsmith at Post No. 2 came in February, 1845, and he drew a stipend of $500 annually. Nancy Timons Samuels and Barbara Roach Knox, *Old Northwest Texas*, (Fort Worth: Fort Worth Genealogical Society, 1981), I-B, pp. 385-388.

    4. Roy D. Holt, *Heap Many Texas Chiefs* (San Antonio: The Naylor Company, 1966), p. 26.

    5. *Old Northwest Texas*, I-B, pp. 385-388. See also T. R. Havins, "Noah T. Byars at Torrey's Trading Post," *Texana*, Vol. VIII, No. 4, 1950, p. 335.

    6. Dorman H. Winfrey, editor, *Texas Indian Papers*, p. 355.

    7. Ibid., p. 322.

    8. Ibid., p. 349.

    9. Ibid., p. 350.

    10. Ibid., p. 327.

    11. Ibid., p. 332.

    12. Ibid., p. 334 and p. 348.

    13. Ibid., p. 366.

    14. Ibid., p. 343.

    15. Ibid., p. 344.

    16. Ibid.

    17. Ibid., p. 370.

    18. Ibid., p. 371.

    19. Ibid., p. 372.

    20. Kenneth Neighbours, *Indian Exodus* (Burnet: Nortex Inc., 1973), p. 36.

    21. Amelia W. Williams and Eugene C. Barker, *The Writings of Sam Houston* (Austin: Jenkins Publishing Co., 1970), Vol. IV, pp. 380-381.

Chapter 18

    1. On August 6, 1841, Jonathan Bird was appointed a major under Gen. Edward H. Tarrant and commissioned to build a fort and settlement on the West Fork of the Trinity River. After some difficulty, he recruited approximately forty men and began work on the site. Harassed by Indians, the men managed to complete a log stockade, a blockhouse fort, and several houses. All supplies for maintaining Bird's Fort were hauled from Bonham at Bird's personal expense. Walter Prescott Webb, editor, *The Handbook of Texas* (Austin: Texas State Historical Association, 1952), Vol. I, p. 163.

    2. Amelia W. Williams and Eugene C. Barker, editors, *The Writings of Sam Houston* (Austin: The Jenkins Publishing Co., 1970), Vol. IV, p. 536.

    3. A native of Virginia, William G. Cooke had entered Texas with a company of New Orleans Greys and had participated in the Siege of Bexar in 1835. He was discharged from the Texas Army in 1837 and went into the drug business in Houston, but in August, 1839, he re-enlisted, receiving a commission as quartermaster general. Following his release from prison following the

Texian Santa Fe Expedition, he was commissioned adjutant general of the militia. Walter Prescott Webb, editor, *The Handbook of Texas*, Vol. I, p. 406.

4. Washington D. Miller, born in Charleston, South Carolina, in 1814, was graduated in engineering from the University of Alabama. He became an attorney in Gonzales, Texas, and later was associated with William H. Cushney in publishing the *National Register* newspaper. Elizabeth LeNoir Jennett, *Biographical Directory of the Texan Conventions and Congresses, 1832-1845*, no place or date of publication cited, p. 140.

5. Amelia W. William and Eugene C. Barker, editors, *The Writing of Sam Houston*, Vol. IV, p. 244.

6. *Journals of the Senate of the Eighth Congress of the Republic of Texas* (Washington: Miller and Cushney, 1845), p. 75.

7. Ibid.

8. Document No. 3301, Andrew Jackson Papers in the Texas State Library.

9. Amelia W. Williams and Eugene C. Barker, editors, *The Writing of Sam Houston*, pp. 536-537. See also *Executive Record Book* No. 40, President Sam Houston, Dec. 1841-1844. No. 2-1/39, Texas State Library.

10. *The Journal of the Senate of the Eighth Congress of the Republic of Texas*, p. 193.

11. John H. Moffitt had come to Texas in 1840 and received title to land near Nacogdoches. He taught school in San Augustine and Nacogdoches until he was named representative. He was in the Senate of the third legislature, 1849-1850, and represented Tyler in the Democratic State Convention of 1857. Walter Prescott Webb, editor, *The Handbook of Texas*, Vol. II, p. 220. See also Elizabeth LeNoir Jennett, *Biographical Directory of the Texan Conventions and Congresses, 1832-1845*, p. 141.

12. Stanley Siegel, *A Political History of the Texas Republic* (Austin: University of Texas Press, 1956), p. 215, citing a correspondent of the Houston *Morning Star*, Dec. 22, 1842. Marquis James, *The Raven* (Garden City: Blue Ribbon Books. 1929), p. 329, says the House met in what had been Hatfield's saloon when Houston had persuaded the group to meet there. Houston convinced the managers of the gambling establishment in the same structure to surrender their quarters to the lawmakers.

13. *The Journal of the House of Representatives of the Eighth Congress of the Republic of Texas*, p. 51.

14. Benjamin F. Parker was born in Illinois in 1833. He moved to Texas with his father and uncles. He taught school and surveyed until elected representative for Anderson County in the Sixth and Eighth Congresses. Ordained Oct. 9, 1864, he continued to preach until his death in 1896. Walter Prescott Webb, editor, *The Handbook of Texas*, Vol. II, p. 335.

15. *The Journal of the House of Representatives of the Eighth Congress of the Republic of Texas*, p. 60.

16. William L. Cazneau, born in Massachusetts, moved to Texas in 1830 to establish a mercantile business. He was appointed commissary general by Mirabeau B. Lamar and represented Travis County in the Seventh, Eighth,

and Ninth Congresses. Walter Prescott Webb, editor, *The Handbook of Texas*, Vol. I, p. 318.

17. John M. Lewis, Montgomery County farmer, came to Texas in 1842 from Virginia. He was an unsuccessful candidate for the United States Congress in 1846. Elizabeth LeNoir Jennett, *Biographical Directory of the Texan Conventions and Congresses*, p. 124.

18. A Elijah Simmons Collard was president of the board of land commissioners of Montgomery in 1837 and served as justice of the peace. Too, a Collards Creek is in the southern section of Madison County, named for John S. Collard, to whom the land was granted originally. Walter Prescott Webb, editor, *The Handbook of Texas*, Vol. I, p. 374.

19. *The Journal of the House of Representatives of the Ninth Congress of the Republic of Texas*, p. 79.

20. Ibid., p. 91.

21. Senator Timothy Pillsbury was born in Massachusetts in 1780. He moved to Maine, where he was a sea captain, John Henry Brown, *History of Texas* (St. Louis: L. E. Daniell, Publisher, 1893), p. 311. He was engaged in shipping. He served in the Maine legislature and was a member of the Executive Council when he made an unsuccessful campaign for Congress in 1834. He moved to Ohio briefly then resided in New Orleans until 1837, when he settled in Brazoria County, Texas, where he was engaged in agriculture. He represented Brazoria in the House of the Fifth Congress and was in the Senate of the Sixth. He served as chief justice of Brazoria County then returned to the Senate of the Ninth Congress. He died Nov. 23, 1858. Walter Prescott Webb, editor, *The Handbook of Texas*, Vol. I, p. 379.

22. *Journals of the Senate of the Ninth Congress of the Republic of Texas*, p. 142.

23. Ibid., p. 157.

24. Ibid., p. 160.

25. Ibid., p. 166.

26. *Telegraph and Texas Register*, March 1, 1845.

27. Benjamin E. Tarver was born May 1, 1802, possibly in Virginia. In 1844 he owned a farm three or four miles north of Brenham, Texas. He represented Washington County in the House of the Third Legislature, Washington and Burleson counties in the Fourth Legislature, and Washington in the Sixth. He died at Brenham on April 22, 1879. Walter Prescott Webb, *The Handbook of Texas*, Vol. II, p. 708. See also Worth S. Rav, *Austin Colony Pioneers* (Austin: The Pemberton Press, 1970), p. 223.

28. Pension Papers, 2-12-370, Texas State Library.

Chapter 19

1. James Smith received title to a league of land on the Colorado Nov. 12, 1832, Bill Moore, *Bastrop County*, p. 30, and served as procuradore on the ayuntamiento. He was associate justice following his appointment in November, 1837. Bill Moore, *Bastrop County*, p. 57.

2. Daniel Gray was granted land by the ayuntamiento in 1835. Bill Moore, *Bastrop County*, p. 38. He came to Texas in April, 1831. During the

Texas Revolution he furnished a steel mill. He died in 1847. Bill Moore, *Bastrop County*, p. 207-8.

3. Bastrop County Deed Book D, p. 158.

4. William Smith sought relief for the heirs of the deceased William H. Smith. Relief was approved Jan. 14, 1840. See *Journals of the Fourth Congress of the Republic of Texas, 1839-1840*, edited by Harriet Smither, (Austin: Von-Boeckmann-Jones, III), p. 253.

5. Bastrop County Deed Book I, p. 181.

6. The first issue of the *Austin City Gazette* appeared October 30, 1839, under the direction of Samuel Whiting, who had moved his press and type from Houston. George K. Teulon served as editor from the first issue until Feb. 2, 1842. John Melton Wallace, *Gaceta to Gazette* (Austin: The Department of Journalism Development Program, The University of Texas, 1966), pp. 5-6.

7. Jacob W. Cruger and George W. Bonnell established the *Texas Centinel* in Austin Jan. 15, 1840, as a rival to the *Austin City Gazette*. A prospectus had called the newspaper *Texas Centinel*. Cruger and Bonnell dissolved their partnership in July, 1840, leaving Bonnell to continue the publication. In December, 1840, however, Jacob Cruger returned to Austin and with Martin Carroll Wing purchased the paper from Bonnell. By the March 25, 1841, issue, the name of the paper had been changed to *Centinel,* and Wing was serving as publisher. Ibid, pp. 48-9.

8. The Battle of Horseshoe Bend was fought in Alabama in March, 1814, and resulted in the destruction of the Creek Nation. John Holland Jenkins writes in his recollections that Col. Neill was wounded in the conflict.

9. *Texas Sentinel,* June 17, 1841.

10. Ibid., August 12, 1841.

11. M. K. Wisehart, *Sam Houston, American Giant* (Washington; Robert B. Luce, Inc., 1962), pp. 17-19.

12. Donald Day and Harry Herbert Ullom, editors, *The Autobiography of Sam Houston* (Norman: University of Oklahoma Press, 1954), p. 15.

13. Thomas Lloyd Miller, *Bounty and Donation Land Grants in Texas, 1835-1888* (Austin: University of Texas Press, 1967), p. 26.

14. Ibid., p. 27.

15. Ibid., p. 42.

16. Ibid., p. 43.

17. Navarro County Deed Book N, p. 554.

18. Bounty Warrant 1396 called for 1280 acres and was awarded Thomas J. Church for military service from Nov. 12, 1836, to Dec. 27, 1837. Six hundred and forty acres in Navarro County were patented to Robert Matthews on April 20, 1849, and 640 acres in Navarro County were patented to Matthews on April 9, 1851. Thomas Lloyd Miller, *Bounty and Donation Land Grants of Texas,* p. 172.

19. Navarro County Deed Book 30, p. 167.

20. James K. Greer, editor, Buck Barry, *Texas Ranger and Frontiersman* (Waco: Friends of the Moody Ranger Library, 1978), pp. 25-33.

Chapter 20

1. Jubilee Lafayette McKinney, a son of John McKinney, was born in Illinois in 1810. He married Elizabeth Clementine Story in Navarro County in December 1852 and died in 1872. Nancy Timmons Samuels and Barbara Roach Knox, *Old Northwest Texas* (Fort Worth: Fort Worth Genealogical Society, 1981), Vol. I-B, p. 514.

2. Jefferson McKinney, a native of Illinois, married Lucinda Sims. It is believed that he was in Texas as early as 1838. Ibid., Vol. I-B, pp. 513-514.

3. Hampton McKinney, a Methodist minister, was born circa 1797 in North Carolina. He was married to Mary B. Clark in 1817 and they were parents of 12 children, eight of whom reached maturity. Ibid., Vol. I-B, pp. 512-513.

4. A married daughter Diadema remained in Illinois. After the death of her husband, Levi Jester, however, she relocated in Texas. Ibid., Vol. I-B, p. 512. Diadema McKinney Jester was the mother of George Taylor Jester, who became lieutenant governor of Texas, 1894-1898, and the grandmother of Beauford Halbert Jester, governor from 1946 until his death in 1949. Ibid., I-B, p. 474.

5. Eloise Baldridge Stover, *Navarro County Before 1900*, Unpublished thesis, East Texas State College, August, 1962, p. 36.

6. Nancy Timmons Samuels and Barbara Roach Knox, *Old Northwest Texas*, Vol. I-B, p. 448.

7. Ibid., Vol. I-B, p. 483.

8. Ibid., Vol. I-A, pp. 34-35.

9. Ibid.

10. Ibid., p. 36.

11. C. C. Taylor was a merchant at Richardson in 1850. He was born in New York in 1815. Ibid., Vol. I-B, pp. 637-638. W. Nicks Anderson wrote March 4, 1847, that he paid Taylor $20 to furnish him with a required map. Ibid., Appendix 6, p. 740.

12. Nancy Timmons Samuels and Barbara Roach Knox, *Old Northwest Texas*, Vol. I-A, p. 37.

13. Miller married Mary H. McKinney, daughter of the Rev. and Mrs. Hampton McKinney. He served in the Union Army. Nancy Timmons Samuels and Barbara Roach Knox, *Old Northwest Texas*, Vol. I-B, p. 537.

14. Roger Quarles Mills, born in Kentucky 1832, served as engrossing clerk for the Fourth Texas Legislature. He began the practice of law in Corsicana. He was elected to the United States House of Representatives and served as chairman of the Ways and Means Committee in 1887. He was elected to the Senate in 1892. Walter Prescott Webb, editor, *The Handbook of Texas*, Vol. II, p. 201.

15. Alexander Beaton, a native of Scotland, was an attorney. He was named county clerk, was agent for the Dallas *Herald*, a partner with Roger Q. Mills, and a Confederate tax collector for District 36. He married Elizabeth Jane McKinney, daughter of the Rev. and Mrs. Hampton McKinney. Nancy Timmons Samuels and Barbara Roach Knox, *Old Northwest Texas*, Vol. I-B, p. 368.

16. John M. Crockett, a native of North Carolina, met with financial re-

verses in Mississippi and decided to cast his lot with Texas. He served as assistant county clerk of Dallas before becoming a commissioner for the Mercer Colony. Walter Prescott Webb, editor, *The Handbook of Texas*, Vol. I, p. 436.

17. John Henninger Reagan served as a member of the Confederate Congress. He was appointed by President Jefferson Davis as postmaster-general of the Confederacy. Walter Prescott Webb, *The Handbook of Texas*, Vol. II, p. 444.

18. *Memorial*, p. 119.

19. Ibid., p. 113.

20. Nancy Timmons Samuels and Barbara Roach Knox, *Old Northwest Texas*, Vol. I-A, p. 81.

21. Ibid.

22. Winkler later married Louisa Smith, Smith's widow. She had been the wife of John C. Neill. The divorce matter of John C. Neill and Louisa Neill came before the Sixth Congress of the Republic of Texas and passed July 18, 1842. Harriet Smither, editor, *Journals of the Sixth Congress of the Republic of Texas* (Austin: Capitol Printing Co., 1945), Vol. III, p. 507.

Louisa was the daughter of Jesse Marshall Bartlett and Frances Callaway Bartlett. She was born in Knox County, Tennessee, September 1818, and married John C. Neill in Washington County, Texas, Sept. 6, 1838. Nancy Timmons Samuels and Barbara Roach Knox, *Old Northwest Texas*, Vol. I-B, p. 366. See also Worth S. Ray, *Austin Colony Pioneers* (Austin: The Pemberton Press, 1970), p. 174. She was married the second time to Thomas Igles Smith and moved to Howe's settlement on Chambers Creek. He died March 1848 and she married Clinton M. Winkler Dec. 24, 1848. Timmons and Knox, *Old Northwest Texas*, Vol. I-B, p. 366. Jesse Bartlett had two daughters, Louisa and Nancy, and a son, Joseph C. Worth S. Ray, *Austin Colony Pioneers*, Vol. I-A, p. 83.

23. Nancy Timmons Samuels and Barbara Roach Samuels, *Old Northwest Texas*, Vol. I-A, p. 83.

24. Ibid., p. 83.

25. Navarro County Deed Book C, p. 372.

26. Timmons and Knox, *Old Northwest Texas*, I-A, p. 86, 89.

Chapter 21

1. David R. Mitchell was born in North Carolina in 1797. He was the son of Andrew and Mary Tate Mitchell, who lived in Maura County, Tennessee, for a time. He married Mary "Polly" Ann Higgins, a native of Georgia. Mitchell served as surveyor for the Robertson Land District and settled in Navarro County in 1847. *Old Northwest Texas*, compiled by Nancy Timmons Samuels and Barbara Roach Knox, (Fort Worth Genealogical Society, 1980), I-B, pp. 538-9.

2. Navarro County Deed Book C, pp. 61-2.

3. Ibid., C-62.

4. John Gillespie, born in Ireland in 1802, was living in the household of Ransome House in Harris County in 1850. He was near the residence of George J. Neill. *Old Northwest Texas*, I-B, p. 546.

5. Navarro County Deed Book C-59.

6. Ibid., C-100.

7. Thomas Ingles Smith had died ten days before Neill and Mitchell was administrator of both estates.

8. Jackson Griffin, ginwright, was on the Navarro County tax rolls as early as 1846. *Old Northwest Texas*, I-B, p. 437.

9. Nathaniel H. Carroll, born in South Carolina circa 1800, lived in Louisiana and Tennessee before settling in Texas in 1837. His will, dated Oct. 17, 1853, was probated in November. Ibid., I-B, pp. 395-6.

10. James Allen Johnson was elected Navarro's first sheriff. He owned land on Pecan (Chambers) Creek by 1850. He was born in Tennessee circa 1812-16. *Old Northwest Texas*, I-B, pp. 475-7.

11. William J. Ladd, an innkeeper, was a native of Indiana. He died in Navarro County circa 1851. *Old Northwest Texas*, I-B, p. 490.

12. Navarro County Deed Book C, p. 89.

13. Ibid., C, p. 152.

14. Ibid., C, p. 100.

15. Ibid., C, p. 173.

16. Ibid., C, p. 172.

17. Ibid., C, p. 173.

18. Navarro County Deed Book C, p. 174.

19. David Laughlin, born in Virginia circa 1794, married the widow Elvira Adams in Navarro County June 12, 1851. His property, one league and one labor, was on Richland Creek, east of the town of Dawson. *Old Northwest Texas*, I-B, p. 493.

20. Navarro County Deed Book C, p. 175.

21. Born circa 1820-1824 in Tennessee, James C. Ragan arrived in Navarro County in 1847. He was married twice, first to Emily, and then to Eliza P. Cockrell. *Old Northwest Texas*, I-B, p. 578.

22. Navarro County Deed Book C, p. 176.

23. Ibid., C, p. 411.

24. Ibid., C, p. 142.

25. Ibid., C, p. 177.

26. Ibid.

27. Ibid., C, p. 178.

28. Robert M. Tyus was a land speculator who lived at Old Franklin and later in Limestone County. Born in Virginia he was 39 years of age in 1850. Usually spelled Tyus, the name appears in some records as *Tyas*. *Old Northwest Texas*, I-B, p. 647.

29. The merchant C. C. Taylor also was a surveyor who gave William Nicks Anderson trouble in the Mercer colony. He was born in New York circa 1815. Ibid., I-B, pp. 637-8.

30. Navarro County Deed Book C, p. 179.

31. Ibid.

32. Ibid.

33. Ibid., C, p. 207.

34. Ibid., C, p. 312.

35. Ibid., p. 213.

36. William B. Pillow came to Texas from Maury County, Tenn., whose census in 1830 gave his age between 30-40. In Navarro County in 1850 he and his two sons, John C. and Henson G., were living in the household of David R. Mitchell. *Old Northwest Texas*, I-B, p. 571.

37. Navarro County Deed Book C, p. 215.

38. Ibid., A, pp. 492-493.

39. Ibid.

40. Ibid., A, pp. 494-5.

41. Ibid., A, p. 495.

42. Ibid., C, p. 216.

43. James Monroe Riggs, born Dec. 15, 1805, in Williamson County, Tennessee, died in Corsicana April 16, 1890. In Williamson County, Tennessee, on Dec. 3, 1835, he married Margaret Catherine Hancock. The Riggs family arrived in Texas in 1846 or 1847 and settled in what is now Ellis County. By 1850 they had relocated in Navarro. Riggs was elected district clerk in 1848 and served ten years. His daughter, Mariah Adelaide, was born June 14, 1837, in Marshall County, Tennessee. *Old Northwest Texas*, I-B, pp. 587-588.

44. Navarro County Deed Book C, pp. 216-7.

45. Ibid., C, p. 239. Why James Clinton Neill singled out Miranda as his only grandchild to be named in his will is not explained. A grandson, John P., son of George J. Neill, was born April 27, 1847, and was still alive when the colonel wrote his will; the baby died August 4, 1848. Mary H. Neill Price and Willis Price had a daughter, Sarah J., born circa 1843-44 in Texas.

46. Navarro County Deed Book C, p. 217.

47. Ibid., C, p. 231.

48. Ibid., C, p. 233.

49. Ibid.

50. Ibid., p. 243.

51. Ibid.

52. Ibid., C. p. 244.

53. Ibid., C, p. 246. Neill had received Bounty Warrant 196 for 1280 acres of land for military service, Sept. 28, 1835, to Oct. 22, 1836. On June 16, 1849, the estate received the warrant for land in Navarro County. Thomas Lloyd Miller *Bounty and Donation Land Grants of Texas, 1838-1888* (Austin: University of Texas Press, 1967), p. 498.

54. Navarro County Deed Book C, p. 247.

55. Ibid., pp. 247-8.

56. William Kincannon's San Jacinto claim of 640 acres, one third of a league in the name of Campbell, one third of a league in the name of Toler located near John Ray's, and one certificate for 1280 acres in the name of Matthews. Anderson and White claimed that all the above claims were "the property of said decedent." Navarro County Deed Book C, p. 282. Thomas Lloyd Miller in *Bounty and Donation Land Grants of Texas, 1835-1888*, cites General Land Office records that William P. Kincannon received Donation Certificate 349 for 640 acres in Hill County. This donation for service in the

Battle of San Jacinto was patented to him Sept. 14, 1849, obviously after the death of Neill. P. 379.

57. Navarro County Deed Book C, p. 268.

58. Ibid.

59. Ibid., C, p. 279.

60. Donation certificate 336 for 640 acres in Navarro County was presented John Huffman for being in the Siege of Bexar. The certificate, dated June 15, 1838, was patended Sept. 28, 1849. Thomas Lloyd Miller, *Bounty and Donation Land Grants of Texas, 1838-1888*, p. 791.

61. The tract known as "George J. Neill Three Hundred and Twenty-Acre Headright" was on the waters of Chambers Creek, approximately 17 miles west of Corsicana. George Neill sold it to John B. Jones for $100. Navarro County Deed Book 33, p. 470.

62. Navarro County Deed Book C, p. 281.

63. Ibid., C, p. 284.

64. Ibid., C, p. 285.

65. Ibid., C, p. 372.

66. Ibid., C, p. 373.

67. Ibid., C, p. 286.

68. Ibid., C, p. 549.

69. Thomas J. Church, by bounty warrant 1396, received 1280 acres on Dec. 28, 1837. The warrant was for service between Nov. 12, 1836, and Dec. 28, 1837. On April 20, 1849, he received 640 acres in Navarro County, but the tract was not patented until April 9, 1851. Thomas Lloyd Miller, *Bounty and Donation Land Grants of Texas, 1835-1888*, p. 172.

70. William Bright, son of Tobias and Jane Ford Bright, was born in Montgomery County, Kentucky, July 9, 1975, and died in Navarro County Feb. 19, 1859. *Old Northwest Texas*, I-B, p. 377.

71. Navarro County Deed Book C, p. 550.

72. James B. (Buck) Barry was born in North Carolina Dec. 16, 1821, and died in Bosque County, Texas, Dec. 16, 1906. He married Sarah Anapolis Matticks in 1847, and in a brief time the couple moved to Texas, settling in Navarro County. Barry was elected sheriff, and the family moved to Corsicana in 1849-50. He served two terms, was elected county treasurer, and again was named sheriff in August, 1854. In July, 1863, he married Martha A. Peveler Search, a widow. James K. Greer, editor, *Buck Barry, Texas Ranger and Frontiersman* (Waco: Friends of the Moody Texas Rangers Library, 1978).

73. Navarro County Deed Book C, pp. 586-7.

74. Robert N. White, born in South Carolina in 1810, lived in Alabama and Mississippi before arriving in Navarro County by 1846. He was the first postmaster of Corsicana, one of Corsicana's first aldermen, and a county clerk. Tradition has it that his son, Thomas Cyrus, was Corsicana's first born baby. *Old Northwest Texas*, I-B, p. 675.

75. Navarro County Deed Book H, p. 47.

76. Ibid., C, p. 217, pp. 405-410.

77. Will H. Mitchell, born in Tennessee circa 1832, was a lawyer. *Old Northwest Texas,* I-B, p. 539.
78. Navarro County Deed Book H, pp. 252-253.

Chapter 22
1. John Holmes Jenkins III, editor, *Recollections of Early Texas* (Austin: University of Texas Press, 1958), pp. 155-156.
2. A. J. Sowell, *Early Settlers and Indian Fighters* (New York: Argosy-Antiquarian Ltd., 1964), Vol. I, p. 58.
3. Memorial and Petitions to the House and Senate of The State of Texas, 2-9/127, Texas State Library.
4. Comptroller Papers, Republic Pension, 3-4-74, Texas State Library.
5. Treasury Papers, Audited Military Claims, 4-85, 370, Texas State Library.
6. Memorials and Petitions to the House and Senate of the State of Texas, 2-9/127, Texas State Library.
7. *Telegraph and Texas Register,* Dec. 17, 1836.
8. Treasury Papers, Audited Military Claims, 4-85, C-12/370, Texas State Library.
9. Hill Moore, *Bastrop County* (Wichita Falls, Nortex Press, 1977), p. 258.
10. Letter from J. S. Jones to M. B. Lamar, April 14, 1839, from Camp near Webber's on the Colorado River. Charles Adams Gulick, Jr., et al., editors, *The Papers of Mirabeau Buonaparte Lamar* (Austin: The Pemberton Press, 1968), Vol. II, p. 529.
11. Letter from W. J. Jones to M. B. Lamar, April 15, 1839, from Camp on Wilbargers' Prairie. Charles Adams Gulick, Jr., et al., editors. *The Papers of Mirabeau Buonaparte Lamar,* Vol. II, p. 530.
12. Albert Clinton Horton was born in George on Sept. 4, 1798, and moved to Alabama in 1823. He served in the Alabama Senate. In 1834 he moved to Texas to open a plantation in Wharton County, but in 1835 returned to Alabama to organize the Mobile Grays. He recruited a cavalry company to assist James W. Fannin, Jr., at Goliad in March, 1836.

He was in the Senate of the First and Second Congresses and was a candidate for vice-president of the Republic in 1838.

He was elected lieutenant governor in December, 1845, but was not inaugurated until May 1, 1846, after a recount showed he had received more votes than Nicholas H. Darnell, whom the Legislature had declared winner.

He commanded troops during the War with Mexico, and from May 19, 1846, to July 1, 1847, was acting governor of Texas.

He was considered one of the wealthiest men in the state but the Civil War wiped out his fortune. He died at Matagorda Sept. 1, 1865. Walter Prescott Webb, editor, *The Handbook of Texas* (Austin: The Texas State Historical Association,1952), Vol. I, p. 840.

13. William Menefee, born in Knox County, Tennessee, on May 11, 1796, studied law before settling in Morgan County, Alabama. In 1830 he came to Texas with his wife and seven children. He served in the conventions of 1832

and 1833 and was a member of the General Council of the provisional government in 1835. He was elected the first judge of Colorado Municipality and was a delegate to the Convention at Washington-on-the Brazos in 1836.

He was nominated secretary of the treasury of the Republic, but his nomination was withdrawn. He represented the Colorado District in the House of the Second, Third, Fourth and Fifth Congresses.

In 1841 he ran against Edward Burleson for the vice-presidency.

He died Oct. 29, 1875, *The Handbook of Texas*, Vol. II, p. 173.

14. Louis P. Cooke, born in Tennessee in 1811, was a student in the United States Military Academy but left before graduating. He arrived in Texas after the Battle of San Jacinto, but went into the army and served as lieutenant colonel during 1836 and 1837.

He was elected to the Third Congress and served as secretary of the navy under President Mirabeau B. Lamar. He represented Travis County in the Sixth Congress.

He and his wife, Mary A. Cooke, died of cholera in Brownsville in 1849, *The Handbook of Texas*, Vol. I, p. 406.

15. Isaac Watts Burton was born in Clarke County, Georgia, in 1805 and educated at West Point. He withdrew in 1823 and came to Texas, where he took part in the battle of Nacogdoches. On Nov. 29, 1835, he was appointed captain of a ranger company but later served as a private in Henry W. Karnes' cavalry company at San Jacinto. Burton's mounted rangers were ordered to scout the coast to prevent the Mexicans from landing, and in doing so captured the *Watchman*, the *Comanche*, and the *Fannie Butler*, earning the nickname The Horse Marines.

Burton practiced law, published a newspaper, and served in the Senate of the First, Second, and Third Congresses.

He died in Crockett in January, 1843, *The Handbook of Texas*, Vol. I, p. 256.

16. Isaac Campbell came to Texas in 1836 and represented San Augustine in the house of the Third Congress. He was married to Elizabeth Holman at San Augustine, *The Handbook of Texas*, Vol. I, p. 286.

17. Deed Records of Bastrop County, Book B, pp. 419-420.

18. Aaron Burleson settled at the mouth of Walnut Creek in 1838. He married Jane Tannehill, whose father Jessee C. Tannehill in 1839 settled on land east of the town of Austin, in what is now Montopolis. He took part in the pursuit of Indians following the raid in 1839 on the home of Captain Robert M. Coleman. Mary Starr Barkley, *History of Travis County and Austin* (Waco: Texian Press, 1963), pp. 4, 33.

19. George Hancock became a property owner in the town of Austin. In 1853 he purchased from the State of Texas the site of the old treasury department, and he and Morgan Hamilton owned a building on Congress and Pecan on one side of which was a general store and on the other the men offered groceries and whiskey. He died in 1879. Mary Starr Barkley, *History of Travis County and Austin*, pp. 47, 53, 66.

20. James and Joseph Rogers settled near Hornsby's Bend, and a cemetery "on a knoll off the road" is the burial place of Joseph, who was scalped by

Indians. The two brothers and Edward Burleson, a brother-in-law, frequently joined other men in patrolling the settlements along the river. Ibid.

21. Jacob Harrell, whose cabin was located on a crossing at the foot of Shoal Creek, Austin, took part in an Indian skirmish on the land around Fort Prairie. With Francis Dieterich he set up a butcher shop on Waller Creek in the vicinity of Twelfth Street, supplying much of the meat themselves. He served as mayor of Austin in 1847 and died August 23, 1853. Mary Starr Barkley, *History of Travis County and Austin,* pp. 6, 53-54, 73.

22. Bartlett Sims was one of Austin's Old Three Hundred colonists, having arrived in Texas as early as 1824. He became a surveyor for the colony. In 1826, however, he was listed in a census as a farmer and stock raiser.

In June, 1826, he was captain of a company fighting the Waco and Tawakoni Indians. In March, 1829, he was captain of the fourth company of militia, and the Convention of 1832 named him a member of the Bastrop committee of safety and vigilance. He was in the Convention of 1833 and at the Consultation of 1835. *The Handbook of Texas,* Vol. II, p. 614.

23. The Little Colony Contract of 1827 shows a James Standiferd as receiving one league of land Nov. 8, 1832. The entry immediately following lists Elizabeth Standiferd as receiving one league of land the same day. A James Standiford served as administrator of the one-third league of land issued Elias McCollom in 1835. Bill Moore, *Bastrop County,* pp. 30, 259.

24. Jeptha Boyce received one-third league of land in 1833. Bill Moore, *Bastrop County,* p. 255.

25. A James Lynn received a second class certificate calling for 1280 acres in 1837. Bill Moore, *Bastrop County,* p. 261.

26. In the May 1840 session of the commissioner's court, Thomas H. Mays reported he had purchased a house belonging to Pinckney Hill for use as the Bastrop courthouse. Bill Moore, *Bastrop County,* p. 163.

27. Bill Moore, *Bastrop County,* pp. 269-270. Deed Records of Bastrop County, Vol. B, pp. 419-420.

28. Bill Moore, *Bastrop County,* p. 271.

29. George J. Neill's petition to the Texas House and Senate, Feb. 3, 1871.

30. A. J. Sowell, *Early Settlers and Indian Fighters,* p. 313.

31. Plug hat was slang for a top hat.

32. Thomas Galbreath, a participant in the Plum Creek Fight, had several comments about the hats. "A hat never becomes a wild Indian," he said. "With his thick, long hair it never fits, and it looks as if he was masquerading with one on. . . ." He also stated, "An Indian's head is not shaped right to wear a hat, and it is hard for him to keep it in place." He remembered seeing friendly Indians serving as government scouts in 1870. They tied their hats on; "otherwise every time their horses jumped or a puff of wind came, off they would go." A. J. Sowell, *Early Settlers and Indian Fighters,* Vol. I, p. 313.

33. James T. DeShields, *Border Wars of Texas* (Waco: Texian Press, 1976), p. 323.

34. A. J. Sowell, *Early Settlers and Indian Fighters,* Vol. I, p. 314.

35. Z. N. Morrell, *Flowers and Fruits in the Wilderness*, (Irving: Griffin Graphic Arts, 1966), p. 129.

36. Highsmith was a private in Captain Jesse Billingsley's First Regiment, Texas Volunteers, seeing action at San Jacinto. Bill Moore, Bastrop County, p. 209. A. J. Sowell, *Early Settlers and Indian Fighters*, Vol. I, p. 1.

37. The son was Benjamin Franklin Highsmith, born 1818 in St. Charles District of Missouri Territory. *The Handbook of Texas*, Vol. I, pp. 808-809. A. J. Sowell, who interviewed Highsmith for a Galveston newspaper, says that Highsmith was born in Lincoln County, Mississippi, on Sept. 4, 1817. A. J. Sowell, *Early Settlers and Indian Fighters*, Vol. I, p. 1. At the age of 15 he joined the company of Aylett C. Buckner to fight in the Battle of Velasco; he was with James Bowie in the Battle of Concepcion, he went with Ben Milam to the siege of Bexar, and he was in the Alamo when William Barret Travis had command. *The Handbook of Texas*, Vol. I, pp. 808-809.

It was Ben Highsmith who left the Alamo with an appeal to James W. Fannin. When Fannin turned him down, the young man began riding back to San Antonio, only to discover that the enemy had arrived. At Powder House Hill he intercepted some Mexicans, who chased him several miles into Gonzales. Walter Lord, *A Time to Stand* (New York: Harper & Brothers, 1961), pp. 133-134.

He served under Capt. William Ware in the Battle of San Jacinto. A. J. Sowell, *Early Settlers and Indian Fighters*, Vol. I, p. 11.

He was a member of the Texas Ranger force during the days of the Republic and in 1842 was with John C. Hayes in the Battle of Salado. He took part in the Sommervel Expedition and later saw service in the Mexican War.

Ben Highsmith married Elizabeth Turner in 1853, and the couple became parents of 13 children. He died near Utopia in Uvalde County in 1902. Bill Moore, *Bastrop County*, pp. 219-220. See also *Frontier Times*, Vol. XV, April 1938.

38. A. J. Sowell, *Early Settlers and Indian Fighters*, Vol. I, p. 1.

39. In letter to Stephen F. Austin, Aylett C. Buckner claimed to have been the first person to build a cabin on the Colorado River. He declared that he had "kept open house ever since he came." Buckner's Creek is in present Fayette County, *The Handbook of Texas*, Vol. I, p. 238.

40. James Curtis had been one of Austin's Old Three Hundred. He received a league of land in Burleson County but moved to Bastrop in 1831. He was the oldest man in the Battle of San Jacinto. Curtis entered service to avenge the death of his son-in-law, Wash Cottle, who had died in the Alamo. Each time Curtis fired a shot at San Jacinto, he shouted, "Alamo! You killed Wash Cottle."

Curtis had three sons and two daughters by his first wife, who died in 1830. He married a woman named Sarah, but by mutual agreement they divorced in 1838. He signed his will in Bastrop Dec. 24, 1846, and died there in 1849. Sam Houston Dixon Louis Wiltz Kemp, *The Heroes of San Jacinto* (Houston: The Anson Jones Press, 1932), p. 164.

41. John Holmes Jenkins III, editor, *Recollections of Early Texas*, p. 157.

42. Some of the Rangers who participated in the battle are named in A. J.

Sowell, *Early Settlers and Indian Fighters*, Vol. II, p. 809. Additional names are in Vol. I, p. 317.

43. A. J. Sowell, *Early Settlers and Indian Fighters*, Vol. I, p. 20-21.

44. Ibid.

45. Sam Luckey, a native of Georgia, came to Bexar County, Texas in 1837. He was in the Congress of the Republic in 1841 and in the Senate in 1845. In the expedition to expel Adrian Woll, he was wounded in September, 1842. He died in San Antonio in October, 1852. *The Handbook of Texas*, Vol. II, p. 92. Nicknamed "Storyteller," he was a tall handsome man. James Kimmings Greer, *Colonel Jack Hayes* (New York: E. P. Dutton & Company, 1952), p. 75.

46. Samuel Hamilton Walker, a native of Maryland, took part in the Indian wars in Georgia and Florida before moving to Texas in 1836. In 1839 he was sent to New York to deal with Samuel Colt regarding the purchase of arms for the Republic of Texas. It was he who suggested certain modifications in the popular "Texas" model revolver.

He fought under Col. Jesse Billingsley against the Adrian Woll invasion forces in 1842 and was a leader who engineered the escape from Hacienda da Salada in February, 1843. Recaptured, he survived the Black Bean Episode.

In 1846 he again was sent to New York to order a thousand revolvers. Returning to Texas, he joined Gen. Zachary Taylor's forces on the Rio Grande. In 1847 he was in Gen. Winfield Scott's army, directing guerilla bands attacking lines of communication between Vera Cruz and Mexico City. He was killed while leading one of the charges into Humantia, Tlaxcala, on Oct. 9, 1847, and his body was returned for burial in San Antonio. *The Handbook of Texas*, Vol. II, p. 854.

47. The name is spelled Peter Fohr throughout James Kimmins Greer, *Colonel Jack Hays*. A. J. Sowell, *Early Settlers and Indian Fighters*, spells the name Peter Fore.

48. Andrew Nelson Erskine, the son of Agnes Haynes Erskine and Michael Erskine, was born in West Virginia on March 18, 1826. With his parents he settled in Seguin in 1840.

A surveyor, Erskine married Ann Theresa Johnson, and the couple lived for a time on Michael Erskine's ranch in Capote Hills. In 1852 the Erskines relocated in Seguin, where Erskine had management of a gristmill and ferry.

He served under John S. Ford in opposing the invasion of Juan N. Cortina on the Rio Grande. In 1862 he enlisted in the Confederate Army, serving in Hood's Texas Brigade. He was killed in the Battle of Sharpsburg (Antietam) Sept. 17, 1862. *The Handbook of Texas*, Vol. I, p. 570.

49. A native of Tennessee, Creed Taylor was at Bastrop when Robert M. Coleman and John James Tumlinson formed a company to take part in the battle of Concepcion and in the siege of Bexar. In January, 1836, he was at San Patricio, on detached duty as a scout or courier. He joined the forces at Gonzales in March, 1836, and then accompanied his mother on the Runaway Scrape.

Taylor was in the Plum Creek fight and in 1841 joined the Rangers under Hays. During the War with Mexico he again served under Hays, taking part in the battles of Palo Alto, Resaca de la Palma, Monterrery, and Buena Vista. He died in his ranch home in Kimble County Dec. 26, 1906. *The Handbook of Texas,* Vol. II, p. 715.

50. A. J. Sowell, *Early Settlers and Indian Fighters,* Vol. I, p. 21; Vol. II, p. 809.

51. James Kimmins Greer, *Colonel Jack Hays,* pp. 48-49.

52. A. J. Sowell, *Early Settlers and Indian Fighters,* Vol. I, p. 315.

53. Ibid., Vol. I, p. 316.

54. D. P. Hopkins in "The Postroad," San Marcos *Free Press,* July 7, 1874, cited in Dudley Richard Dobie, "The History of Hays County, Texas," unpublished thesis, The University of Texas, Austin, August, 1932, pp. 39-40.

55. Dudley Richard Dobie, "The History of Hays County, Texas," unpublished thesis, p. 84, based on an interview Feb. 27, 1932, with Sam R. Kone.

56. A. J. Sowell, *Early Settlers and Indian Fighters,* Vol. I, p. 259.

57. Ibid., Vol. I, p. 257.

58. Letter, Frances Hicks, Utopia, Texas, to Peggy Neill, Feb. 6, 1984.

59. "All Around the Canyon," unidentified clipping in possession of Peggy Neill, Pharr, Texas.

60. Letter, Frances Hicks, Utopia, Texas, to Peggy Neill, Feb. 6, 1984. Also letter, Peggy Neill to C. Richard King, April 4, 1984.

Chapter 23

1. Duncan Robinson, *Judge Robert McAlpin Williamson,* Austin: Texas State Historical Association, 1948, p. 129. Robinson suggests that Tumlinson's ranger company was organized to patrol Brushy Creek, p. 130.

2. John James Tumlinson immigrated to Texas from Tennessee in 1821. The General Council elected him in November, 1835, to head the corps of rangers, with whom he participated in the siege of Bexar. He was a private in the Battle of San Jacinto, but in 1840 commanded a group of volunteer rangers pursuing the Comanche Indians after the raid on Linnville. *The Handbook of Texas,* Vol. II, pp. 807-808.

3. Sam Houston Dixon and Louis Wiltz Kemp, *The Heroes of San Jacinto* (Houston: The Anson Jones Press, 1932), p. 334.

4. Noah Smithwick, *The Evolution of a State* (Austin: Gammel Book Company, 1900), p. 124.

5. Smithwick calls him Jim Edmunson. John Holmes Jenkins III, editor, *Recollections of Early Texas,* p. 245, identifies him as James Edmondson. He served under Mark B. Lewis in the Archives War of 1842. He moved to California during the Gold Rush days and spent the remainder of his life there.

6. Ganey Crosby, known as "Choctaw Tom," was a nephew of Colonel Ganey of revolutionary fame, not an honor of which "Choctaw Tom" cared to boast; Ganey was one of the Tories who gave General Marion so much to do in South Carolina. Noah Smithwick, *The Evolution of a State,* p. 207.

7. Martin J. Wells received one-third league of land in 1829, p. 259. On October 29, 1832, he received title to a league of land on the Colorado River,

p. 29. He was born Dec. 9, 1774, in Lincoln County, Tennessee, and was married to Sarah (Sally) Boyd before coming to Texas. Bill Moore, *Bastrop County*, p. 221.

    8. Noah Smithwick, *The Evolution of a State*, p. 126.

    9. Smithwick says that Curtis was "one of the first white settlers in the colony and had had many brushes with the Spanish authorities." Noah Smithwick, *The Evolution of a State*, p. 127. Curtis was the eldest man to take part in the Battle of San Jacinto. John Holmes Jenkins III, editor, *Recollections of Early Texas*, p. 243.

    10. In 1834 Andrew Dunn received deed to land from the ayuntamiento of Bastrop. Bill Moore, *Bastrop County*, p. 38.

    11. Jimmy Leach and Andy Dunn were reported by Smithwick as having drowned during this ranger expedition. Without horses, they had constructed a raft. Noah Smithwick, *The Evolution of a State*, p. 180.

    12. Now known as Brenham.

    13. Noah Smithwick, *The Evolution of a State*, pp. 128-129.

    14. An Andrew Neal received 320 acres of land in Montgomery County on Dec. 30, 1840. *First Settlers of the Republic of Texas* (Austin: Cruger & Wing, Publishers, 1841), Vol. II, p. 55.

    15. High Childress was a native of Tennessee. A Methodist minister, he had a reputation as a fiddler, dancer, hunter, and Indian fighter. John Holmes Jenkins III, editor, *Recollections of Early Texas*, p. 241.

    16. John Holmes Jenkins III, editor, *Recollections of Early Texas*, pp. 41-43.

    17. Service Record, No. 558, cited in *The Heroes of San Jacinto*, p. 175.

    18. Edward A. Lukes, *DeWitt Colony of Texas* (Austin: Jenkins Publishing Company, 1976), p. 63. Also John Henry Brown, *History of Texas* (St. Louis: L. E. Daniell, Publisher, 1892), Vol. I, p. 124.

    19. John Henry Brown, *History of Texas*, Vol. I, pp. 126-127.

    20. Anson G. Neal received one third league of land in Gonzales County May 5, 1838. *First Settlers of the Republic of Texas*, Vol. I, p. 132. He was a first lieutenant in Grumbles Company, wrote Mirabeau B. Lamar, captain commanding the garrison at Laredo, May 30, 1847. Charles Adams Gulick, Jr., et al., editors, *The Papers of Mirabeau Buonaparte Lamar* (Austin: The Pemberton Press, 1968), Vol. VI, pp. 99-105.

    21. Francis Berry received a league of land in Gonzales County. James Berry received one third league of land. *First Settlers of the Republic of Texas*, Vol. I, p. 128.

    Anson G. Neal took part in the battle of the Alamo River, frequently called the battle of Alcantro or El Cantaro. In reporting to Mirabeau B. Lamar, Neal explained that Antonio Canales may have decided against launching a full-scaled attack on Matamoros because his horoscope was not right for such action. Or, he may have played a game he frequently performed. He would divide a piece of paper into sections, upon which he sketched a lion, an eagle, a sheep, and a dove. Then, blindfolded, he would prick a section. "If the warlike bird or animal was pricked," Neal reported to Lamar, "he argued favorably; if the lamb or dove, he argued otherwise."

Neal also told of the appearance of a baker in camp. He wanted to sell bread to the soldiers, but Canales feared it might be poisoned. He told the baker to eat three loaves before he would permit it to be sold in camp. The baker objected to having to eat so much, and the Mexican general took his objection as proof that the poison was slow acting. Joseph Milton Nance, *After San Jacinto* (Austin: University of Texas Press, 1963), pp. 236, 234.

Chapter 24
1. William E. Rogers was listed on the tax roll of Navarro as a land owner in 1847 and in 1849 was overseer of some road work. Nancy Timmons Samuels and Barbara Roach Knox, *Old Northwest Texas*, Vol. I-B, pp. 727, 730; Vol. I-A, p. 202, iii.
2. Travis County District Court Records, Vol. M., p. 38, Feb. 23, 1876.
3. John C. Wilson has not been identified.
4. Thomas E. Stanley has not been identified.
5. Don Wilson had a dry goods and clothing store on Congress Avenue, Austin, opened in 1886. Mary Starr Barkley, *History of Travis County and Austin, 1839-1899* (Waco: Texian Press, 1963), p. 143.
6. Zachary Taylor Fulmore was the son of Zachariah and Sarah Bethea Fulmore. He was born November 11, 1846, in Robeson County, North Carolina. After serving in the Confederate Army, he moved to Texas and was admitted to the bar. He served on the board of trustees for the Texas School for the Blind and was a member of the commission appointed to select a site for and to organize what later became the Texas Blind, Deaf, and Orphan School. He served as chairman of the board of managers of the Confederate Home for Men and was a charter member of the Texas State Historical Association. He was author of *The History and Geography of Texas As Told in County Names*, published in 1915. He was a member of the state bar association. *The Handbook of Texas*, Vol. I, p. 655.
7. Nathan George Shelley joined John Hancock and George Moore in establishing a law office in Austin in 1856. Mary Starr Barkley, *History of Travis County and Austin, 1839-1899*, p. 76. Shelley was a director of the Austin Graded School, founded in 1876. This association organized graded schools, for which tuition was charged, p. 75.
8. Moore belonged to the law firm established by Nathan George Shelley and John Hancock. Ibid., p. 76.
9. In the Alamo Papers file in the Texas State Archives is a letter William J. Cannon wrote from Soldiers Home, Leavenworth, Kansas, on August 3, 1892, and a statement of June 9, 1893, saying that his family lived on Onion Creek, approximately four and a half miles south of Austin, where he was born March 16, 1821. He was the son of William C. Cannon and Martha Cannon. He states that his father came from Tennessee in 1815 and established a small trading post where the Caddoes, Lipans, Tonkaways, and Comanches came in small parties to trade. Mary Starr Barkley, *History of Travis County and Austin*, p. 8. Bill Moore's *Bastrop County* (Wichita Falls: Nortex Press, 1977), p. 254 shows that the land commissioners of Bastrop County issued a certificate for one

labor of land to William Cannon in 1835. Page 260 shows a William Cannon serving as administrator of one-third league of land, the title of which was in the name Charles M. Cannon.

10. Robert L. Redding was an associate justice in Bastrop County in 1841, after having served as a justice of the peace in the second district in 1839. He was chief justice in 1846. Bill Moore, *Bastrop County*, pp. 57, 58, 59.

Robert Love Reding, the son of Maximilian and Mary Love Reding, came to Texas in 1835. He was born in Davidson County, Tennessee, in 1810. He was in the Battle of Goliad, was a signer of the Goliad Declaration of Independence, and in 1837 became a merchant in Bastrop. He was one of the incorporators of a steam mill company operating a saw mill, grist mill, and planing mill. He was married to Elizabeth Jane Perry in 1839. He died in Bastrop in 1849, p. 217.

11. Preston Conley, a native of Tennessee, was born 1798 and emigrated to Texas in 1833, settling in what is now Bastrop County. Following service in the Battle of San Jacinto, he was elected sheriff of Bastrop County and was in office ten years. He resumed farming and stock-raising. Sam Houston Dixon and Louis Wiltz Kemp, *The Heroes of San Jacinto* (Houston; The Anson Jones Press, 1932), p. 162.

12. Neill made his home on Spring Branch of Rocky Creek, approximately four miles due north of Anderson, in Grimes County at the time of his death. Letter, Peggy Neill to C. Richard King, April 1, 1986, based on an interview with clerks in the Grimes County courthouse. He moved from Montgomery County in 1848, George Neill further testifies.

13. James Clinton Neill signed his will March 28, 1848, attesting at the time that he was "sick in body but of perfect mind and memory." He died three days later. The probate court met July 31, 1848, to settle Neill's estate.

14. On April 6, 1875, W. E. Rogers of Bosque County sold to H. C. Ford of Hill County land approximately five miles west of Austin on Williamson Creek, the said being a part of the William Cannon league. Involved was one-fourth interest in and 1800 acres sold to James C. Neill in 1845 and afterward conveyed to Mrs. Mary H. Price, less the one-half interest, approximately 225 acres, already conveyed to J. E. Preston of Travis County.

On Feb. 15, 1850, George J. Neill of Travis County sold to Benjamin Choate of Bastrop County land on Williams Creek granted to William Cannon and bounding Robert L. Reding's and Williams Creek and to the road from Austin to San Marcos. The land crossed the creek in one place.

On August 8, 1879, Benjamin and Mary Choate deeded 40 acres of this land to their son, Frank F. Choate. The property was described as lying a few yards east of the Austin-San Antonio road.

15. The Tehuacana Hills are in northern Limestone County, *The Handbook of Texas*, Vol. II, p. 719. A post office called Tehuacana Springs was established here, but a settlement called Tehuacana Hills was established after James M. Love set up a blacksmith shop in 1848. The village was named for the escarpment, but the post office drew its name from the water in the area.

16. James E. Rector, with Joe A. Bowers, Joseph Harrell, Thomas F.

Mitchell, E. J. Moore, William O. Thomas, and Ben Thompson, were charter members of the Star State Savings Association, chartered in Austin in 1871. Mary Starr Barkley, *History of Travis County and Austin, 1839-1899*, pp. 108-109.

17. A. M. Jackson was president of the Star State Savings Association of Austin. Mary Staff Barkley, *History of Travis County and Austin, 1839-1899*, pp. 108-109.

Chapter 25

1. Letter, Donald E. Brice, reference specialist, Texas State Library, to Peggy Neill, Feb. 10, 1984. The 36th often is referred to as the 32nd Texas Cavalry.

2. Carl L. Duaine, *The Dead Men Wore Boots* (Austin: The San Felipe press, 196), p. 107.

3. Letter, Monte D. Tomerlin to C. Richard King, April 16, 1981.

INDEX

Acaquash (chief), 126, 128, 132, 139-140, 141, 143, 145-146, 147, 151-152
Ackland, Kit, 194
Aedh Reamhar the Stout, 2
Alabama legislature, 22-29, 30
Alabama Militia, 1, 21
Alamo, 73, 74, 78, 82, 86, 87-88, 90, 98-99, 100, 101, 102-104, 106, 114, 127, 169
Alexander, Amos, 46
Allen, J.M., 107
Alps, 44
Anadarko, 126, 137, 144, 147, 151, 162
Anahuac, 34, 53
Anderson County, 167, 186, 187
Anderson, Dr. William Nicks, 182, 183, 184-185, 186, 187
Andrews, Richard, 67
Archer, Branch T., 39, 40, 69, 70, 91
Ardmacha, Domnall, 3
Arndt, E.L., 181
Arnold, Hendrick, 71-72
Auger, Joseph, 23
Austin, Stephen F., 32, 33, 34, 36, 37, 42, 62, 63, 65-68, 69, 70, 91, 122
Austin, Texas, 122
Austin, William T., 73, 108
Ayish Bayou, 119

Badgett, Jesse, 93
Bagenal, Mabel, 4
Bagenal, Sir Henry, 4
Baker, Nathan, 23
Bandera, 193

Bank of Tennessee, 99
Barnard, George, 134
Barnett, Dr. George W., 48, 50
Barragan, Marcus, 113
Barrett, Don Carlos, 71, 79
Barrett, T.F.L., 76
Barry, Buck, 173
Barry, James B., 186
Barton, Dave, 135
Barton, R.A., 148
Bastrop, 46, 55, 200, 201
Bastrop County, 45, 189, 190
Baugh, John J., 98
Baylor, Judge R.E.B., 122
Beal, J.A., 30, 31
Beasley, Maj. Daniel, 16
Beaton, Alexander, 176
Beazley, B.F., 30, 31
Bedford County, Tennessee, 10, 18
Bee, Bernard E., 184
Bee, Hamilton, 129
Bell, Thomas, 180
Berry, Francis, 204, 205
Berry, John Bate, 47
Berry, Sarah, 204, 205
Bexar, Siege of, 64-68, 71-75, 172
Bintah (chief), 126, 137, 139, 162
Bird, Jonathan, 164
Bird's Fort, 145
Black, John S., 124
Black Knee, 2, 3
Bledsoe, A., 189
Bloodgood, William, 179, 181
Bobo, W., 186
Bonham, J.B., 93
Booker, Dr. Shields, 113
Bouldin, Amanda, 206

Bowie, Col. James, 65, 66-67, 69, 70, 80, 82, 87-88, 93, 98, 99
Boyce, Jeptha, 190
Boyd, John, 180, 182, 187
Boyne, Battle of the, 6
Bradburn, John Davis, 32
Brazoria Gazette, 94
Brazos River, 46
Briar Creek, 183
Brigham, Asa, 117-118
Bright, William, 186
Brooks, Zack, 185
Brown, Col. Richard, 20
Brown, Jeremiah, 34
Brown, John, 190
Brown, Joseph Porter, 190
Bryan, William, 107
Buckman, Oliver, 49
Buckner, Aylett C., 193
Bucksnort Falls, 150
Buffalo Bayou, 113
Buffalo Hump, 152, 159
Bufford, Philip T., 180
Bunton, J.W., 48
Bureau of Indian Affairs, 124
Burleson, Aaron, 190
Burleson, Edward, 47, 48, 70, 71, 72, 74, 75, 79, 81, 83, 103, 114, 123, 191
Burnet, David, 38, 39, 41, 108
Burnham's Crossing, 96
Burns, Cynthia, 58
Burnt Factory, 8
Burton, Isaac, 190
Butler County, Alabama, 25
Butler, Pierce, 124, 125
Buttler, Hattie Lou, 199
Byars, Noah Turney, 159

Caddo, 46-51, 131, 137, 139, 144, 147, 151, 162
Cahawba, 24
Caldwell County, 169
Caldwell, Mathew, 191, 195
Calhoun, John C., 23
Caliman, Joseph, 21
Cameron, John, 95
Campbell, G.A., 177

Campbell, Isaac, 190
Canary Islands, 78
Cannon, William, 169, 207, 208-210
Canoma, 46-48
Carey, William R., 86
Carner, John, 180, 182
Carpenter, Bejamin, 29
Carrig, Edenduff, 4
Carrol, N.A., 180
Carrol, N.H., 181
Carroll, Abner, 186, 187
Carroll, Elias, 185
Castaneda, Lt. Francisco, 56-58, 60-61
Castleberry, Martin, 23
Catawba River Valley, 11
Catfish Bayou, 180
Cazneau, William L, 167
Chambers, B.J., 176
Chambers Creek, 176
Chambers, Dr. Henry, 22
Chambers, Ed, 197
Chambers, Talbot, 45
Cherokees, 95, 151, 162, 195
Chester County, Pennsylvania, 8, 9
Childress, George C., 99
Childress, High, 203
Chisholm, Jesse, 127, 139, 141, 148
Chisholm, Richard, 58
Chitwood, Capt. John, 18
Choctaw Tom, 48
Cholocco Litabixee, 19
Church, Thomas J., 173, 186
Cibolo crossing, 65
Cincinnati, Ohio, 108
Claiborne, Gen. Ferdinand, 16
Clare, County Down, Ireland, 8
Clarke County, Virginia, 8
Clay, Nestor, 41-42
Clayton, Elizabeth, 11
Clayton, George, 11-12
Clayton, Hannah, 11
Clayton, Lambert, 12
Clayton, Sarah Lambert, 11-12
Clear Fork of the Brazos, 128
Clements, Joseph C., 57
Clifton, John, 180, 181
Clinton, Archibald, 9

Clinton, Sarah, 9
Clopton, B.M., 190
Clotworthy, Dame Mary, 7
Clotworthy, Sir Hugh, 7
Clotworthy, Sir John, 7
Coahuila, 40
Cobb, Henry A., 117
Cocke, John, 18
Coffee, Brig. Gen. John, 19-20, 21
Coheen, Captain, 48
Coleman, Robert M., 44, 48, 49, 50, 55, 66, 67
Collard, Jonathan, 167
Collin County, 181
Colorado River, 34, 46
Columbia, 52, 117
Comal County, 198
Comanches, 41, 83-84, 128, 132, 135-138, 140, 142-143, 146, 147, 148, 150, 151, 152-156, 158, 159-163, 191-192, 193
"Come and Take It" flag, 58, 65
Committee of Safety, 48, 52, 55
Conley, Preston, 208-210
Conner, John, 129, 156, 157
Constitution of 1824, 60, 75
Constitution, Republic of Texas, 38-39
Cook, Ann, 12
Cooke, Louis P., 190
Cooke, William G., 158, 165
Coopwood, Thomas, 25
Coosa River, 19, 28
Copano, 90
Cornells, Jim, 17
Corry, William M., 108
Corsicana, 173, 178, 182
Cos, General, 66, 68, 72, 74, 75
Cotton Grove, 21
Crawford, J.B., 101
Creeks, 17-20, 19, 134
Cribbs, J. J., 31
Crockett, Davy, 97, 110
Crockett, John M., 176
Cromwell, 6
Crosby, Ganey "Choctaw," 202, 203
Cross, Sterling C., 184, 186
Crowley, James T., 23

Culp, Daniel D., 160
Cunningham, L.C., 190
Curtis, James, 193, 202, 203
Cuthbert, Price, 23

Darst, Jacob, 58
Davidson, Henrietta, 12
Davis, George W., 55
Davis, Nicholas, 25
de la Garza, Antonio, 71
de la Garza house, 73, 74
De Leon, Cpl. Casimiro, 53, 54, 56, 57
Delawares, 126, 131, 133, 137, 138, 140, 143, 147, 151, 152, 160, 162
Delett, James, 25
Delgado, Col. Antonio, 114
Denton, J.B., 120-121
Department of Brazoria, 69
Department of Brazos, 54
DeWitt Colony, 56
DeWitt, Evaline, 58
DeWitt, Green, 53
Dickinson, Lt. Almeron, 58, 64, 78, 99, 103
Dickinson, Susanna, 103, 104
Dixon, A.J., 182
Domnall, 1-2
Dooley, Capt. William, 18
Drake, Dr. Daniel, 108
Dunbar, William, 179, 181
Dungannon Castle, 5
Dunn, Andy, 203
Durbin, Bazil, 204-205
Durst, 154
Dysart, John, 14

Eberly House, 123
Edmondson, Jim, 201
Edmundsen, William, 7
Eggleston, Horace, 101
Eldridge, Joseph C., 124, 128-129
Elizabeth I, 4
Elliott, James D., 180, 181
Elosua, Gen. Altonio, 53
Ephraim, U.I., 173
Erskine, Andrew, 195
Evans, Moses, 124

Exeter, England, 7

Falls, Capt. Gilbreath, 10-11
Falls of the Brazos, 130
Falls Treaty, 150-157
Fannin, Col. James W., 66, 67, 69, 76, 79, 81, 103, 105, 203
Fannin County, 180
Farmington, 15
Farrar, General, 28
Fisher, George, 34
Fitch, Lt. Tony, 79, 100
Fitzgerald, Nancy B., 205
Flight of the Earls, 5
Flores, Gasper, 83, 93
Fluker, William, 29
Fohr, Sam, 195
Forbes, John, 95
Fort Defiance, 105
Fort Groce, 37
Fort Mims, Alabama, 16-17
Fort Strother, 19
Fort Williams, 19, 171
Fox, Martha, 23
Franklin, Alexander, 118
Franklin Turnpike Co., 99
Frazier, James, 24
Friday, 135
Fry, Samuel, 118

Gaines, James, 119
Galbreath, Thomas, 194, 196
Galveston Bay, 38
Galveston Island, 111
Gambrell, Herbert, 127
Gardiner, George, 173
Gayle, John, 30
Gazette, 170
General Consultation, 68-70, 76, 172
General Council, 85-86, 90-91, 103, 172
General Land Office, 172
Gillespie, John, 120, 121, 179
Gilliam, John, 175
Goacher's Trace, 46
Goliad, 105
Gonzales cannon, 53-61, 64-65, 78, 86, 103

Gonzales, Rafael, 204
Gonzales, Texas, 100-101, 102, 104, 204
Gooding, Sallie, 199
Goswell, E.B., 160
Grant, Dr. James, 73, 79-81, 82, 90, 95, 131
Granville, John Karl, 9
grass fight, 71, 198
Graves, F.A., 181
Gray, Daniel, 169
Greeley, Horace, 111
Green, Ed J.S., 198
Green, Pvt. Thomas, 110
Greene County, Alabama, 21, 22, 23, 24, 25, 26, 188
Greene County Gazette, 30
Greene, Gen. Nathaniel, 22
Griffin, Jackson, 179, 181
Grimes County, 178, 179
Groce, Jared, 37
Groce, Leonard Waller, 37
Groce's Retreat, 108
Groos, C.A., 198
Guadalupe County, 169
Guadalupe River, 53, 56, 101

Had-dah-bah, 137, 144
Hales, Col. Charles, 108
Halifax, Lord, 8
Hall of Tara, 1
Hancock, George D., 190
Handy, R.E., 104
Hanks, Wyatt, 121
Harlin, John A., 175
Harney, 135
Harrell, Jacob, 190
Harris, Martha, 111
Harris, Pvt. Thomas, 111
Harris, Rev. Buck, 198
Harris, Temple O., 111
Harrisburg, 112
Harrison, Charles L., 173
Hays County, 198
Hays, Capt. John C., 110, 191, 193-194, 195
Heard, L.F., 199
Hegns, Joel, 118

Henderson County, 181, 184
Henderson, J. Pinckney, 131
Henderson, William F., 177
Henny, Thomas, 45
Henry VIII, 3
Heremon, 1
Herndon, T. H., 31
Hicks, Frances, 199
Highsmith, Abujah M., 192
Highsmith, Ben, 193, 194-195
Highsmith, Deborah Turner, 192
Highsmith, Mary A., 192-193
Highten, James, 181
Hill, Dr. Benjamin Washington, 130, 131, 136, 137, 138, 140
Hill, George W., 147, 151
Hill, Harry, 99-100
Hill, William Pinckney, 190
Hinds, Geron, 204, 205
Hines, Dr. B.M., 199
Hockley, Col. George W., 95, 103, 105, 112
Holtham, John G., 33
Hopkins, Archiband Henderson, 29
Hopkins, D.P., 196
Hopkins, Dennis, 29
Hopkins, Elizabeth, 29
Hopkins, Hardy, 29
Hopkins, Joseph Carpenter, 29
Hopkins, Mary, 29
Horn, Elisha T., 23
Hornsby, Smith, 50
Horseshoe Bend, Battle of, 1, 20-21, 44, 49
Horton, Albert C., 190
Horton, Alexander, 120
Houston, Mrs., 123
Houston, Sam, 20-21, 38, 39, 41, 42, 69-70, 71, 77-79, 80, 81, 82-83, 93, 94-95, 102, 104, 105-106, 107-110, 111-112, 117, 122-129, 135-136, 137-140, 142, 143-144, 145, 146, 150, 151-157, 163, 164-168, 170-172, 176, 195
Howe, William R., 176, 177
Hubbard, S.A., 199
Hudson, Dr. S.B., 199
Huffman, John, 185

Huges, Joseph, 23
Hunt, Capt. John C., 189
Huntsville, Alabama, 23, 27
Huston, Almanzon, 69, 70, 120
Huston, Col. A., 107, 109
Huston, Felix, 131
Hutchins, Amanda, 23

Indian Bureau, 130
Indian Depredations in Texas, 48
Ingram, John, 198
Invincibles, 86
Ioni, 151, 162
Iredell, North Carolina, 10
Irvine, R.B., 121

Jacks, William H., 63
Jackson, A.M., 211
Jackson, Andrew, 16, 17-18, 19-20, 23, 171
Jackson County, Alabama, 24
James II, 6
James VI, 5
Jameson, Green B., 77-78, 93, 98, 103
Janiculum Hill, 6
Jarrett, John, 186
Jarrett, Sarah Ann, 186
Jenings, John W., 31
Jenkins, John Holland, 44, 49-50, 188, 193, 203-204
Jim Second Eye, 129
Johnson, Alfred, 180
Johnson, Col. Frank, 51, 72, 73, 74, 75, 77, 80-81, 82, 90
Johnson, James A., 177, 180
Johnson, Thomas, 181
Jones, Anson, 129, 158, 160, 163, 167
Jones, Benjamin, 25
Jones, H.J., 181
Jones, J.S., 189
Jones, Landey, 118
Jones, Oliver, 38
Jones, W. Jefferson, 189
Jordan, Isaac, 25
José María (chief), 126, 137, 144, 156, 160

Karnes, Henry W., 66, 74, 104
Kattenhorn, Henry, 161
Ke-chi-ka-roqua, 143, 145
Keechi, 48, 137, 139, 143, 151, 152
Kendall, Eleanor, 175
Kendall, Elizabeth Diadem, 175
Kendall, Fenwick Robert, 175
Kendall, George W., 111
Kendall, Joseph, 175
Kendall, Martha, 175
Kendall, Mary, 175
Kendall, Nancy McKinney, 175
Kendall, Susan, 175
Kennedy, Caesar, 24
Kennedy, Capt. Thomas, 10
Kennedy, Charlie, 199
Kennedy, Dosa, 199
Kennedy, Edna, 199
Kennedy, Houston Taylor, 197, 198, 199
Kennedy, Kate Neill, 198-199
Kennedy, Katie, 199
Kennedy, Lula, 199
Kennedy, Maud, 199
Kennedy, May, 199
Kennedy, Morris, 199
Kennedy, Sam, 199
Kerr, James, 38, 204
Killeleagh, Baronet of, 6
Kincannon league, 185
King's Mountain, Battle of, 9, 11
Kinney, Thomas, 169
Kiowa, 145
Knox, Jane, 23

La Grange Intelligencer, 167
Labadie, Dr. N.D., 113
Ladd, William J., 180
Lafayette, General, 23, 24
Lafayette Lodge No. 26, 30
Lamar, Mirabeau B., 123
Lambert, John, 11
Lambert's Creek, 9
Lame Arm, 152
Laredo, 87, 88
Laughlin, David, 180
Leach, Jimmy, 203
Leach, Rachel, 177

Lee County, Texas 34
Leiper, Allen, 14
Leiper, James, 14
Leon Creek, 193
Lessassier, Luke, 38
Lewis, John M., 167
Lewis, Moses, 31
Lewis, William M., 29
Liberty, Texas, 32
Limestone County, 180, 181, 182, 186, 187, 207
Linney (chief), 125, 126
Linnville, 191
Lipan, 162
Lockhart, John Washington, 124
Lockhart, Texas, 191
Louisiana Purchase, 17
Love, James M., 180, 181
Love, William M., 180, 182
Lovejoy, John L., 180
Luckey, Sam, 194
Ludlow, Israel, 108
Lynch, J.D., 181
Lynch, John L. 189
Lynch, Joseph, 183-184
Lynch's ferry, 113, 115
Lynchburg, 113
Lynn, James, 190
Lyttle, Robert F., 108

M'Vay, Zaddock, 29
MacManus, Seumas, 2
Macomb, D. B., 76
Madero, Juan Francisco, 32
Madison County, Alabama, 24
Magill, William, 50
Manchola, Rafael, 36
Marlin, John, 147-148, 150, 161
Marsh, John, 118
Marshall County, Tennessee, 10
Martin, Capt. Albert, 55
Martin, John, 29
Martin, William B., 25
Mason, Charles, 117
Masons, 120
Massey, John, 29
Matamoros expedition, 79-81, 91, 94-95, 131

Matamoros, Mexico, 79-80
Matthews, Flora Ann, 173
Matthews, Robert, 173
Mays, A., 190
McAlpin, Jefferson C., 30
McBride, George, 14-15
McClure, ——, 105, 182
McCrory, Col. Thomas, 18
McCulloch, Henry, 191
McCulloch, Pvt. Benjamin, 110, 191
McDonald, D., 121
McDowell, Capt. Joseph, 10
McDowell, Col. Charles, 10, 11
McFall, Samuel, 46, 47
McFarlain, W. Z., 123
McFarland Lodge, 120
McFarland, William, 120
McGregor, Martha M., 111
McKean, Timothy, 169
McKinney, Hampton, 175-178
McKinney, James P., 198
McKinney, Jefferson, 175
McKinney, Jubilee, 175
McKinney, Lucinda, 175
McNeal, Samuel L., 206
Meeks, John, 31
Melton, Ethan, 177
Menefee, William, 190
Mercer, Charles Fenton, 176
Mercer Colony, 176
Merriwether, Zachary, 24
Milam, Benjamin Rush, 43-44, 45, 46, 64, 72, 74
Milam Colony, 43-46
Military Plaza, 74
Millard, Henry, 76
Miller, J.C., 187
Miller, James B., 42, 54
Miller, James H.C., 50-51
Miller, John L., 176
Miller, S.R., 190
Miller, Washington, 165
Millican, Ira, 180
Mills, Roger Q., 176
Mims, Samuel, 16
Mina, 44-45, 48, 49
Miranda's expedition, 41
Mission Concepcion, 66

Mission Refugio, 83
Mission San Francisco de la Espada, 65
Mission San Jose, 75
Mitchell, David R., 177, 178, 179-187
Mitchell, Will H., 187
Mobile, Alabama, 17
Mobile Bay, 28
Moffitt, John H., 167
Montgomery Patriot, 111
Moody, J.W., 118
Moore, Allen M., 180
Moore, Jim, 175
Moore, Col. John H., 49, 55, 56, 58-59, 60-61, 106, 110, 191
Mopechucope, 160
Morehouse, Edwin, 148, 151, 156-157, 158, 160, 161, 162
Moreland, Capt. Isaac N., 110
Morgan, James, 181
Morison, Joseph, 179
Morris, John D., 116
Murphy, John, 24
Muscle Shoals, 28, 29
Muskogee, 134
My Eighty Years in Texas, 102

Nacogdoches County, 167
Nacogdoches Telegraph, 94
Nacogdoches Volunteers, 73
Nancy Gillespie v. Andrew S. Gillespie, 24
Nangle, William, 127-128
Narhashtowey, 144, 146, 155
Natchez, 17
Navarro County, 179, 183, 186
Navarro, Jose, 71, 90
Navarro, Texas, 178, 181
Navasota River, 48
Ne-est-choo, 137
Neal, Andrew, 203
Neal, Anson G., 205
Neal, Lourahama, 205
Ned, Jim, 146, 159
Neely, Richard W., 169
Neill, Abjah Morris, 198, 199
Neill, Agnes Snoddy, 11

Neill, Alexander (son of James Neill), 13
Neill, Alexander (son of Capt. Wm.), 9
Neill, Amanda (Miranda), 212-213
Neill, Andrew (son of James Neill), 9, 10, 13
Neill, Ann, 12
Neill, Archibald, 9
Neill, Betty, 12
Neill, Cynthia Forgy, 11
Neill, Elizabeth, 7, 8, 9
Neill, Esther Reford, 7
Neill, George Clayton, 14-15
Neill, George Jefferson (son of J.C.), 33, 44, 169, 182, 183, 184, 185, 188-199, 200, 208-211, 212
Neill, Gilbreath Falls, 9, 10-11
Neill, Hannah Clayton, 9, 11, 12, 13
Neill, Harriet, 33, 188, 198, 209
Neill, Harvey, 198
Neill, Itasca Perkins, 198
Neill, James (son of Capt. Wm.; father of J.C. Neill), 9, 10, 11, 13-14
Neill, James Clinton: in Alabama militia, 21; as Alabama representative, 24-29; ancestry of, 1-12; at Bexar, 64-68, 73-75, 79, 81-82, 84-90, 92, 94, 95-96, 97-98; birth of, 13; as commissioner, Indian Bureau, 130-163; death of, 178, 210-211; discharged from army, 21, 55-56, 117-118; enlists in army, 18, 49-51; farm of, 29, 30; at Gonzales, 55-56, 59-61; issued league in Texas, 34, 44-46; as justice of peace, 23-24; as judge of Mina, 44; leaves Bexar post, 98; as lt. col., artillery, 76, 103, 112, 117-118; marriage of, 15; as Mason, 120-121; military background of, 1, 49, 71; obtains supplies for Alamo, 101; relief request of, 165-168; and Sam Houston, 20-21, 42, 107; at San Felipe convention, 36-42; and slavery, 37-38; and smallpox vaccine, 50; surveying business of, 172-174; to Texas, 32-34; and Twin Sisters, 107-115; will of, 178, 179-187; wounded, 115-116
Neill, James C. (grandson of J.C.), 198
Neill, James W., 205
Neill, Jane, 13, 205
Neill, Jemima, 205
Neill, John, 7-8, 9, 11
Neill, John Lambert, 13
Neill, Kate, 198
Neill, Lewis (son of John), 7-8
Neill, Lourahama, 205
Neill, Marcella Jones, 191
Neill, Margaret Harriet, 12, 15, 211
Neill, Mary (daughter of James), 13
Neill, Mary (Polly) (wife of Capt. Wm.), 9
Neill, Mary (daughter of Samuel), 205
Neill, Mary E. (daughter of George J.), 198, 212
Neill, Mary Harriet (daughter of J.C.), 33, 207-211
Neill, Mary Highsmith (wife of George J.), 192-193, 197-198
Neill, Miranda, 183, 205, 209
Neill, Nancy Fitzgerald, 205, 212
Neill, Robert, 9, 10, 12
Neill, Samuel (son of George J.), 198, 199
Neill, Samuel (son of Capt. Wm.), 9
Neill, Samuel (son of James), 13
Neill, Samuel C. (son of J.C.), 33, 169, 182, 200-206, 210, 211, 212
Neill, Sarah (Sally), 8, 9, 11, 198, 209, 212
Neill, Sarah Scott, 12
Neill, Thomas, 7
Neill, Capt. William, 7-10
Neill, William David, 14-15
Neill, William James, 12
Neill's Creek, 9
Neill's Gap, 15
Nelson, Captain, 11
Nelson, Horatio, 180-181
New Orleans, 28

Newland, William, 101
Niall Black Knee, 2, 3
Niall of the Nine Hostages, 2-3
Nichols and McGee, 196
Nichols, Q. J., 196
Niul, 2
Noel, Theodore, 30
Nolan's River, 154

O'Banion, Jennings, 101, 189
O'Cahan, Rory Dell, 5
O'Neill, Claneboy, 4
O'Neill, Con, 3-4
O'Neill, Hugh, 1, 4-6
O'Neill, Mabel Bagenal, 4
O'Neill, Owen Roe, 6
O'Neill, Shane, 4
O'Neill, William, 7
O'Neill Dragoons, 6
O'Neills, 3-8
Old Mill, 68, 72
Oldham, William, 76
Oliphant, Lambert, 12
Oliphant, Rebecca Neill, 12
Oliver, Elizabeth, 204
Oliver, John, 204
Ortiz, Jesus, 177
Osburn, James M., 180, 181

Pace, Alfred E., 186
Pacer, Bob, 203
Pah-hah-yuco, 128
Park, William A., 115, 116
Parker, Benjamin F., 167
Parker's Fort, 48
Parkham, William, 99
Parrish, Capt. Joel, Jr., 18
Patton, William H., 131
Peach Creek, 105
Pennsylvania, 109
Pentill, T.M., 207
Peoples, Jehu, 177
Perkins, George, 197
Peruzzi, 6
Peters Colony, 176
Petty, Lt. George, 203
Peyton, Angelina, 36-37
Pharsa, Phenius, 2

Philip II, 5
Pickens, Israel, 22, 23, 24
Pillow, William, 182, 183, 186
Pillsbury, Timothy, 168
Pilot Grove, 180
Piombo, Sebastino del, 6
Plum Creek Fight, 110, 191
Pochanaquarhip, 153
Pollard, Dr., 93
Ponton, Andrew, 54-55, 57
Porter, R.N., 150
Porter, Robert E., 169
Portis, D.T., 210
Powell, Joseph, 29
Price, Andrew (Drew), 207
Price, Drury, 207
Price, James K., 207
Price, Mary H., 182
Price, Mary Neill, 207-211
Price, Mary R., 207
Price, Rebecca Harriet, 207
Price, Sarah, 207
Price, Willis A., 180, 181, 182, 183,
   184, 207, 209
Pullen, Asa, 183

Quinn, Edmund, 168

Rabb, Andrew, 44
Ragan, J.C., 180
Ragsdale, Samuel, 10
Ramsour's Mill, Battle of, 10, 11
Raney, Matthew F., 26, 29, 30, 31
Rangers, 193-196, 200-204
Raymond, J.H., 163
Reach, Hiraim, 168
Reagan, John H., 176
Rector, James E., 211
Red Bear (chief), 43-44, 128, 137,
   139, 144, 146, 154
Red River Herald, 95
Redding, Robert, 208-210
Redlander, 119
Reed, John, 14
Reford, Dorothy Till, 7
Reford, Robert 7
Rhodes, Henry S., 29
Richardson community, 177

Richardson, Matilda, 23
Riche, Eilenor, 23
Richland, 177
Ricks, Joseph, 31
Riggs, James Monroe, 177, 178, 183, 186
Roasting Ear (chief), 126, 152
Roberts, Capt. John S., 73
Roberts, Mark F., 183
Robertson County, 173, 175, 176, 177
Robinson, James W., 69, 76, 83-84, 86, 89-90, 91-92
Robinson, William, 35-36
Rock Creek, 14
Roden, John C., 29
Roemer, Ferdinand, 133
Rogers, James, 190
Rogers, Joseph, 44
Rogers, William E., 207
Ross, Alexander, 8
Routh, James, 113
Rowan County, North Carolina, 9, 13
Ruis, Francisco, 83
Rusk, Thomas J., 111
Rutherford, Col. James, 11
Rutherford, Robert S., 169

Sabinal Cemetery, 199
Sabine River, 119
Sabine, 34
Sah-sah-rogue, 143, 144
Samamigey, 134
San Antonio, 195; *also see* Bexar
San Antonio de Valero, *see* Alamo
San Augustine, 119-121
San Felipe convention, 93-94
San Felipe de Austin, 88
San Felipe Inn, 36
San Felipe Telegraph, 94
San Felipe, Texas, 33, 36, 37-42, 45, 52, 68-70
San Jacinto, 112-115
San Jacinto River, 113
San Saba silver mines, 65
Sanchez, Luis, 127, 130, 137, 140-142
Sand Bar Fight, 65

Sanderford, Joseph, 29
Sandies Creek, 65
Santa Anna (chief), 159
Santa Anna, Antonio Lopez de, 36-37, 52, 59, 80, 90, 96, 104, 111, 113, 114
Scott, Frances T., 29
Scurry, Richardson A., 111
Seaman, Nathaniel, 108
Seguin, Erasmo, 42
Seguin, Juan, 93, 105
Sesma, Gen. Joaquin Ramirez y, 87
Shane's Castle, 4
Shaw, Jim, 129, 141, 156, 160
Shaw, John, 14
Shawnee, 125, 126, 131, 140, 147, 151
Shea, John, 116
Shelby, Colonel, 11
Shenandoah Valley, 8
Shepherd, Jacob H., 66
Sherman, Sidney, 112, 114
Sibley's Brigade, 111
Simmons, Benjamin, 14
Sims, Bartlett, 46, 190
Sims, Julius, 24, 26
Singleton, Philip, 115
Six Mile Creek, 180
Sloat, Benjamin, 130, 131, 142, 143, 147, 148-149, 150, 160
Smith, Ashbel, 131
Smith, D.W., 101
Smith, Deaf, 88, 104, 113, 189, 204, 205
Smith, Dr., 59-60
Smith, Erastus, 204
Smith, Henry, 39, 69, 77, 80-81, 82, 89, 90-91, 92, 93-94, 95, 96, 98, 99
Smith, James, 44, 169
Smith, John W., 83, 84, 86, 100
Smith, Pulaski, 108
Smith, Rev. W.P., 58
Smith, Stephen, 101
Smith, Thomas I., 124, 141, 148, 151, 156, 158, 176, 177, 178, 179, 181
Smithwick, Noah, 62, 63, 65, 66, 67, 201, 202, 203

Society of Friends, 7
Solygay, 135
Sowell, Andrew, 191
Sowell, John, 58
Spanish National Church of San Pietro, 6
Spout Spring, 8
Spring Hill, Tennessee, 99
St. Louis (chief), 137, 138-139, 140, 144, 159
St. Patrick, 3
Standoford, James, 190
Stanley, Booker F., 208
Stanley, Elias S., 208
Stanley, George F., 208
Stanley, John, 118
Stanley, Mary E., 208
Stanley, Thomas E., 207-208
Steele, Col. Robert, 18
Stephens, C.R., 44
Stewart, James, 5
Stivers, Dr. Samuel, 121
Strait, Margaret, 23
Stroud, 154
Sturtevant's Creek, 25
Sublett, P.A., 76
Succat, 3
Summerville, Alabama, 24
Sutherland, Dr. John, 99
Swearingen, Lemuel, 114
Swearingen, W.C., 114
Swisher, John, 196, 198

Talladega, Battle of, 19
Tally, Ephraim, 119
Tannahill, Jessie C., 44
Tarbox and Brown stage, 196
Tarver, B.E., 168
Tawakoni, 129, 140, 141, 143, 145, 146, 147, 148, 151
Taylor, Christopher C., 176, 181, 184
Taylor, Creed, 58, 65
Taylor, Creek, 195
Taylor, General, 174
Taylor, J.M., 198
Taylor, John, 18, 182
Teel, Benjamin, 212

Tehaucana, 140, 151
Tehaucana Creek, 124, 132, 134
Telegraph and Texas Register, 52, 111, 189
Tennessee Militia, 18, 21
Tennessee River, 28
Tennessee Volunteers, 97, 171
Teran, 33
Terrell, George W., 124-125, 151
Terrell, George Whitfield, 124
Texas Almanac, 114
Texas Army, 62-63, 69, 76, 77, 81, 84, 87, 94, 100, 104, 105-106, 107-108
Texas Declaration of Independence, 92
Texas Gazette, 41
Texas National Register, 158
Texas Sentinel, 170
Texas State Library, 56, 116
Thorn's Branch, 204
Thornton, James I., 26
Tomerlin, Bennet, 212
Tomerlin, Miranda Neill, 212
Tomerlin, Monte, 213
Tonkawa, 162
Torna, 3
Torrey brothers, 130, 151, 156, 160, 161
Torrey, Thomas, 134
Torrey Trading Post, 133, 142
Toweash (chief), 162
Travis County, 198, 207
Travis Guards, 122
Travis, William B., 51, 53, 76-77, 78-79, 96, 98-99, 102
Treadwell, John, 180
Tumlinson, Capt. John J., 200
Tumlinson, James, 53
Tuscaloosa County, 24
Twiggs, Gen. D.E., 110
Twin Sisters, 107-115
Tyrus, R.M., 181

Ugartechea, Col. Domingo de, 53, 54, 55, 56, 58, 70, 74
Union County, Kentucky, 11
Uvalde, Texas, 199

Vandeveer, Logan, 190
Vasquez Expedition, 110
Velasco, Battle of, 69, 79
Veramendi, Maria Ursula de, 65
Veramendi palace, 71, 73
Viesca, José María, 32
Vuavis, Lieutenant, 72

Wacos, 48, 49, 126, 139, 140, 141, 146, 147, 148, 151, 152, 155
Wade, Pvt. John M., 111
Walker, Sam, 195
Wallace, J.W., 58, 59
Walnut Creek, 181
Ware, Capt. William, 11
Warren, R.H., 24
Warren's Trading Post, 129
Washington County, 34, 168, 190, 203, 205
Washington-on-the-Brazos, 77, 123, 158
Waterloo, 190
Watson, Harris E., 120
Watson, Mr., 157
Wavell, Arthur Goodall, 43
Wells, Marty, 202
Wells, Wayman F., 198
Western, Maj. Thomas G., 130-140, 147, 148, 150, 158, 160, 161
Wharton, John A., 108, 109
Wharton, William H., 36, 37, 70, 91, 100
White Feather (chief), 152
White, J., 30, 31
White, R.N., 186
White, William, 182, 183, 184-185, 186
Whiteside Hotel, 37
Whitesides, J.T., 130
Wightman, John, 204
Wilbarger, J.W., 48

Wilcox County, Alabama, 25
Will Bryant v. Rhody Bryant, 24
Williams, Samuel May, 33, 34, 134, 136, 137, 138, 140, 141, 147, 154, 155
Williams, F.S., 180
Williams, Francis F., 180-181, 187
Williams, Ira, 181
Williams, John A., 119
Williams, Leonard H., 130, 131, 159, 160, 161
Williams, Samuel, 51
Williamson, Capt. Robert McAlpin, 38, 40, 45-46, 48, 51, 55, 120, 201, 202, 203, 205
Williamson, H.J., 93
Wilson, David M., 208
Wilson, Don, 208
Wilson, John C., 207-208
Wilson, Rhoda, 208
Wilson, Robert, 151
Wilson, Thomas W., 208
Winkler, Clinton M., 176-177
Winn, Walter, 139
Wolfenbarger, Samuel, 44, 48
Woll, Gen. Adrian, 195-196
Wood, Joseph, 207
Woodfolk, Maj. William, 21
Woodruff, Edward, 108
Wright, Joseph Michael, 6
Wyman, E.S., 161, 180

Yegua Creek, 44
Yellowstone, 108
York Creek Cemetery, 198

Zambrano Row, 74
Zavala, Emily, 115-116
Zavala, Lorenzo de, 52, 115-116
Zuber, William Physick, 102-103, 106

www.ingramcontent.com/pod-product-compliance
Lightning Source LLC
Chambersburg PA
CBHW052103230426
43671CB00011B/1915